Tactical Fly Fishing

TACTICAL FLY FISHING

*for Trout and Sea Trout
on River and Stream*

PAT O'REILLY

The Crowood Press

First published in 1990 by
The Crowood Press
Ramsbury, Marlborough
Wiltshire SN8 2HE

British Cataloguing in Publication Data
O'Reilly, Pat
Tactical fly fishing: for trout and sea trout
on river and stream.
1. Trout. Fly fishing
I. Title
799.1'755
ISBN 1-85223-294-3

Line-drawings by David Batten

Typeset by Inforum Typesetting, Portsmouth
Printed in Great Britain by
Butler & Tanner Ltd, Frome

To the people of the Teifi Valley,
who made me so warmly welcome.

Contents

Preface   9
Acknowledgements   11

PART I   FOR BEGINNERS TO RIVER FLY FISHING

1   Trout and Trout Streams   15
2   Insects and Other Food of River Trout   33
3   Tackling Up   48
4   The Gentle Art of Casting   63
5   Fly-Fishing Techniques for River and Stream   78

PART II   SPRING TACTICS

6   Spring Trouting on Lowland Rough Streams   93
7   Late Spring on Hill and Mountain Streams   105
8   Spring Tactics for Spate River Trout   117
9   Early Days on a Chalk Stream   126
10 The Early Runners   135

PART III   SUMMER TACTICS

11 High Season on a Rough Stream   153
12 Small Stream Nymph Fishing by Night and by Day   162
13 The 'Dog Days' on a Chalk Stream   171
14 Things that go Bump in the Night   180
15 Fresh Tactics for 'Halfling' Sea Trout   192

PART IV   AUTUMN TACTICS

16 September on a Rough Stream   205
17 Autumn Miscellany on a Chalk Stream   215
18 Indian Summer Wine   224
19 Sea Trout in Coloured Water   231

PART V   WINTER ACTIVITIES

20   Winter Work on the River   241
Appendix: Trout and Sea Trout Flies   254
Bibliography   261
Glossary   263
Index   267

Preface

I fish alone – not always, of course, but most of the time – alone, the river and I. Over the years many rivers and streams have taught me about the wild things of the water – the plants and the animals; the insects and the fishes. My ever-patient tutors have rewarded my successes as fairly as they have punished my failings. At first I learned quickly, or at least thought I did. Then came a period of frustration, a period in which I began to realise how much there was to learn in order to become a good fly fisher. Now, I am more at peace with the river, reconciled to being a first-form pupil to the end of my days. Ambition is still there, but it is of a different kind. No longer do I count as good a day in which many fish, or even large fish, come to my net (pleasant though such days are). Rather it is a day when I solve some age-old problem, or tempt a very difficult fish – difficult because of acquired cunning or the near impenetrability of his feeding lie.

Throughout my angling days, one subject has greatly intrigued me – the intricate relationship between migratory and non-migratory trout. Fresh-run sea trout behave rather like nocturnal salmon, and respond to similar angling tactics. After many months in a river, they become more like their non-migratory cousins, in both appearance and behaviour, and trouting tactics can bring about their downfall. However, little has been written of the in-between or 'halfling' stage when sea trout are most difficult to tempt. But with the right tactics they can be caught.

There are still more angling questions than answers, and long may it remain that way. A few problems have been avoided by improving on tackle. Rather more were solved by improved casting and fishing technique – getting the best out of the tackle. But by far the majority of problems – solved and unsolved – are to do with tactics. These are the minute by minute decisions of angling: exactly how and where to cast a fly, what type of fly to use and, most particularly, how the fly should behave in or on the water. Of course, tactics are also about the behaviour of the angler and this is often the crucial factor in determining success or failure. These matters are the essence of tactical fly fishing, and the theme of this book.

Part I is included primarily for those new to fly fishing on rivers and streams. It provides an introduction to the behaviour of trout and sea trout, the food upon which they feed and the tackle and basic fly-fishing techniques for their capture. Parts II, III and IV cover a range of tactics for trout and sea trout in spring, summer and autumn respectively. Winter need not be a time of hibernation for the fly fisher. Part V includes a chapter on river bank maintenance and on observations which can enhance the quality and enjoyment of fishing in the season ahead. There is also an appendix giving tying details for the artificial flies mentioned in the book, a list of recommended reading, and a glossary of common fly-fishing terms.

There is a kind of magic in river fishing – the anticipation and tension, frustration and disappointment, and (thankfully) the occasional triumph would seem guaranteed to drain the nervous system of its last drop of energy. Yet, strangely, for many of us, fly fishing has the opposite effect. Come failure or success, a few hours by the riverside brings with it an engulfing peace of mind. If this book helps its readers to some share of this, then I will be well satisfied.

Pat O'Reilly
West Wales, 1990

Acknowledgements

Preparing a book of this sort involves teamwork; and I have been fortunate to receive help from a valued team of friends who have given generously of their expertise and their time.

I am particularly grateful to Bob Carr, Max Davies and Peter Gathercole for their help and advice with photographs; to David Gardner, Principal Fisheries Officer with the National Rivers Authority in Wales, for advice on migration habits of sea trout; and to Derek Hoskin, my fellow instructor at West Wales School of Fly fishing, for tying many of the flies in the colour plates. My thanks also to Dennis Smith, Merlin Jones, Mike Davies, Rob Salt and Tony Summers for inviting me to their waters and advising me during my fishing trips to gather material for the book.

To Sandy Leventon, editor of *Trout and Salmon*, and to Chris Dawn, editor of *Trout Fisherman*, many thanks for granting me permission to quote from several of my articles published over many years in their magazines.

Finally, a special thank-you to my wife, Adrienne, a most constructive critic of my literary efforts, for her patience in reading so many drafts, and for her encouragement and advice.

PART I
FOR BEGINNERS TO RIVER
FLY FISHING

1
Trout and Trout Streams

Brown trout, born and reared in a hatchery and grown on in stew ponds, are stocked into an upper tributary of the River Severn. Each carries a Severn-Trent Water Authority tag. The intention is to supplement the river's stock of wild trout, and to provide improved sport for local anglers. The following spring, on the River Towy in South Wales, an angler lands a sea trout, bright and silver, fresh up on the morning tide. A green tag shows it to have been one of those brown trout stocked into the Severn system, having completed a journey of several hundred miles. What made that fish choose a nomadic existence?

On a small Devon river the final phase of a dam is completed. A new reservoir is formed and the passage of migratory fish up or down the stream is restricted. But sea trout are already up above the dam. What will happen to them after they have spawned? The answer: they survive, eventually toning in so closely with the colour scheme of local resident trout that only an expert eye can identify those which were once sea trout.

A trout, it appears, is a sea fish in the process of evolving into a freshwater fish. (The Atlantic salmon is going through a similar process, but to date its progress is somewhat less than that of Salmo trutta.) *To the biologist, there is no difference between brown trout and sea trout (the same can be said about the rainbows and steelheads of North America), but to the fly fisher, brown trout and sea trout are quite different. Not only are sea trout generally much bigger, but the two species look so different one from the other . . . usually! In most respects they are a separate 'species', responding differently to a fly and, on being hooked, each behaving in its own characteristic way. A sea trout will leap and cavort on the surface in spectacular fashion, while a brown trout will more often make for deep water, fighting doggedly for the safety of a bolt-hole.*

At any point in time, I suggest, a particular fish may be a resident brown trout or a sea trout, or it may be somewhere between the two – a sort of halfling, bearing some characteristics of each. As anglers, we will do well most of the time if we treat them as separate species. But we should keep in mind the Jekyll and Hyde nature of Salmo trutta.

THE SALMONIDS

The salmon family includes not only the Atlantic salmon but also grayling and various species of char and trout. River fly fishers are generally most interested in brown trout (*Salmo trutta*) and, occasionally, rainbow trout (*Salmo gairdneri*). Both these species are widely distributed throughout the rivers and streams of North America, where the brown trout was introduced over a century ago. The brown trout is a native of European and Asian rivers, where rainbow trout rarely thrive and have to be supplemented with hatchery stock. Notable exceptions are the River Chess in Buckinghamshire and the River Wye in Derbyshire, where rainbow trout have successfully established themselves on certain stretches. By and large, however, it is safe to assume that rainbow trout found in British rivers are the result of the work of trout farmers.

Brown Trout

Salmo trutta is a versatile creature, adapting its livery to suit its habitat and growing to a size determined by the amount of food available. The trout of a peat-stained spate river may be predominantly olive and gold with bright crimson spots, while its chalk stream brother may take on a coat of light brown and silver with spots of a darker brown, almost black. At one time it was thought that there were many more species of trout. Special scientific names were allocated to the brown trout of Loch Leven, to the slob or bull trout of the estuaries, and to the enormous trout which inhabit the depths of certain of the great lakes of Ireland. All of these, as far as the biologist is

Fig 1   A brace of brown trout, the larger of which weighs just over 2lb.

Fig 2   On larger rivers, trout spawn in the gravelly stretches, most notably on the upper reaches and the tributaries. This is the River Cothi, a major tributary of the Towy.

concerned, are strains of *Salmo trutta*, differing only in their behaviour. From our point of view, as fly fishers, there is a great deal of difference between the brown trout of a mountain stream, of a lowland brook and of a chalk stream. In this book, they are each treated separately, as different animals sharing only the same name.

Life Cycle

Brown trout spawn in winter, seeking shallow gravelly stretches in which to lay their eggs. The hen fish uses her tail to scoop out a depression, called a redd, into which the eggs (as many as a thousand or more) are deposited. The eggs are fertilised when the cock fish covers them with his milt. The ova develop and hatch in spring. Trout go by various names during their early development from alevin to fry and thence to parr. Young trout are constantly preyed upon by other animals – birds and fishes, including their own kind. After three or four years, perhaps only one or two from the brood will have survived to adulthood. In a tiny mountain stream, a four-year-old trout could weigh less than an ounce, whereas it might reach 4lb under the more ideal conditions found in an alkaline chalk stream. The size of the river and the available food supply determine how big a brown trout is likely to grow. On a mountain stream a half-pounder might be classed as a specimen, while the catching of a chalk stream brown trout of five times this weight would not justify any great clamour. (If people were endowed with similar properties some of us would be over 30ft tall!) For me, the

17

point of river trouting is not really about how big the trout are, but how well I have done in relation to the norm for the fishery and the prevailing conditions.

Sea Trout

Young trout which yield to some primeval urge to leave the river and run away to sea, will return at a later date to spawn in the same or some other river. (Sea trout cannot match the legendary homing instinct of the salmon, which generally do return to spawn in the rivers of their birth.) It is these returning fish which we call sea trout. There are various regional names for the migratory strain of *Salmo trutta*. Peal (in the West of England), white trout (in Ireland) and sewin (in Wales), are just a few examples. Small sea trout are sometimes referred to as whitling or finnock; large sea trout at the fishmonger's shop as salmon-trout (the prefix is an unnecessary entice-ment for anyone who has enjoyed the delicate flavour and texture of a freshly caught spring sea trout).

Identification

Large sea trout are sometimes mistaken for salmon. To distinguish a sea trout:

1. The caudal fin (tail) of a salmon is usually forked, while that of a sea trout is more or less straight edged.

Fig 3   A sea trout from the River Conwy. The large spots which extend to below the lateral line are usually enough to identify a sea trout.

2. The upper jaw-bone of a salmon rarely extends behind the eye, while that of a sea trout does.
3. Both salmon and sea trout have between 120 and 130 scales along the lateral line, but in the salmon only ten to thirteen scales are behind the adipose fin (the small fleshy fin on the back of all salmonids between the dorsal and caudal fins) and the tail. Sea trout have between thirteen and sixteen such scales.
4. Salmon have fewer spots than sea trout, and rarely do they occur below the lateral line.

Although any single test may be inconclusive, in practice it is rarely difficult to distinguish the species. Sea trout, even the bright silver dream fish of early spring, have an overall different 'look' about them that is hard to describe. I can only hope that you get plenty of opportunities to learn from first-hand experience the difference between these two great sporting fish.

Life Cycle

In the British Isles, sea trout spawn from later October to the end of November, always provided the water level is high enough for them to run up into the brooks and head-waters. Usually under cover of darkness, the hen fish cut their redds in gravel beneath swiftly flowing water a foot or so in depth. Once fertilised by the cock fish (which may be a migratory *or a non-migratory* specimen of *Salmo trutta*), the eggs are covered and the adult fish quickly make their way back to sea – a factor which must contribute to the much higher survival rate of spawning sea trout compared with salmon.

Salmon kelts can remain in the river for weeks and even months, losing condition and risking fungal infection of fins damaged during upstream migration and spawning. A 5lb sea trout will have made three or more spawning runs; a salmon of the same weight will almost certainly be a first-year spawner, a grilse or maiden fish which has spent just one winter at sea. Sea trout have been known to spawn more than ten times. Very few salmon spawn more than twice, and the vast majority perish on their first return to the river.

After two to three years' feeding in the river, during which time they are not distinguishable from the non-migratory brown trout, the young sea trout lose their parr marks and turn bright silver. In late winter these 'smolts' run down to the sea where they feed in the rich estuarial and coastal waters. The proportion of young which become migratory varies from river to river, but generally it is higher in waters where food is scarce. The ratio of migratory females to males also varies across the regions, but it is not unusual to find twice as many females as males taking to sea feeding. Later the same year, many of these young fish, which migrated as smolts in the spring, return as 'whitling' weighing about half a pound. They run up river, and the larger of the whitling spawn with the mature sea trout. Thereafter, most sea trout spawn each year. In Wales, sea trout typically put on between one and two pounds of weight between spawnings. Fish of around fifteen pounds are taken most seasons on the rivers of Wales and the west of England. Many Scottish rivers and lochs are equally renowned for their sea trout fishing. In south-west Ireland, the sea trout are generally smaller, but there are some exceptional specimens which buck this trend.

Sea trout, like salmon, do not feed when first they enter the river. They can live on the energy stored as muscle (the part we eat). However, unlike the salmon, they can lose their resolve and certainly do feed in fresh water, most notably towards the end of the fishing season. After several weeks in the river, their flanks change from silver to a dull brown, and their spots begin to turn brown or even red. In fact, they look very much like a brown trout, for which they are sometimes mistaken. What is particularly important to the fly fisher is that *these sea trout behave very much like brown trout*, and they can be caught by the use of tactics generally associated with trout fishing.

Early in the season and again towards the close are times when you have the best chance of catching a really big sea trout. On many Welsh rivers the fish of March and April generally run between five and ten pounds in weight with the occasional specimen well above this size. These spring fish are far from plentiful, and are usually taken by anglers fishing for salmon. In many regions, June is considered the start of the 'serious' fly fishing for sea trout. Then the fish are plentiful, although the average size is reduced compared with the spring run. In September and October some rivers have a second run of large sea trout mixed with the shoals of whitling. These are not the bright silver fish of spring, but they can provide a spectacular close to the season.

Fig 4   A 2lb rainbow trout from the River Test. The tails of rainbow trout are covered in tiny black spots; these are rarely present on the tails of brown trout.

Rainbow Trout

Rainbow trout (*Salmo Gairdneri*), native to the Pacific basin, were imported to European rivers about the turn of the last century. They pose problems to the river keeper because of their tendency to run downstream in shoals. On rough streams liable to flooding it is doubtful whether stocking with this species can be justified. However, in suitable conditions rainbow trout grow much more quickly than brown trout and are less expensive to rear. They reach maturity earlier than our native trout and, although shorter lived, can attain similar weights. A 2lb wild fish is a very good one on any of the few British rivers in which rainbow trout breed successfully, but pond-reared fish can attain weights of 20lb or more with careful rearing. Rainbow trout have such distinctive colouring that it is difficult to imagine how they could be confused with brown trout, but one certain means of separating the species is by the tail fin. That of a rainbow trout carries numerous black spots, while the tail of a brown trout is without any spots.

THE FACTORS OF LIFE

Throughout its life in the river, a trout's behaviour is largely dictated by four factors. The first three are essential needs for survival and growth: oxygen, food, and safety from predators, and the fourth is its own laziness.

The requirement for a constant supply of oxygen means that trout must face upstream when resting in flowing water. Young trout need food frequently, and in small amounts. When necessary, larger fish can go for several days between meals, and quite often they will fast through the day, ignoring all offers of food until the sun has set. Nevertheless, it is considerations of food supply which ultimately dictate where in a river a trout will choose to lie. The best fish get the best lies, and, therefore, the most plentiful supply of food.

An important influence on the lifespan of a trout is the risk of predation. A shallow water lie, albeit in the path of a plentiful supply of food, may offer little protection against herons and other predators from above. These lies hold short-term tenants which do not grow large. The presence of a bolt-hole near to the food path makes a lie attractive and relatively safe; large trout often live in such inaccessible places.

Finally, the laziness factor! Trout do not enjoy battling against a strong current. Indeed, it is just as well, as they would not be able to sustain themselves. The amount of energy a trout takes in is the calorific value of its food *minus* the energy it uses up in holding station and in collecting the food. Trout grow more quickly in gently flowing water, and they seek out 'easy' lies whenever possible.

Awareness of these four factors will help you locate, approach and tempt the larger-than-average trout of a river or stream. And at least three of the factors are important when sea trout fishing. Sea trout have little need of food while they ascend the river. However, when they stop to rest, they take up lies which afford sufficient oxygen, security and a reprieve from the hard work of battling upstream against a heavy current. There are certain times when sea trout will feed on surface or sub-surface flies.

A TROUT'S SENSES

Trout have a full complement of senses: smell, taste, touch, hearing and sight, but they are not all well-developed. Trout also have the ability to remember their reactions to previous situations. They will dart away from a shadow cast upon the water, and will ignore certain types of flies if a more palatable alternative is available. This selective feeding is not uncommon. Indeed, were it so there would be little justification for the wide variety of artificial flies which anglers have devised over the centuries.

Hearing

A trout detects sound waves in the water by means of its ears, buried beneath the skin above and to the rear of its head, and of vibration-sensitive organs along the lateral line (the line of dots starting behind the gill covers and running back to the tail). Fortunately, when you talk on the river bank virtually all the sound energy is reflected at the surface, and the fish do not hear you. Not so, however, if you scrape and stamp your feet on the bank or the bed of the river. These vibrations are transmitted very efficiently into the water. Tumbling mountain streams or weir pools are noisy places where your own stumbling may be masked, but you will need to walk and wade more carefully on quiet pools and gentle glides. Likewise, gravel and rock beside a spate

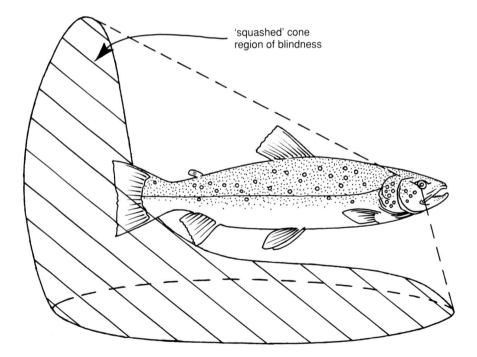

'squashed' cone region of blindness

Fig 5   A trout has a very wide angle of vision, with only a narrow region of blindness below and to the rear.

22

river will transmit vibrations through to the river bed rather better than will the soft boggy soil of a water meadow.

Taste and Smell

Many sea fish and some freshwater species – eels and pike, for example – have a sense of smell far more developed than that of the trout, and can detect the odour of an angler's bait at great range. Trout need to be much closer before they will respond to the same offering. There have been attempts to produce substances which, when applied to an artificial fly, will induce trout to take more readily. As far as I know, none of them really work, and I hope all such future attempts are equally unsuccessful, since fly fishing made easy would be both a travesty and a tragedy.

Sight

Crucial to its survival, the vision system of a trout is both sensitive and versatile. The only light available to the trout is that which penetrates from air to water; but, due to reflection at the surface, the water is a much darker environment than the air above it. Yet, in this dimly lit underwater world, both brown trout and sea trout are able to detect movement on the banks at considerable distances. After sea trout fishing, I often hear brown trout rising to take moths from the surface of a pool when it is so dark I have to use a torch to find my way safely along the bank.

Sea trout, which shun the bright light of day, emerge after dark and cruise around the pools. They can be tempted with an artificial fly on even the blackest of nights. I think it likely that sea trout rely on a combination of sight and hearing to locate the fly, initially by homing in on the vibrations caused as the fly swims through the water, and then by switching to sight as the range closes.

Trout have much wider angles of vision than we do. They have binocular vision both in front of, and above, their heads. They can see with one eye or the other in all directions save for an arc of about 30° behind and below them. Since they spend most of their time on or very near the bed of the river, the only area of vulnerability is that cone of blindness to the rear. River trout must fan their tails to hold station, and as a result the head rocks slightly from side to side. This further reduces the size of the blind spot.

The easiest way to approach a trout without being seen is from downstream, and how close you can get before giving the game away is a relatively simple calculation, provided that the trout remains stationary! Most of what we learn in angling is by experience, of course, but there is a logic to it. When light waves travel from air to water they slow down, and this causes the rays to bend or refract towards the vertical. The shallower the angle of incidence, the greater is the refraction. At the same time, more of the incident light is reflected at the surface until, at a grazing angle of around 10°, all of the light is reflected. To the trout, it appears that it is looking up at a circular window cut in a poorly reflecting mirror. In this window it sees a distorted image of things outside the water. Beyond this 'magic circle' all the trout can see at the surface is a dim reflection of objects on the river bed. To us, this would be a most

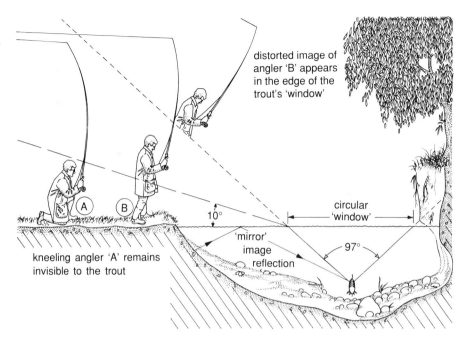

distorted image of angler 'B' appears in the edge of the trout's 'window'

circular 'window'

10°

97°

'mirror' image reflection

kneeling angler 'A' remains invisible to the trout

Fig 6   The trout's distorted view of the river bank through its circular window. Outside the window it sees a dimly lit reflection of the river bed.

confusing world, but trout get used to seeing things suddenly appear and disappear as they drift across the window. John Goddard and Brian Clarke have shown in their book, *The Trout and the Fly*, that a fly drifting towards a trout is seen first as a set of points of light where the legs of the insect distort the surface of the mirror. As the fly approaches the magic circle, first its upright wings become visible and then the body appears in the window. Surface turbulence due to conflicting currents or strong wind distort what the trout sees both by reflection in the mirror and by transmission through the window. The edge of the window becomes a moving pattern of fragments of mirror interlaced with fragments of transparent window. Breezy days make it much harder for the trout to see the angler *and vice-versa*.

How close must you cast a fly before a trout will see it? This all depends upon the diameter of the window, which, in turn, is determined by the depth of water in which the trout is lying. In shallow water your casting must be more accurate, but you will be able to approach a little closer than you could a fish lying in deeper water. All this assumes a flat surface, of course. If there is a ripple, then this will cause further distortion. Large objects seen through the edge of the circle will appear chopped up with the pieces constantly dancing about. When you fish a dry fly on the surface, your fly line and nylon leader will be less likely to startle the trout if there is a good surface ripple, but your fly may have to be cast nearer to the trout before it is seen. (In flowing water, this gives less time for the trout to inspect the fly for authenticity!)

TROUT RIVERS

Trout are amazingly versatile creatures. They cling tenaciously to life in tiny mountain torrents, survive the force of a mighty spate river in full flood, and thrive on the abundance of a graceful chalk stream. This says much about the quality of the water in these courses, for, despite the widely varying terrain through which they flow, they must all provide sufficient oxygen and minerals to support plant, insect and trout life.

Oxygen

Trout need well-oxygenated water. On many larger rivers, such as the Severn and the Thames, the upper reaches are the domain of the trout, while coarse fish, which can survive lower dissolved oxygen concentrations, populate the slower-flowing lowland stretches. Three variables dominate in determining the level of dissolved oxygen in running water. The first is turbulence. The surface ripple on windy days, the presence of waterfalls and rapids, all help water to absorb more oxygen. The second key factor is temperature. Although they become inactive, trout can survive for long periods in water close to freezing, but as the water warms up it gives off oxygen. As the temperature rises beyond 16 °C feeding activity declines, and around 20 °C brown trout become very distressed and soon die. Most other salmonids suffer a similar fate at or around 20 °C. A third, and possibly the most worrying, factor is the demand for oxygen from other substances and organisms in the water. Inadequately treated sewage places a high biological oxygen demand on any watercourse into which it is discharged. Certain industrial chemicals, agricultural sprays and seepage from silage pits kill fish and other water creatures, not necessarily because of their toxicity, but because of their oxidising properties. They combine with, and hence reduce the amount of, dissolved oxygen in the water.

Where the ability of a stream to support trout life is already marginal, many other factors – including the types of plants bordering or growing in the stream – influence the dissolved oxygen levels. A screen of deciduous trees planted on the southern side of the stream will provide shade in summer. Of course, to make a detectable difference to water temperature and dissolved oxygen level, such a planting scheme must be extended over several miles of river.

Acidity and Alkalinity

Trout prefer water which is slightly alkaline. They can tolerate moderately acid conditions, but neither they nor the creatures upon which they feed really thrive in acid water. Consequently, streams which run through peat bogs and pine forests (both major contributors to acidity) contain mainly small trout, whereas water flowing through chalk or limestone country is likely to hold trout of a much larger average size. Chalk streams, with their relatively high alkalinity (a Parts Hydrogen or pH measure of greater than 7), are more able to tolerate pollution in the form of acid rain. In contrast, many European hill streams, whose pH is naturally low, have suffered to the extent that they are now unable to support trout life in their upper reaches. The

River Towy, in South Wales, is one such example. In contrast its neighbour, the Teifi, runs through more fertile land and has not suffered to anything like the same extent.

ROUGH STREAMS AND SPATE RIVERS

The trout and sea trout waters accessible to the majority of fly fishers are rain-fed rivers. These waterways receive most of their water by means of run-off from the surrounding land. In the south-east of England the rain-fed rivers flow very slowly through flat terrain, and provide a habitat more suited to coarse fish than to trout. (Surprisingly, some of these drain-like rivers have sparse runs of sea trout to over twenty pounds.) Elsewhere in the British Isles, faster-flowing streams and spate rivers abound, and virtually all hold stocks of wild brown trout. All of those with free passage to the sea are also likely to have runs of sea trout.

These rain-fed rivers begin as tiny runnels and becks cascading down the hillsides before settling into a more gentle meander through lowland valleys and plains. The level of water in such a river, and hence also the strength of current (as well as its pH), vary greatly throughout the year. After periods of heavy and prolonged rain, rough streams may rage fiercely, bank-high with brown water. Some spate rivers frequently burst their banks, the larger rivers remaining unfishable for days or even weeks at a

Fig 7 The upper Towy, now too acidic for resident brown trout to thrive, is arguably Britain's premier sea trout river. Each year the River Towy yields several dozen fish above 10lb.

time. Fortunately, at such times fishing can usually be found on the smaller tributaries. In contrast, during a dry spell a stream may dwindle to barely a trickle between near-static pools.

A Welsh Spate River

Rising as a series of runnels draining a boggy catchment high in the Cambrian mountains, the River Teifi holds both resident brown trout and sea trout (or sewin as they are called in Wales). At its source, nearly 1500ft above sea level, the Teifi is dammed to form Llyn Teifi, one of a small group of lakes known as 'Teifi Pools'. On a fine day, these are wild and beautiful fisheries set in an awe-inspiring landscape. The pools hold small, brightly marked brown trout averaging around six ounces. They rise freely to the sparse fly-life (mainly terrestrial insects blown off-course by blustery winds). Via the dam, the river begins its descent through a series of narrow gulleys and boulder-strewn gorges through which the peat-stained water cascades in confusion. Falling 500ft in the first two miles, it is not surprising that there is little plant life in this part of the river except for lichen and mosses clinging to exposed boulders. There, tiny trout feed avidly on the most meagre of rations: a four-year-old fish may weigh no more than an ounce. Survival must be quite a struggle, but somehow in that rushing torrent the trout manage to find quiet pockets of water, little eddies amongst boulders or behind rocky outcrops, from whence they dart rapidly to intercept every passing morsel of food.

As the Teifi drops down to 400ft above sea level it becomes a steadier stream hurrying along between grassy banks. Much of these upper waters are not heavily wooded, and it is possible to fish the river without wading. The head-waters are slightly acid, since, near the town of Tregaron, they flow through a 2000-acre peat bog known as Gors Coch Glan Teifi – the red bog. Bends in the course of the river result in continual erosion as, over the centuries, the bed shifts like a slowly writhing snake. Aquatic weed, such as water crowfoot (*Ranunculus*), and a variety of marginal plants now harbour a greater abundance of insect life. From Tregaron down to Llandysul, the native trout reach an average of 8–10in at maturity but with the best fish topping 2lb.

By the time the Teifi has fallen to 250ft above sea level its nature has changed yet again. The valley has narrowed and, except after heavy rain, the river drifts lazily through long glides and deep pools linked by shorter runs of tumbling rapids. Soft bedrock has been eroded over the years to leave waterfalls cascading through narrow gorges – spectacular surroundings in which to fish. Salmon and sea trout must leap over these obstacles to reach their spawning grounds. On the middle Teifi, a wide range of aquatic insects feature increasingly in the diet of the trout. For the most part, however, hatches of flies are sparse and terrestrial insects remain important items of trout food. Weed growth, while rarely prolific on this type of river, is more plentiful in the middle reaches of the Teifi, where it provides shelter both for trout and for the insects upon which they feed.

For a river of this size (the Teifi carries more water to the sea in a year than the River Thames), the Teifi has a very short tidal region. The five-mile tidal stretch is

Fig 8   The dam at Llyn Teifi.

characterised by high reeds and mud flats at low water. Sea trout and salmon drift in and out with the tide, often running a mile or two up the river before returning to the estuary to wait their 'turn'. Here, particularly when the summer is a dry one, they suffer heavy predation by commercial seine nets.

Much of the fishing on the Teifi is controlled by angling associations. At the time of writing (1989), there are waiting lists for full membership of the main angling associations; but applicants rarely have to wait longer than twelve months. Day tickets are available on a few stretches, and holiday visitors can always gain access to association beats by purchasing weekly permits from local tackle shops.

Less than 100 years ago, sea trout were all but absent (only three were recorded in twenty years), and the Teifi was a famous salmon river. Today, stocks of salmon and sea trout fluctuate cyclically, one waxing as the other wanes. Some things never change, however. Writing in *The Salmon Rivers of England and Wales* in 1904, Augustus Grimble said of the River Teifi: 'Over-netting and poaching are the drawbacks to Teifi angling, and if these evils were mitigated then the Teifi would be one of the best salmon rivers.' Today, given a wet spring and summer, it outshines all other Welsh rivers; but in low water its light remains hidden under a monstrous bushel of nets.

CHALK STREAMS AND LIMESTONE RIVERS

Chalk deposits, the calcified remains of countless sea creatures which lived many millions of years ago, are extremely porous. When rain falls on chalk hills it is quickly

*Fig 9   Cenarth Falls on the River Teifi. The middle and lower reaches of this
spate river are characterised by narrow gorges and spectacular waterfalls.*

absorbed in the subterranean 'sponge' through which it gradually filters to emerge in
lowland streams. Although the majority of chalk streams are in the south of England,
there are spring-fed rivers in many parts of the world which flow through limestone.
Their waters have much in common with chalk streams: high pH, an abundance of
plant and animal life and a temperature which fluctuates little throughout the year.

An English Chalk Stream

It takes several months for rain falling high on the South Downs to emerge as spring
water entering the bed of the River Itchen. The near constant flow of this famous
chalk stream contrasts with the widely varying levels of a spate river. Beloved of that
great angling writer of yesteryear, G.E.M. Skues, the Itchen rises from the chalk of the
South Downs near the village of Cheriton, six miles east of Winchester. The source of
this splendid river is a mere 250ft above sea level. The flow is rapid and is continually
supplemented by fresh water entering along the river bed. As a result, the temperature
of the water rarely varies outside the range 6–10 °C. Within 200 yards of its source,
the Itchen is a swift stream with enough food to maintain a population of wild brown
trout. The water is alkaline and contains sufficient calcium for crustaceans, such as
crayfish, to thrive. Three miles from the source of the Itchen; is its confluence with

29

Fig 10   The River Alre, on the upper Itchen system.

the Alre, just below Old Alresford. Between this point and Eastleigh is some of the best river trout fishing to be found anywhere in the world.

Not surprisingly, it is rarely easy to obtain a rod (the right to fish) on the Itchen; the clubs and syndicates have no shortage of candidates for their waiting lists. It is usually easier to get a day on one of the many tributaries of the Itchen. Even these smaller chalk streams hold some mighty wild brown trout. Pressure of fishing means that pond-reared fish have to be imported to supplement the natural stock of this (and just about every other) chalk stream. On many stretches shoals of rainbow trout share an uncomfortable coexistence with the more solitary brown trout. Not all of the Itchen's brown trout are native to the river; many will have begun life in a trout farm.

The River Itchen falls 100ft in the first five miles, by which time it has reached Itchen Abbas and the famous Avington fishery. Further down, the gradient eases slightly, but at no point can this river be termed, 'a gently drifting stream'. The presence of submerged weeds – particularly water crowfoot but also huge beds of Canadian pondweed in places – results in upwelling currents which cause severe surface turbulence. This gives the chalk stream fly fisher perhaps his major problem – that of drag. An insect falling on to the surface is swept this way and that, entirely at the mercy of the surface currents. An artificial fly should ideally behave in the same way, but it cannot. Attached to a nylon leader which itself is lying on the surface of the water, the fly is constrained, and often cuts across the surface currents in an unnatural manner. Wise old trout are rightly suspicious of such things!

Weed growth is so prolific on the Itchen that if it were not controlled, the main

Fig 11   The River Itchen, near Botley, beloved of that great tactician, G.E.M. Skues.

channel of the river would be unable to carry the water. The surrounding meadows would then flood until eventually the river would carve a fresh channel. To avoid this problem, the weed is cut on particular dates through the growing season. Co-operation between landowners ensures that the disturbance of silt, and the inevitable abundance of floating weed trimmings (which make fly fishing all but impossible) are restricted to just a few days during the season.

The biggest threat to this great fishery must surely be pollution, aggravated by excessive borehole abstraction and the consequent reduction in water flow. The Itchen, like its sister river, the Test, is vulnerable to agricultural, and particularly fish farm, pollution. The clarity of water in these great chalk streams, while still excellent by spate river standards, is not what it used to be, and a remedy has yet to be found.

Most of the fisheries on the Itchen are very well tended. Many of the trees have been pollarded to provide shade throughout the day. There are foot-bridges over feeder streams and the banks are trimmed regularly to within 2 yards of the water's edge, giving the fly fisher every chance of a clear back cast. Wading is not necessary and on most beats it is forbidden, since bank damage and weed disturbance would inevitably result.

All this might make it sound as if catching trout on a chalk stream is simplicity itself. Far from it! The clarity of the water, the strength of the current and the ever-present surface drag problems are but some of the contributors to the challenge of chalk stream fly fishing. Further obstacles to success are the superabundance of natural food and the intense pressure of fishing. Chalk stream trout can become both discerning and very wary. Why should they bother to go out of their way for a poorly cast artificial fly when with far less effort they can browse contentedly on the real thing?

The Itchen is a much shorter river than the Teifi, in fact little more than 20 miles in total, and the volume of water it carries to the sea each year is very much less. However, during most of the fly fishing season these two rivers are of similar water flow. But what contrasting fishing they offer! Not surprisingly, they require quite different approaches for best results with the artificial fly, and in later chapters we will consider tactics best suited to the trout and sea trout of these contrasting environments.

2

Insects and Other Food of River Trout

It was going to be another blank, and I had only myself to blame. Trout had risen sporadically throughout the afternoon, and I had missed a couple of good chances. Then, as the sun dipped over the horizon, a most amazing evening rise had developed. Trout were now rising upstream and down as far as I could see. Not just a few fish, but dozens, and there were some big trout amongst them. There was only one problem: they wouldn't take my artificial fly.

When this happens the sensible thing to do is to watch the surface, to see what flies hatch from or fall on to the surface. I had done that. There were midges, upwinged flies, sedge flies and several terrestrial insects borne on the gentle evening breeze. I watched an upwinged olive fly as it drifted towards me. It fluttered its wings, rested a few seconds and fluttered again before getting airborne. The trout resolutely ignored it, although I could not be sure they were as clement towards all others of its kin. A daddy-long-legs struggled and died, trapped in the surface film. No trout came to put it out of its misery. No wonder my artificial daddy-long-legs was treated with disdain.

I had started with a Greenwell's Glory, a pattern which rarely lets me down on rough stream or chalk. Within an hour I had worked my way through half the patterns in my fly box. In desperation, I had even tried a weighted nymph, but with little optimism, as I could see that the trout were feeding at the surface. Soon it would be too dark to see to tie on another fly. The feast would be over and the only rises would be to the occasional sedge fly returning to lay her eggs. Many of the sedges are nocturnal creatures. They hatch in the evening, and return to lay their eggs after dark, when anglers and trout are tucked up in their respective beds.

That was it! Emerging sedge pupae. Of course! The sedge flies I had seen were not returning to the river to lay their eggs; they were newly hatched insects. In that case the trout must be taking them from just under the surface, before breaking through the surface film. I tied on my only remaining sedge pupa and suffice it to say that, before I lost it in a hawthorn bush that crept up on me unnoticed, it transformed my catch from a humiliating blank into a brace of fine wild brown trout topping 3lb in total.

THE OMNIVOROUS TROUT

There can be few creatures more catholic in their tastes than a hungry trout; and most trout would seem to be hungry most of the time. When food is scarce, they will try to eat anything that moves, and quite a lot that doesn't. Sticks, stones and even coins have been found inside trout being prepared for the table. On the other hand, trout soon learn what they prefer, and given a choice of menu with adequate quantities, they can feed very selectively at times.

Trout find most of their food *below* the surface of the water. Aquatic mites, worms, beetles, snails, crustacea, small fish, and the larvae and nymphs of insects which live in the river bed and amongst submerged weeds make up the core of their diet. In addition, they will readily accept terrestrial flies, caterpillars and a multitude of other creatures which fall or are blown onto the surface of the stream. As a fly fisher, you must try to imitate the appearance and behaviour of these various food forms with what, euphemistically, we call artificial 'flies'.

The parr of salmon and sea trout are (from a sporting point of view) of no interest to fly fishers. It appears, however, that the young of the migratory salmonids enjoy very similar diets to the adult resident trout, and this poses us with quite a problem. We wish to avoid catching parr when fishing for adult fish. Selective fishing is more about knowing *where* to fish than choosing the right flies. However, to catch trout which are feeding on a specific type of fly you may have to imitate the insects hatching at the time.

It would seem logical to discuss the main species of flies chronologically, as they hatch through the year. Unfortunately, this is not really practicable. For one thing, hatches of some species occur at widely differing times depending on the river and from year to year. Secondly, there are several flies which hatch early in the season and then reappear later as the water temperature falls again. For these reasons I have chosen to group the flies into their biological categories or 'orders', with an additional section for the 'bits and pieces' which do not really fit anywhere in particular. My list is far from complete, but includes a selection of flies which are usually to be seen on chalk and rough streams through the season.

THE UPWINGED FLIES (EPHEMEROPTERA)

Perhaps the best known of the angler's flies, upwinged flies are the dayflies, or mayflies as they are sometimes loosely termed. (In this book I reserve the name Mayfly for just two species of very large flies.) The upwinged flies are important in spring on all lowland streams, and are of paramount importance to the chalk stream fly fisher. The order includes minute species such as *caenis*. This is a pale fly little more than an eighth of an inch long and not too affectionately known as the Angler's Curse. This is because it is beyond most fly dressers to tie a representation small enough to pass muster under the scrutiny of the ultimate judge (the trout!). At the other extreme is *ephemera danica*, the Mayfly, which can have a body length in excess of an inch.

An upwinged fly begins its life on the bed of a stream, as an egg from which a tiny

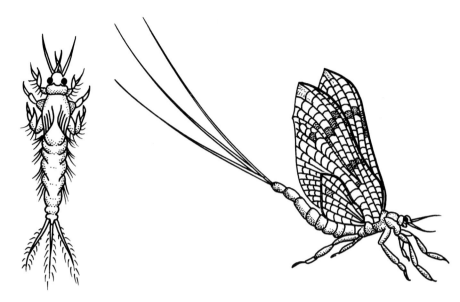

*Fig 12   Mayfly (*Ephemera danica*) and its nymph.*

nymph hatches. Some species of nymphs are slow crawling insects, burrowing in the silt or hiding in dense weed. Another group is able to brave the elements by holding fast to stones on the river bed even in the swiftest of currents. Others are quite strong swimmers, able to move freely in the water throughout the period of their nymphal development. When nymph fishing, we can imitate not only the form of these insects but also their behaviour, ranging from the 'slow crawlers' to the 'agile darters'.

After about a year the nymph ascends to the surface where the outer skin splits and a winged fly – a sub-imago, or dun – emerges. The duns of most species need to rest briefly on the surface of the water before their wings dry and become strong enough for them to fly off. At this stage they are particularly vulnerable to predation by eager trout, who may take either the rising nymphs or the hatching duns. It is important to be able to discern which of these forms the trout are, in fact, taking, as imitating the other would result in lost sport.

After resting for several hours on vegetation near to the river, the flies undergo yet another metamorphosis. The dun sheds a layer of skin, and the insect which emerges is an iridescent imago, or spinner. During this final moulting, the forelegs and the tails grow noticeably longer. Gone are the dull wings and drab colouring of the dun. Shining like a star, its wings reflecting the evening sunlight, this is the mature adult, ready to fulfil its final role as procreator.

Mating is generally accomplished while airborne. The male ephemerids die soon after mating. Of more interest to us are the females, which return to the water to lay their eggs. Several species crawl down plant stalks to deposit eggs, attaching them to plants or stones. Some fly upstream, hovering above the water to drop their eggs like bombs. Others dip down to the water, placing their eggs delicately onto the surface

Fig 13   Nymphs of upwinged flies have three tails, like this Ecdyonurus *nymph found clinging to a stone on a hill stream. Many, like the species pictured here, retain only two tails when they hatch into the winged form.*

Fig 14   A Blue Winged Olive spinner about to shed the last of its sub-imago shuck.

film to be swept by the current to their final resting place amongst bank-side weeds. (Presumably, any species which habitually flew downstream have long since become extinct, or are now acclimatised to salt water conditions!) The adult flies live just a day or two. Hence the name, from the Greek 'ephemeros' – living for one day. The nymphal form thus represents over 99 per cent of their lifetime, and it is not surprising that nymphs constitute a large proportion of the diet of trout. The colour of nymphs does not vary anything like as much as that of the adult flies – particularly the spinners – and it is usually sufficient just to copy the general size and shape (and of course the behaviour) of a particular nymph in order to deceive the trout consistently. Remember, though, that nymphs are a developing insect, and they are smaller and paler in colour when young. Most of the time, it is the nymph near to or entering the sub-imago stage that you will choose to imitate.

Of the adult flies, you will be interested in both male and female duns, and of the spinners, more particularly in the female. In most cases it is quite difficult to distinguish between male and female duns, and extremely unlikely that the trout do so. In certain species spinners differ quite markedly between the sexes, and in these cases it is normally the female which is imitated by artificial flies. Below are described some of the more important species of the upwinged flies.

March Brown (*Rithrogena germanica*)

One of the early season flies, the March Brown, is not found on all rivers and streams, but it is widely distributed in the north of England and also quite common in Wales. The patterns I use to imitate the March Brown are called by the same name. I fish the March Brown Spider as both a nymph and a wet fly (to represent an emerging dun) in sizes 14 to 16.

Large Dark Olive (*Baetis rhodani*)

A fly not put off by the chilly winds of March and April is the evening-hatching Large Dark Olive. The nymph is a dark brown agile darter, and is well represented by a Pheasant Tail. The duns hatch in early spring and again as autumn approaches. I find a size 14 Greenwell's Glory imitates both the dun and the spinner very well.

Iron Blue (*Baetis niger, B. muticus*)

Yet another fly which is not put off by a cold blow, the Iron Blue, has much wider distribution than the March Brown, with closely related species appearing on both chalk streams and spate rivers. It is a small fly with unmistakable inky blue wings. No fly box should be without a few Iron Blue Duns, for they hatch from late spring through summer and into autumn. A Red Spinner, in sizes 14 and 16, imitates the imago quite effectively.

Medium Olive (*Baetis tenax, B. buceratus, B. vernus*)

A fly for late spring (May and June), the Medium Olive hatches at various times through the day, often in heavy rain. Once again, Greenwell's Glory is a superb pattern with which to match the dun. A size 14 Lunn's Particular is a good imitation of the spinner of this olive (and the spinners of several other related species).

Pale Watery (*Baetis fuscatus*)

A summer through to autumn fly hatching from mid-afternoon onwards, the Pale Watery is a particularly important fly on the chalk streams. The Ginger Quill is reputed to be the only close representation for the dun of this fly. I do not think many trout are aware of this, as several other olive patterns seem to work reasonably well on both spate rivers and chalk streams. It is a small fly, so sizes 14 and 16 can be worth a try.

Mayfly (*Ephemera danica, E. vulgata*)

The Mayfly is by far the largest upwinged fly seen on rivers in the British Isles. The main hatch occurs from mid-May to the second or third week in June, although it can

Fig 15   The Mayfly is much larger than other upwinged flies, and large trout which ignore olive duns and spinners will often exert themselves to rise during a Mayfly hatch.

be up to two weeks later than that if the weather remains wintry. On some rain-fed rivers I have seen a second sparse hatch towards the end of summer. The greedrake or dun has a cream abdomen with brown markings. The large veined wings act like ships' sails as the duns turn in the wind, drifting downstream before making their maiden flights. At this time, they are at the mercy of the trout, and even large canibal trout have been known to change their eating habits to try a few Mayflies just once a year.

At the beginning of the hatch I have most success imitating the emerging nymph. The Mayfly nymph is one of the very few for which I would bother to use a specific representation – Richard Walker's Mayfly Nymph. There are also several patterns which represent the dun, and my preference is for a hackled fly without wings. I get just as many rises to the hackled version but am able to hook a higher proportion than when I use a winged fly. For the dead spinner (often called a 'spent gnat') I do recommend using a winged fly, since, with the Mayfly lying dead on the water, the wings must be clearly visible to a trout from whatever direction it approaches the fly. Another reason for choosing a closer imitation at this stage is that the rise to a spent fly is usually a more leisurely affair – the fly will not escape. And, since falls of spinners during the Mayfly 'carnival' are quite prolific, there are more than enough to go round so there is no need for the trout to fight over their food.

Because these are such large flies, it would not be unreasonable to represent them by an imitation on a size 6 hook. I find the trout more responsive, however, if my artificial fly is rather smaller than the real thing, so I tie my Mayflies on size 10 hooks.

Blue Winged Olive (*Ephemerella ignita*)

From June onwards this is a very important fly on just about every river in the British Isles. The duns hatch in the afternoon. Blue Winged Olive duns and spinners are so

Fig 16   A male spinner of the Blue Winged Olive. The forelegs and tails are much longer than those of the dun.

eagerly sought by trout that it is well worth finding an imitation that closely matches the flies on your particular rivers. Both at my home in West Wales and also on the chalk streams of Hampshire, I use the Sherry Spinner; but my choice of duns differs between the two waters. I use Gold Ribbed Hare's Ear (GRHE) on the River Test, but prefer a darker and more buoyant Blue Winged Olive Dun on the Teifi. All these flies are tied on size 14 hooks.

Angler's Curse (*Caenis*)

This little fly usually hatches early in the evening, and it is one I do not try to copy. Instead, when trout are taking *Caenis* to the exclusion of all else, I offer them something really shocking, like a daddy-long-legs. If that doesn't work I go home and read a book!

Yellow May Dun (*Heptagenia sulphurea*)

I mention these beautiful evening flies simply because I have wasted many a summer evening trying to tempt trout with imitations of the Yellow May Dun. My efforts have met with little success, or perhaps it was success, for, in his *Waterside Guide*, John Goddard suggests that trout rarely take this fly.

Regional Variations

I have listed just a few of the more common upwinged flies, but there may be others of greater importance on the rivers you will fish. I have noticed that most olive duns are lighter in colour when first they hatch, and that rough stream flies are often darker than flies of the same species which hatch on chalk streams. Careful observation should help you select patterns which more accurately match the natural flies on your river, and this can only improve your chances of success.

General Representations of Upwinged Flies

Unless the fish are being particularly selective I am quite happy to fish a general representation of all of these flies. For the duns I know of no more effective a pattern than Greenwell's Glory. I use this fly extensively on rough stream and chalk, and sizes 12 to 16 are always in my fly box. For the olive spinners, a good general-purpose fly is the Sherry Spinner, which most closely matches the Blue Winged Olive and is a reasonable imitation of the other olives. It is an excellent taker of trout on the fast rivers of Devon, where sizes 14 and 16 are my preference. I like these flies dressed with two or even three turns of best-quality pale ginger cock's hackle, as this helps to keep them floating high.

THE STONE-FLIES (PLECOPTERA)

Stone-flies thrive in clean, well-oxygenated water. They occur in chalk streams and also in upland rough streams, but are seldom found in muddy or slow-moving rivers. Their geographical distribution is patchy, but where they do occur there are often vast numbers of them, and in such rivers they are an important part of the diet of trout.

The life cycle of stone-flies is similar in most respects to that of the upwinged flies. There is no sub-imago form, but – as if to make up for this oversight – the nymphs themselves moult many times during their development. Adult stone-flies live for a few weeks. The males have tiny wings and spend most of their time crawling amongst stones and weeds on the river bank. The females fly around the meadows in a haphazard fashion, often getting blown onto the water in breezy weather. Mating takes place on vegetation rather than in flight, and the females get their eggs into the water by the various methods described for the upwinged flies.

Stone-Fly Nymphs

All stone-fly nymphs have two tails and two long antennae at the head. When the adult fly emerges, the tails are lost in several species, but the antennae are always retained. Some of the nymphs – for example, the nymph of the Yellow Sally, which in the adult has flat wings and retains its tails – are ideally equipped for clinging to

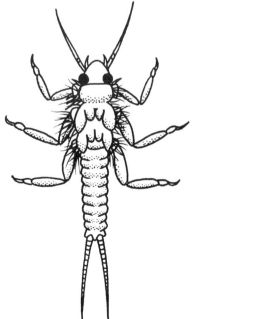
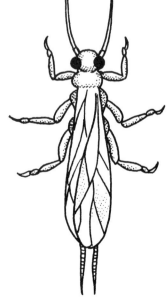

Fig 17   A stone-fly and its nymph.

stones in fast currents. Their bodies are flattened in the vertical direction and the legs are strong, enabling them to hold securely to rocks or weeds in mountain streams. Other species bury themselves beneath the stones and gravel of the river bed, from where trout extract them by turning over stones with their noses.

Adult Stone-Flies

One group of stone-flies, which includes the needle fly and the willow fly, wrap their wings closely along their thin bodies and look rather like miniature cigars. Others, such as the February Red and the Large Stone-fly, lay their wings flat along the top of their bodies.

Yellow Sally (*Isoperla grammatica*)

Unlike most stone-flies, which emerge in autumn and winter, the Yellow Sally and its relative, the Small Yellow Sally (*Chloroperla torrentia*), are spring and summer flies. Imitate these with Taff Price's Yellow Sally pattern in sizes 12 to 16.

General Representations of Stone-Flies

Most species of stone-flies are brown, have thin needle-like bodies and wings of brown with a tinge of grey. Trout appear to feed on them unselectively, and so specific imitation (apart from the two yellow flies mentioned above) is unnecessary. Traditional general representations of stone-flies include the 'spider' patterns such as the Partridge and Orange and the Black and Peacock Spider. I use each of these patterns tied in a range of sizes from 10 to 16. Finally, to the stone-fly imitator *par excellence*, the Grey Duster. A heavily hackled size 14 will skate across the surface in an autumn breeze and trout will chase and slash at it as confidently as they do at the real thing.

SEDGE FLIES (TRICHOPTERA)

I think of sedge flies as the 'sweet course' of the trout's menu. Although there is considerable variety amongst the dozen or so sedges of interest to river fly fishers, trout take them so avidly that once a sedge hatch begins, almost any pattern of artificial sedge fly seems to do the trick.

The sedge or caddis flies include an extra stage in their development. The eggs hatch as larvae which live in the river for a year – sometimes two – prior to a second metamorphosis which produces the pupae. The pupal stage usually lasts about two weeks and the insect is at its most vulnerable as it ascends to the surface in preparation for emerging as an adult fly. When they get the opportunity, trout will eat the larvae, the emerging pupae and the adult caddis flies.

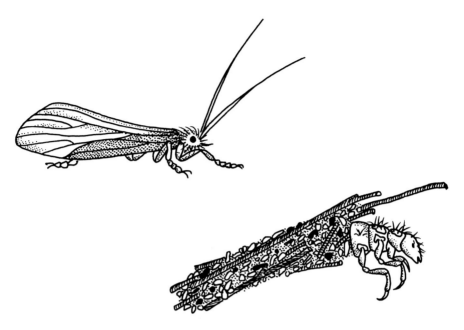

Fig 18   A sedge fly and its nymph. The majority of sedge fly larvae construct shelters from sticks, stones and leaves collected from the bed of the stream.

Sedge Larvae

Many sedge larvae (caddis grubs, as they are sometimes known), make shelters from bits of reeds, sticks and small pebbles. They crawl along the river bed complete with their camouflaged homes, and it is only their movement which gives them away. Trout are quite prepared to eat the grubs complete with their cases. Artificial flies have been devised to imitate the free-crawling and the encased types of larvae. The best sedge nymph imitation I have come across was devised by Tom Chapman, when he was head bailiff at the Peckham's Copse fishery in West Sussex. Tom produced several variations of his Green Nymph using an olive seal fur body. The secret, as with all nymphing, is in the way this fly is fished. It should be allowed to sink on to the bed of a slow-moving pool, before being inched along very slowly. A trout may follow the nymph for some time before deciding to snap at it.

Sedge Pupae

Once fully grown, the larvae seal themselves into their cases and the pupae begin to take form. Body, antennae and wings gradually develop, all folded within the pupal case, while the legs grow outside the shuck. When ready to hatch, some species swim ashore while others hatch at the surface. At this stage they are vulnerable to predation, and can be readily imitated. A good pattern is Richard Walker's Longhorn Pupa.

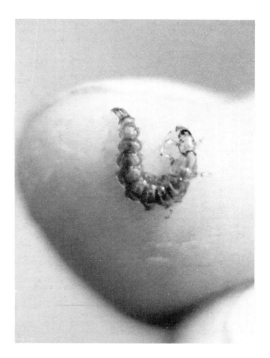

Fig 19 A free-crawling caddis or sedge larva. This one will hatch into a Sandfly (Rhyacophila dorsalis).

Adult Sedge Flies

I have yet to find a river which has a head of trout and does not have hatches of sedge flies. Several species – generally the smaller varieties, such as the Grannom, which emerges in spring – can be seen around rivers throughout the day. The majority of large sedge flies are nocturnal, however, emerging as the light fades and continuing their weak, fluttering flights across and into the river long after dark.

At dusk, it can be difficult to differentiate between the sedges and the many nocturnal moths whose flight and airborne appearance are quite similar. At rest, however, sedge flies are quite distinctive, with their very long antennae, no noticeable tails, and wings which cover the body like the pitched roof of a house. Wing coloration varies from a dull silver or cinnamon gold through all the browns and to a dark reddish. The body is generally a little darker than the wings.

A workable selection of sedge fly imitations would include the Grannom, Cinnamon Sedge, and Silver Sedge patterns. The latter accounts for more than 60 per cent of my chalk stream brown trout taken during the evening rise. The Silver Sedge is a pleasant fly to fish since it remains visible at reasonable range when viewed against the dark surface of water overhung by trees. Another excellent pattern, which I use to imitate the Sandfly and the various light brown and red sedge flies, is the orange G and H Sedge. This fly is tied with deer hair whose hollow fibres provide extra buoyancy in the rough and tumble of a hill stream. Apart from the Grannom and the Silver Sedge, for which size 14 is large enough, the other patterns can be tied on hooks as large as size 10.

FLAT-WINGED FLIES (DIPTERA) AND VARIOUS TERRESTRIALS

There are several thousand species of Diptera in Britain and they are characterised by possessing only one pair of wings. (Some of the upwinged flies have such tiny rear wings that they are invisible except under microscopic inspection, so they may also appear to have just one pair of wings.)

Hawthorn Fly (*Bibio marci*)

This large black fly is a welcome visitor on lowland rivers. Hatching in late April and early May around mid-morning, huge swarms of these flies can be seen struggling against the breeze with their long legs dangling like helicopter winch wires. Any large black pattern with heavy hackles will take fish during a fall of hawthorn flies, but some close copies have been devised and are not difficult to tie.

Midges (Chironomids), Reed Smuts (*Simulium*) and Black Gnats (*Bibio*)

In this group are several species of aquatic and land-based flies which we generally call buzzers, smuts and gnats. Their larvae are equally diverse and include the bright red 'bloodworms'. When trout are feeding on these tiny insects (the term 'smutting' has been coined to describe the act of sipping large quantities of reed smuts or similar small flies from the surface) imitative fly fishing is very difficult. Hatching midges can be imitated with a range of patterns based on the Blagdon Buzzer. For the adult flies try a Black Gnat tied on a size 18 hook – even smaller if you have the eyesight to manage it!

Crane-flies (*Tipulae*)

The daddy-long-legs family is a large one, with over 300 species known in Britain. Only a few of these are truly aquatic, but all are poor fliers, at least in windy conditions, and drop in regularly for supper on the river. The larvae of the crane-flies are well known to gardeners as the 'leather jackets', but it is the adult fly which interests the trout fly fisher. Not perhaps the easiest of flies to tie, the distinctive long thin wings and trailing legs are copied to near perfection by some expert fly dressers, and when these flies are on the water the imitations are readily accepted by even the most discerning of trout.

It is often said that the daddy-long-legs is an autumn fly. Certainly the larger varieties are plentiful at that time, but I have found crane-flies in the meadows below my cottage during every month of the year. On windy days these flies will find their way into the trout's pantry, and are well worth imitating from May onwards. It is the smaller versions, tied on size 12 or 14 hooks, which catch best during the summer.

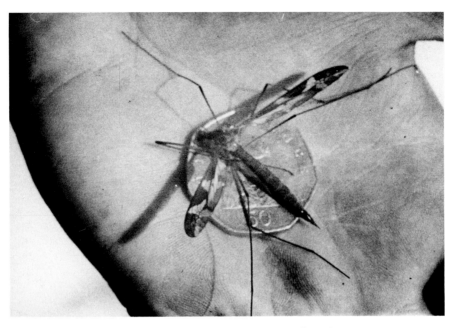

Fig 20   The distinctive long thin wings and trailing legs of the crane-fly can be copied to near perfection.

Damselflies (*Zygoptera*) and Dragon-flies (*Odonata*)

What a picture the damselflies make as they dart to and fro amongst the reeds, the sunlight glinting on their iridescent blue, green or brown wings and abdomens. And yet, in my experience, they are generally poor insects to copy for river trout fishing. Dragon-flies, in particular, are rarely seen on the surface of the water, and I have watched a spent damselfly drift 50 yards through a pool of rising trout without one of them poking a nose at it. Paired flies can be seen sweeping across the water, the female with her abdomen bent double to accept fertilisation by the male. Thereafter, the females (and occasionally both partners, still in the tandem position), fly low across the water, depositing eggs on to the surface.

Some species of damselflies lay their eggs underwater, the females crawling down reed stalks to deposit their eggs on submerged aquatic plants. On their return to the surface, they must wait a few moments for their wings to dry. Then, as they prepare for take-off, they often flutter on the surface like the dun of an olive, and I have occasionally seen trout take them at this stage. On a warm summer afternoon when very few flies can be seen hatching, I have met with a little success fishing an imitation damselfly twitched on the surface beside reed beds.

Fig 21   Turn over a stone in any fertile stream and you should find signs of life. Snails, freshwater shrimps, bloodworms and nymphs of caddis and stone-flies were found on this piece of slate from a Welsh mountain stream.

OTHER FORMS OF TROUT FOOD

Trout readily accept creatures with more than six legs. This is fortunate, since the hackles of imitation flies must create the equivalent of several dozen legs! Caterpillars, especially the furry types, are very easy to copy, and so are spiders. Beetles are not so easy, but reasonably successful patterns have been devised – the Coch-y-Bonddhu is one such example. Shrimps inhabit most fast-flowing alkaline rivers and streams. Their colouring varies considerably, from a translucent cream or orange to very dark brown. They crawl slowly among the gravel and weed, but are capable of amazing bursts of speed, swimming on their sides. There are many excellent patterns for imitating this crustacean, and on some streams there is no better way to tempt a trout from a deep lie.

Finally, we should not forget that trout are not averse to eating other small fishes – even their own young. Many of the wet flies – lures of the flashy type such as the Teal, Silver and Blue, Silver Doctor and Alexandra – are meant to represent various types of fry. More obviously acting as fish imitators are the streamer flies, ghost and tube flies which have become popular in recent years for sea trout fishing.

Part of the pleasure of fly fishing is the imitation of nature. It is important to use a fly which, to the trout at least, looks like food. Much more important, however – indeed, the essence of tactical fly fishing – is the reinforcement of this illusion by control of the behaviour of the artificial fly.

3

Tackling Up

No waxed cotton coat, no waistcoat with twenty pockets, not even a salmon fly in his hat, but there he was ahead of me, on the stretch of Devon hill stream I had set my mind on fishing. In grubby old jacket and patched wellies, fly fishing was clearly his intention. I stood there, dismayed, as he untied a battered cane rod from the crossbar of his 'sit-up-and-beg'. He was obviously one of the youngsters, up from the village (three miles, but he'd have had a hard pull, up hill all the way).

But what about that rod! Its cork handle sported more holes than the 'twenties' section of a competition darts board – the result, I had no doubt, of securing flies the lazy way. The top joint had a set which, in another limb, could have got a doctor struck off the register for gross incompetence; the spiggot joint was so worn that he had to pack it with not one but two blades of grass. In no time at all he had threaded a line through the rings and was tying on a small dark fly. Curiosity got the better of me and I ambled across.

'What fly?' I enquired. I could see, now, he was no youngster – middle-aged, more like. He didn't look up, but shook his head vaguely.

'Dunno. Fair copy o' these midges, though. Try one!' He thrust a tiny black and white fly into my hand. It didn't look like anything in particular, but local knowledge should always be welcomed, so I thanked him, adding, 'What do they eat when they can't get humans?' It was plagiarism, of course but good enough to stand re-cycling. The urchin paused with a knot half completed. His brow furrowed and he looked straight at me. He was older than I had thought, much older, probably nearer seventy than the seventeen I had credited him with at first sight. His wrinkled leathery face beamed.

'Tolkien?'

I nodded, and he finished the knot. 'These things are no problem, son, once you get going.' And with that he got going, off across the stream, hopping from one boulder to another until, with the sun on his right shoulder, throwing a long evening shadow on to the far bank, he began fishing. The tired old cane rod flicked gently back and forth, the motion smooth and flowing, seemingly effortless. Periodically, the fly would alight on a tiny patch of relative calm, searching some eddy or swirl between the cascades of white water. He needed no more than ten minutes to cover the 30 yards that took him round a bend and out of my sight. In that time he had hooked and brought to hand half a dozen yellow-bellied trout which he quickly released to rejoin their brethren. And all the while I could hear his chuckles of delight, so full was he of the joys of fly fishing.

I soon lost the little black and white fly, but I will always cherish the memory, and the lesson he gave me: what matters most about your tackle is how you use it.

A MATTER OF PRIORITY

The most important parts of a fly-fishing outfit are those nearest to the fish. The reel and the rod are of secondary importance, so I see no reason for following tradition and discussing them first. Let's start at the business end.

FLIES

Be very careful if you buy cheap flies – they are often badly tied from inferior materials and on poor-quality hooks. Even if you tie your own flies, it will pay you to check each hook for temper before dressing a fly on it. Place the hook in the vice and, with your thumb-nail, try to bend the point away from the hook shank. If the point breaks off at the barb, or if the bend unfolds and does not return when you release the pressure, reject the hook. Professional fly dressers know that their reputations depend upon the quality of their flies. They use good-quality hooks and tying materials. Mass-produced flies, the majority of which are imported, are very variable in these respects. Some are excellent, and good value for money, but many are very poor and fall apart.

Winter is the time when many fly fishers get down to stocking their tackle boxes with flies for the coming season, but for those not into fly tying, here is a small 'starter' selection, obtainable at most tackle shops. Alternatively, you could place an order with a fly tying professional.

Name	Type	Hook Sizes
Mallard and Claret	wet fly	12, 14
Butcher	wet fly	10, 12
Sherry Spinner	dry fly	14, 16
Black Gnat	dry fly	16, 18
Greenwell's Glory	dry fly	14, 16
Mayfly	dry fly	10
G and H Sedge	dry fly	12
Daddy-Long-Legs	dry fly	8, 10
Pheasant Tail	nymph	14, 16
Mayfly Nymph	nymph	10

Even with this small selection, and assuming you settle for just a couple of each type and size, that is still quite some investment. An economy list, with which I would be happy to fish the season, would be the Mallard and Claret and the Butcher wet flies, the Greenwell and the Sedge dry flies, and the Pheasant Tail nymph. In later chapters I will recommend some other trout and sea trout flies for particular situations. The tying details for all the patterns mentioned are contained in Appendix I.

Storing Flies

The most important features of a fly box are that it should allow the flies to dry out quickly and should then keep them secure and dry until next required. If flies are

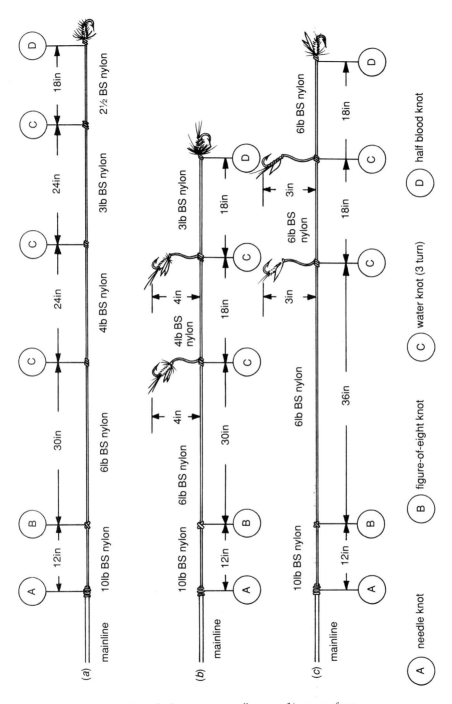

Fig 22   Leader design: (a) dry fly for trout on a small stream; (b) a team of wet flies for spring river trouting; (c) a team of wet flies for summer sea trout.

stored wet, the hooks are likely to rust and the fur, threads and feathers to rot. Dry flies need to be stored so that they keep their three-dimensional shape, and the special boxes with individual hinged compartments are ideal, although rather expensive, for this purpose. For wet flies and nymphs, boxes with metal clips are available at little cost, and these generally contain ventilation holes to help speed up the drying process. Boxes with plastic foam inserts are suitable for both dry flies and wet flies.

LEADERS

The leader, or cast as it used to be known, is the nylon connection between the main line and the fly itself. A properly constructed leader helps transfer power from the line to the fly so that you achieve delicate presentation. The leader has to be long enough to keep your fly line well out of sight of the trout, and it should be fine enough not to frighten the fish as it alights on the water. Usually, this means that your leader must be at least as long as your rod, but there are times when we can get away with less, and others when a leader of twice the rod's length improves results. (Casting with a very long leader is difficult, and certainly not recommended for beginners.)

That part of your leader where it joins the main line must be thick to transmit power smoothly from the fly line. The nylon to which you attach your fly should be very fine and, ideally, invisible to the fish. So the leader must taper down, either gradually or in discrete sections. The ultimate is a factory-made continuously tapering leader, onto which a short length of fine nylon, called the 'point', is attached. If you get your fly stuck in a tree, the leader should break at its weakest link, the point.

There is another reason for using tapered leaders. When fishing the dry fly you will want your imitation to alight gently upon the surface. If it splashes down heavily, followed by a bundle of tangled nylon, no self-respecting trout will give it further consideration. Your leader must, therefore, straighten out just before the fly touches the surface of the water, and the taper helps ensure that this happens. Most river fly fishers make up their own leaders and carry spare nylon to replace the point as required. To make your own stepped taper leaders you will need spools of supple nylon in ratings of 6, 4, 3 and 2lb breaking strain.

Leader Knots

To attach leaders repeatedly to a fly line would cause damage to the end of the line. Instead attach a foot or two of 10lb nylon permanently to the fly line and tie a loop onto the nylon for joining your leaders. Where two or more wet flies are to be used, 'droppers' are required on the leader. Suitable knots for these joints, and for attaching your flies, are shown in Fig 24. Once you have formed a knot, wet the nylon before pulling it tight. This ensures that the individual turns bed down fully without melting under the heat of friction.

Some of the cheaper brands of nylon are far too springy for use as leader material. Not only do they have a 'memory' of the radius of their spool, tending to lie in coils on the water, but they may also display marked variations in knot strength. Nylon is

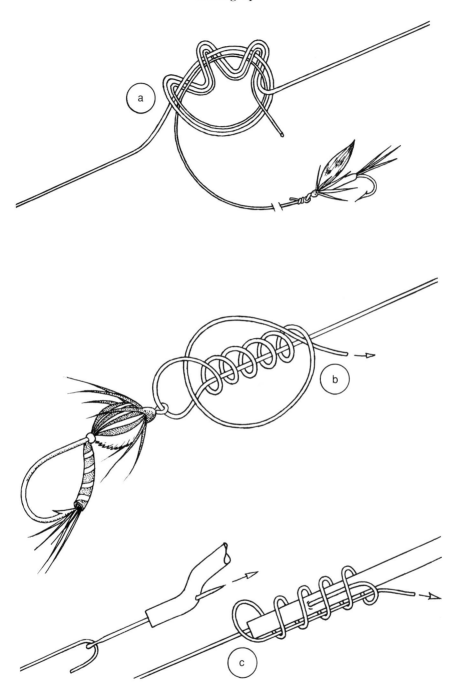

Fig 23   Knots for leader and fly connections: (a) water knot for joining lengths of nylon and for forming droppers; (b) tucked blood knot for attaching flies; (c) needle knot for joining leader to main line and main line to backing.

relatively inexpensive and it pays to go for good quality. Be wary of cut-price offers on bulk spools. Unless clearly marked with a quality brand name, they are likely to be very poor material and will detract significantly from the pleasure of fishing.

LINES

Most modern fly lines have a braided dacron core around which there is a flexible plastic coating. By varying the density of the plastic, the lines can be made to float or sink at varying speeds. The floaters are coded F and the sinkers S. Intermediate lines (coded I) have almost neutral buoyancy, and drift through the surface very slowly. They have most of the characterstics of a floating line plus the advantage of minimal surface wake when they are retrieved through the water. Lines with high-density plastic over a few yards at one end are called 'sink-tip' lines, and are coded F/S. I use floating lines for most of my river fishing.

The profile of the line affects its casting characteristics. Level lines are very cheap to produce, but, as it is impossible to cast a fly delicately with such a line, they are rarely used in river fishing. The double-taper line (coded DT) provides for delicate fly presentation and is ideal for fishing the dry fly. Weight-forward lines have a shorter belly followed by a long running line. They are better suited to casting on larger rivers. With care, a dry fly can still be presented well using a weight-forward line. Finally, the shooting-taper (ST) or shooting-head line is used when fishing a wet fly at very great distances. There are occasions when you may want to use a shooting head

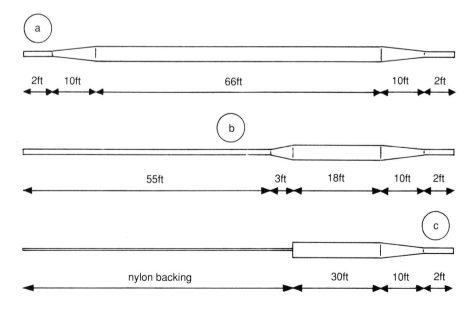

Fig 24   Popular fly line profiles: (a) double-taper; (b) weight-forward; (c) shooting head.

on large spate rivers, but for the present we will concentrate on more conventional river lines – the DT and WF types. So, the overall coding system must include both density and profile information.

Many river anglers have a preference for double-taper lines. For accuracy and delicacy of presentation at moderate range they are unbeatable. However, a weight-forward line allows the beginner to cast a greater distance when his timing and action are less than perfect. It also casts reasonably well with just a short length of line out of the rod tip. More importantly, the weight-forwards line flows well through the rod rings when you use the 'double haul' (a casting technique which will be discussed in detail in Chapter 4). With practice, a weight-forward line enables you to turn your fly over at long range with the wind against you.

Finally, to the weight of the line. The American Fishing Tackle Manufacturers Association has produced specifications for the weights of fly lines, so that a number 5 line, for example, will have the same weight over the first ten yards of the body of the line (*see* Fig 25) irrespective of the brand name. Larger numbers indicate a heavier line, with which a more powerful rod can cast a heavier fly over greater distances. For trout and sea trout fishing, lines in the range 4 to 8 are normally used. So, for instance, a weight-forward floating fly line of AFTM rating number 6 would be coded WF6F.

Line Quality

Modern plastic-coated lines do not rely on surface tension to stay afloat; they are less dense than water. This is achieved by the incorporation into the plastic coating of numerous tiny air bubbles. It is difficult to control the manufacturing process to prevent the air bubbles drifting out to the surface of the plastic coating, and cheap floating lines often have a rough surface finish. The effect is that the line does not slide easily through the rod rings, and in a very short time can cause damage to the rings. I would have nothing at all to do with cheap floating lines. If you need to economise, it would be better to do so when looking for a sinking line, but do check any such purchase thoroughly for any flaws in the plastic coating.

Trout will be alarmed by a fly line – whatever its colour – if it splashes anywhere near them. To be successful, you must cast your fly in such a way that the line stays well away from the trout. So, for a floating line you can safely choose a light colour that you can see easily at dusk. (White is ideal.) Sinking lines are thinner than floaters of the same rating and, therefore, make less splash if cast correctly. Nevertheless, they can disturb fish below the surface, and I opt for sinkers of a dark colour to provide some sort of camouflage against the background of the river bed.

Backing

Before winding your line on to the reel, pad out the spindle with 10 yards of wool and then attach at least 50 yards of backing line. This is a monofilament or braided synthetic fibre. It further increases the spindle diameter and also provides extra line length should a fish make a particularly long and powerful run. On the few occasions when the backing is taken out by a strong fish you will want to be confident that the

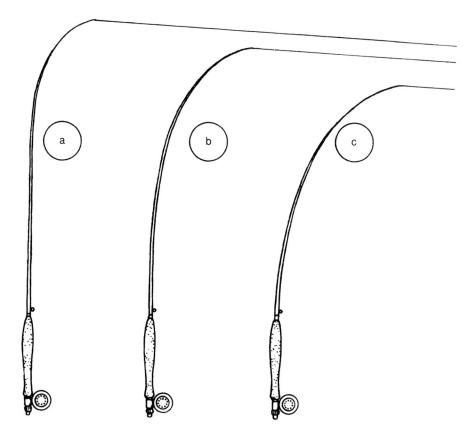

Fig 25 Rod actions: (a) a tip- or fast-action; (b) a medium- or middle-and-top-action; (c) a through or slow action. A middle-and-top-action is a good compromise between the needs of casting and fishing.

joint between main line and backing is secure and can flow freely through the rod rings.

RODS

A fly-fishing rod is a multi-purpose tool. The choice of a rod is inevitably a compromise, and it must fall somewhere between rods best suited to casting, to hooking a fish, and to playing and landing a fish. Each of these factors is further complicated by the need to consider the size and nature of the river, and of the fish you expect to catch. A 6ft brook rod well-suited to casting for ¼lb trout on a hill stream would be poor equipment for tackling sea trout on the River Dovey, for example.

For ease of casting, particularly in windy conditions, a rod which is stiff, flexing only at the tip, would be the preferred choice. A very stiff rod allows you to set the hook very quickly, but when using a fine nylon leader the risk of it snapping during the strike is a serious one. A softer rod, which flexes through both the middle and tip regions, would be superior in this respect. Finally, when playing a fish which leaps or makes surging runs towards an obstruction, you need to apply controlled pressure. A very soft rod, which flexes from tip to butt, absorbs shocks well, and allows you to apply a larger average level of tension to turn a running fish.

So what is the ideal fishing rod? I suggest that you compromise in favour of safe fishing, and use rods of softer action which reduce the chance of a leader breakage resulting in a trout being left with a fly in its jaws. A satisfactory compromise, then, for river and stream fishing is the middle and top action. Several manufacturers produce carbon or graphite rods to this specification. Built cane rods, which are somewhat heavier and generally more expensive than carbon rods, have a natural tendency towards soft action, and a 6–7ft built-cane rod can be the heart of an ideal brook fishing outfit.

As an indication of the weight of fly line they are capable of casting, modern rods are marked with their AFTM rating. A rod marked AFTM5 is designed to be fully loaded, and hence to cast best, with 10 yards of AFTM5 fly line extended beyond the rod tip. A shorter length of heavier line would give the same loading, and a longer length of lighter line could achieve the same purpose, of course. Thus, if you use a double-taper line, you have the opportunity of varying line length. Most manufacturers now show the recommended range of lines by marking their rods with more than one AFTM number. For example, AFTM4–6 would indicate that the rod would be fully loaded by 10 yards of AFTM6 line extended beyond the rod tip. You could obtain the same loading, and hence line speed, with 12 yards of AFTM5 line or about 14 yards of AFTM4 line. So a beginner should always use a line of the highest rating marked on the rod. Indeed, rarely in river and stream fishing would I choose any other, unless I anticipated the need for long-distance casting, when the lower line rating would allow me to aerialise more line. All this assumes you are using a double-taper line. The situation is more straightforward if you use a weight-forward line. Remember, the weight-forward line has most of its weight in the thick belly of the first 10 yards or so. This is followed by a thin running line. So in our example, extending 14 yards of an AFTM4 weight-forward line beyond the rod tip would not achieve the full loading of the AFTM–6 rod. Indeed, you would be likely to damage the running line after a short period, because it only has a thin plastic covering.

Whenever possible, try out a sample rod, with its matching line, before buying, to make sure you can cope with it. Many people buy rods which are too powerful for them. This 'try before you buy' suggestion may not seem particularly helpful if you are new to fly fishing, but you might be able to get an experienced fly fisher of similar build to yourself to come along and help you. Most mail-order tackle firms will put together a set of matching tackle (rod, reel and line) to your specification, and they have expert staff who really do understand such matters as 'rod action' and AFTM ratings. Not all small tackle shops can provide this sort of expert guidance, (the proprietor may be a sea or coarse angler, for example), so it pays to ask a few questions before spending money on a fly rod.

Fig 26 Modern fly reels (bottom row) are available in either plastic or alloy construction. They owe much to the design of early brass reels (pictured above).

REELS

Simplicity and reliability are the main requirements of reels. They come in various sizes to suit the line rating. It is usually the width of the spool which the manufacturer varies to produce lightweight, regular and king-size reels of a given pattern. A spare spool is very useful as this will enable you to change quickly from one type of line to another. For small stream fishing a centre-pin reel with a simple drag mechanism or ratchet (to prevent tangles when line is pulled from the spool) will do nicely. On larger rivers you may appreciate the advantages of a multiplying fly reel, particularly when trying to gather in line quickly in order to follow a running sea trout. On the heavier rods normally used for sea trouting, the extra two ounces in weight is no disadvantage. (It may lessen the apparent weight of the rod in your hand when fishing, since it brings the centre of balance nearer to the wrist.)

LANDING NETS

Much of my river trouting is done without a net, but some river banks are so high that it would impossible to lift out or release a fish by hand. When sea trout fishing, a landing net is just about essential, as lifting out a sea trout by hand can be difficult in daylight, and much more so in the dark. Rigid frame nets are simple and inexpensive, but large ones can be more awkward to carry. On 'wilderness fisheries', folding nets can get tangled and refuse to unfold at the crucial moment. On balance, I prefer fixed frame nets, especially when fishing for sea trout in the dark.

EYE PROTECTION

Even an experienced caster can misjudge the effects of the wind on his line. To hear a fly clatter against the lens of your glasses is proof for life that wearing eye protection when fly fishing makes very good sense. I usually wear polarised spectacles which help reduce the effects of reflections from the surface and allow you to see more of what is happening on the river bed.

ESSENTIAL ACCESSORIES

These are few and not costly, and they can all be fitted into your pockets:

1. A tin of leader grease, such as Mucilin. Apply this to all but the last 9in of the leader to help it stay afloat when fishing the dry fly.
2. Fly floatant. Various sprays and dips are available. I prefer the small bottles of light oil because, apart from the concern about the effects of aerosols on the ozone layer, you can see how much is left in a dip and avoid running short of floatant during a day's fishing.
3. Leader sinkant, or simply a wad of soft felt soaked in washing-up liquid. Use it to remove grease from the leader when fishing wet fly.
4. Small, blunt-nosed scissors. Attach these via twine to a ring on your jacket or waistcoat.
5. A priest, or weighted cosh, to kill any trout you decide to keep. Hold the trout (while still in the landing net if you use one) with one hand and strike it sharply above the eyes with the priest.

CLOTHING

Warm woolly socks and wellies (without holes!) are essential. Waders are not a necessity if you intend to fish chalk streams (where wading is often prohibited), but they do help keep legs warm and dry on wet and windy days. For spate river fishing, waders are extremely useful, as they help you get into position to cover fish which you would otherwise not be able to. For small stream fishing, thigh waders are all you will need, but on larger spate rivers a pair of chest waders would be worth the extra investment if you intend fishing for sea trout and salmon.

Apart from the quality of materials, waders differ in the design of the sole of the boot. For general use, those with metal studs inserted into rubber soles are very good. They provide reasonable grip on rocky river beds and are sufficiently flexible to avoid

Fig 27   Everything you need for small-stream fishing can be fitted into the pockets of a waistcoat except for your rod and, if required, a landing net.

undue discomfort when walking across meadows. (Do not walk any distance along made up roads wearing studded waders or you will very quickly spoil them.) Other designs have cleated rubber, crepe or rope soles, all of which allow you to wade with less likelihood of fish being disturbed by the noise of your boots scraping on the river bed. None of these materials is ideal for gripping and it is all too easy to lose your foothold on the kindest of river beds when your attention is on the fishing.

Chest waders allow you to fish from deeper water, but remember that your weight on the river bed will be gradually reduced, and it becomes increasingly more difficult to hold position in a strong current as the depth increases. I would advise non-swimmers not to fish in water where chest waders are required. Another sensible rule is not to wade if the water is so coloured that you cannot see the river bed.

Fishing waistcoats and waxed cotton jackets are good long-term investments. They are designed with numerous pockets, pouches, rings and other fittings to help you keep scissors, priest, landing net, etc. secure and ready to hand. In warm weather I fit everything I need into the pockets of my waistcoat, carrying just my rod and, if the size of my quarry justifies it, a landing net slung behind me. In spring and autumn, I manage to pack all I need into the pockets of my waxed coat. Spare rods and reels have to be left in the boot of the car, of course, but I like the freedom of not having to carry a bag, which I am quite liable to put down and leave behind on the river bank.

MATCHING THE TACKLE

No single outfit can be ideally suited to all requirements but, like very other sport, you have to start somewhere. Your quarry and its river environment dictate the weight of line and the size and power of rod you will need. Below are described two outfits

Fig 28   A modern built-cane Martindales brook rod. At short range, cane rods can present a fly accurately and with great delicacy.

which between them should suit most of your river fishing needs. You will probably start with just one of these, chosen according to the waters available to you.

Small Stream Outfit

My idea of the perfect brook and small stream outfit is lightweight and extremely portable. Everything should fit into waistcoat or jacket pockets except the rod itself. Tackling up for small stream fishing is the least expensive way of getting started as a fly fisher, but I should say at the outset that it is a style of fishing which does not suit all temperaments. If you prefer wide open spaces where you can cast with ease, or if you are unable to scramble over rough ground, amongst boulders and through bushes, then do not rush out and buy the outfit described below. It is for the loner, the explorer, the wilderness fly fisher.

Rod   7ft long, middle and top action, AFTM4–5 carbon or built cane.

Line   Double-taper AFTM5 floating line.

Reel   Simple lightweight trout fly reel for AFTM5 line plus 50 yards of backing.

Leader   8ft long, stepped from 10lb to a 5lb, 3lb or 2lb point according to size of trout anticipated.

Flies   A small selection of dry flies and nymphs in a pocket-sized floating fly box.

Priest   Essential if fish are to be taken for the table.

Net   Rarely required, but a small fixed frame net on an elastic cord is preferable to the folding frame type which tends to get caught in brambles and refuses to open when required.

Spate River Outfit

If you are likely to fish extensively on powerful spate rivers then you would not thank me for setting you up with the tackle outlined above. A longer rod matched to a slightly heavier line will make it easier for you to cover the distances you may sometimes need to cast, although it is surprising how often you can catch good fish within a few yards of where you are standing if you have not already 'put them down'. With this tackle you will also be equipped for the windy conditions which can prevail in more exposed situations.

Rod   9½–10½ft long, middle and top action, AFTM6–7 carbon.

Reel   Single action or (my preference) multiplying regular trout reel for AFTM7 line plus 100 yards of backing.

Line   AFTM7 weight-forward floating line (white, moon-glow or ivory). Optional AFTM7 sink-tip or medium sinker on spare spool.

Leader   10ft of level 10lb nylon for spring and autumn (high water) sea trout. 10ft of level 6lb nylon for summer sea trout. Stepped taper leaders with 2lb, 3lb or 5lb point strength to suit size of trout anticipated.

Flies   A pocket-sized box of dry flies and a second box containing wet flies for trout and sea trout. Keep these small boxes topped up from a 'master store' kept at home or in the boot of the car.

This outfit would cope with both trout and sea trout and would give you more than a fighting chance of beating the occasional salmon under all but the most adverse of conditions. If salmon from large spate rivers are your main interest then a more substantial rod (and a different book!) will be required.

4

The Gentle Art of Casting

It was a losing battle! Try as I would, I could not get my fly to turn over properly in the gusting east wind. Not surprisingly, the trout resolutely ignored a fly which drifted downstream perched upon a nest of curled-up nylon. On this unseasonably cool July morning, very few fish were rising on the tiny lowland rough stream, and I could little afford to make a clumsy cast; today I seemed unable to make any other. I knew this to be the most productive stretch of the beat. I also knew I would have to give it best. My casting simply was not up to it!

I decided to try the 'dog-leg', a gentle 's' bend where I might just find a rising trout and some shelter from the malevolence of the wind. On arrival, things looked encouraging. Hard against the high east bank a neb broke the surface. It was no steady riser, but I watched it take a couple of olive duns as they skated slowly in the lea of the bank. Fortunately I had a clear back cast, so at a range of some 15 yards covering the fish would be easy. Or so I thought! My first attempt landed amongst weeds on the shingle beach, disturbing nothing but a pair of damselflies which sped off upstream. In half a dozen attempts, using a variety of casting methods, I failed to get my fly within 2 yards of my target. The judge's decision: not near enough!

The wind swirling across the high bank was causing turbulence, and although my line went where I wanted it to, the fly just would not *follow. A really slamming cast would have put the fly down in the desired spot; it would have put the trout down, too. This was my last chance, as the sun would soon be too high for serious fishing with the dry fly. I sat and pondered.*

Finally, it dawned on me; the answer was simple. I used a slanting cast, neither overhead nor horizontal, to power my line and leader upstream and across so that they bounced off the vertical face of the high bank. As gently as thistle down, the fly settled on the surface just inches from the edge. Up came the trout, a beautiful quarter-pounder, and the deception was complete. I was delighted, and a bigger fish could hardly have added to the sense of achievement. As so often on river and stream, this was no textbook technique, but a hybrid – a concoction to suit a particular situation. Textbooks and professional tuition can help develop the basic skills – the tools of the trade – but the gentle art of casting a fly on the river is all about how *these tools are used.*

VERSATILITY IS THE KEY

If you have taken up fly fishing recently, or your experience is limited to fishing on lakes or reservoirs with relatively clear banks, then many of the casting techniques described below may be new to you. They are all useful when fishing rivers and streams. Indeed, as you gain the confidence to fish in confined spaces you will further adapt your casting to suit various situations. Often this means departing from 'text book' techniques and improvising to cover fish which have taken up particularly awkward lies.

If possible, get a qualified instructor to help you get started. Professionals qualified via the National Angling Council, the Welsh Salmon and Trout Association or the Association of Professional Game Angling Instructors have to pass stringent tests both on their own technique and their ability to pass on their knowledge and skills to others. At my own fly-fishing school we make extensive use of video cameras and slow-motion play-back to help beginners develop the basic skills of casting, and the self-taught to identify and iron out their problems.

It is easier to start right than to correct faults which have become habits. Unfortunately, some people cannot get away for a few days at a time to attend a course of instruction. They may not find it easy to attend a casting clinic even for a couple of

Fig 29   A casting clinic at West Wales School of Fly Fishing.

Fig 30 Alternative grips on the rod butt.

hours. I have, therefore, included here a description of how to make some of the casts which are most useful in river fishing. With a note that the descriptions in this chapter assume a *right-handed* angler, you might like to set up your tackle and try some of the methods described below.

Always practise on a lawn or meadow. Never cast a fly line onto an abrasive surface such as concrete. In place of the fly, tie on a small tuft of wool. Strip off about 8 yards of line from the rod tip and lay it out in front of you. Pick up the rod in the right hand with your thumb along the top of the butt. If, after half an hour's casting, you find this grip uncomfortable, try the alternative methods shown in Fig 30. Some anglers prefer to place the forefinger along the line of the rod, instead of the thumb, while others find it more comfortable to hold the rod in the 'V' formed between thumb and forefinger. Choose the method which affords you a secure grip without any discomfort.

Tuck the butt close in beneath your wrist and position your feet comfortably. For greatest accuracy your right foot should be forward of the left, so that you can aim in the required direction more easily. When distance casting, you may find it easier to keep your balance with your left foot leading. For now, choose the option you find most comfortable, but remember that you may have to use either stance at the river (and a great many others), according to the positions of boulders or other obstructions under foot.

THE OVERHEAD CAST

You are now ready to make your first cast. Keep your left hand comfortably by your side, holding the line to prevent more being pulled from the reel as you cast. Start with the rod tip close to the ground. Keeping your right arm and the rod in a straight line, raise the rod slowly at first and then progressively increase the speed from the 10 o'clock position until the butt is vertical. Stop the backward motion at this point and the line will be projected backwards.

As the line straightens out, let the butt break away just an inch or two from your wrist, allowing the rod to drift back to the 1 o'clock position. This is the moment to begin your forward push. Again, make it a smooth, progressive movement. (You *must* avoid snatching.) Accelerate the forward motion until the butt is in the 11 o'clock position, at which point push forward sharply to straighten your wrist, bringing the rod in line with your casting forearm. The rod should now be at the 10 o'clock position where it will straighten, giving up its stored energy. This will further accelerate the line in the forward direction. Your fly line should follow the rod, straightening out in front of you. Finally, as the line falls to the surface, smoothly lower your rod to the horizontal to 'follow through'.

If you have timed your push correctly, the line will land nice and straight in front of you, and the piece of wool should drift down gently at the end of an extended leader. If, after a few attempts at the overhead cast, you are not getting good results, check for one or more of the following mistakes:

1. Using too little effort on the back cast.
2. Using far too much effort and snatching on the forward cast. Once the rod has been 'loaded' (like a spring under compression) on the back flick, all you need do on the forward push is to determine the direction and height at which the line travels.
3. Letting the rod go well beyond the vertical behind you, in which case the line will either hit the ground or will be projected skywards on the forward push to fall all around you in an untidy heap.
4. Pushing the rod too far down in front of you, which causes the line to slam down heavily without properly extending the leader.
5. Not waiting until the line has straightened out behind you. As you cast longer distances, you will have to allow more time before commencing the forward push.
6. Allowing the left hand to follow the rod, thereby losing much of the stored energy. If you find you have this tendency then put your left hand – holding the line, of course – into a pocket, and keep it there while casting.

It helps to have an observer point out the faults in your casting. If you have access to a video recorder and camera then you can be your own critic, analysing your faults on the playback before trying to rectify them. To show how it should be done there are some excellent video films available, illustrating a range of casting techniques.

'Shooting' Line

Gradually extend the amount of line out of the rod tip in order to increase your casting distance. The pause before changing direction will have to be increased as you lengthen the line (just as the period of a pendulum increases with its length). There will come a point, however, probably at between 15 and 20 yards, where any further increase in line length results in disaster. You will have overloaded the rod and will be unable to achieve sufficient line speed to aerialise the line, which will collapse about your ears in an untidy mess. Once you have exceeded the casting potential of the rod, you will have to shorten the line and begin again. Do not wind in this extra line. Instead, leave it coiled loosely beside you on the ground and cast once more. This time, open your left hand to release the coils just as the line is about to straighten out in front of you. If the line is travelling fast enough it will pull on the coils of spare line causing them to 'shoot' through the rod rings, extending your casting distance.

Long-Distance Casting

The distance a stone can be thrown is determined mainly by four factors: the weight of the stone, its shape (which governs the wind resistance), the angle at which it is launched and the speed at which the stone leaves the hand. The same applies when casting a fly line. Heavier tackle (higher AFTMA rating) can be cast further than light tackle, provided that you have the strength to load the spring of the rod fully. But for maximum distance you must also get those other factors right.

Fig 31   The overhead cast: (a) Peel the line smoothly from the water to minimise disturbance, accelerating smoothly to push the line high above any obstructions.

(c) A smooth forward acceleration to 11 o'clock and rapid closing of the gap between wrist and forearm will send the fly across the water so that the line straightens out a foot or two above the surface.

(b) Pause at the vertical (12 o'clock) position, allowing the wrist to break slightly and the rod to drift to 1 o'clock as the line straightens out behind.

(d) Allow the rod to drift down with the line to follow through ready for fishing.

Fig 32   European casting champion, Hywel Morgan, demonstrates the properties of built-cane, glass-fibre and carbon-fibre rods. The slow action of the cane rod casts a wide loop, while the faster carbon rod casts a tighter loop which suffers less drag as it travels through the air.

As the line travels through the air, you will notice that it forms a loop, the front face of which suffers considerable drag as it cuts through the atmosphere. Weather conditions must, therefore, influence casting distance. A far more important factor is the diameter of the loop. A wide loop gives a great deal of air resistance, while a narrow loop gives far less. To cast a narrow loop, you must apply the power as the rod moves through a small arc around the vertical.

A soft, through-action rod has to be moved through a relatively wide arc in order to load it fully, whereas a fast, tip-action rod can be fully stressed by rapid acceleration through a narrow arc. For this reason, distance casting rods are usually quite long and are of fast action. River fishing is not a casting tournament, of course, and in practice the middle-and-top-action rods recommended in Chapter 3 are, for most purposes, a satisfactory compromise between the ultimate casting tool and the ideal equipment for hooking and playing a fish. Whatever rod you use, the loop size will vary according to your casting technique, with rapid acceleration through a relatively narrow arc giving better results when you reach for distance.

Try to achieve a launch angle of about 45° and, at the same time, to maximise the speed of the line on the final launch forward. As you try for increased distance, you will reach a point where putting more effort into the forward push gives little or no benefit: the rod has reached its limiting velocity and, for the weight of line involved, no further increase in line speed is achievable.

False Casting

Once you are getting reasonable results try keeping the fly line in the air instead of letting it fall to the surface at the end of your forward push. To do this bring the rod forward to the 10 o'clock position and then, instead of following through on the forward push, simply repeat the back flick and keep the line moving backwards and forwards above your head. This is known as 'false casting'. When applied with a very short length of line beyond the rod tip, vigorous false casting is a simple and effective way to dry a fly which has become waterlogged.

False casting has another quite essential role – it enables you gradually to extend the amount of line you cast with. To do this, pull off a foot or so of line from the reel at the beginning of each back-push and let it flow through the fingers of your left hand as the line travels forward. Continue false casting and extending line until you have sufficient to reach the distance you require. With practice you will soon feel the line shooting out under power from the rod. Should you release the line at the wrong moment you will waste most of the rod's stored energy and the line will fall in a heap.

Timing is the essence of good casting, and in due course you will acquire a feel for when the tackle is working properly. Practice and yet more practice are the means to perfecting your technique. Do not worry about distance – that will come all too easily once you have mastered the basics. In any case, river fishing rarely requires a cast of more than 12 yards, and you will very quickly reach that standard. Within your first season you will probably be able to cast up to 15 yards with the lightweight outfit described in Chapter 3, and nearer 20 yards with the longer rod. Do not worry if you achieve somewhat less than this, as accuracy and delicacy in presenting the fly are much more important. If you want to become a really accurate caster, practise aiming towards a target such as a dinner plate. When you can land your fly on the target 50 per cent of the time on a calm day, from a distance of 10 yards, you are a fine technician of the art.

It is advisable – especially if you are using the heavier of the two outfits described in Chapter 3 – to limit your practice sessions to no more than an hour or so at a time at first. Beginners invariably try to make up for inexperience by putting extra effort into their casting, and this can put quite a strain on shoulder muscles, which are quick to complain. Once you have mastered the basics of casting you will be able to fish for many hours without even noticing a twinge. It is all a matter of timing, not power.

THE DOUBLE HAUL

There is a way of increasing line speed beyond the speed of the rod tip, and this involves using the left hand to further accelerate the line at the peak velocity points on both back and forward casts. Not only does the double haul provide greater distance, but it can also increase casting accuracy at short range, since it enables you to use a narrower loop to cut sharply through the air in windy conditions. When casting in a confined space, this technique allows a tighter loop and hence access to lies which would otherwise be unfishable.

Double hauling demands co-ordination. For each forward and back cycle of the rod, the left hand must make two complete cycles of movement towards and away from the bottom rod ring, so that your hands are at maximum separation when the rod is at its fully forward position *and* at its fully back position. The peak line speed is thus the sum of the speeds of the rod tip *and* the left hand.

Make a few false casts using the ordinary overhead technique before introducing the double haul action. The most important haul is that made to launch the line on its way to the target, so at this point you should power forward with the rod and pull down line with your left hand. At the end of the haul, open your left hand to allow line to shoot. If you time the haul and the final release correctly, you should be able to shoot several yards of line.

THE SIDE-CAST

Similar to the overhead cast, but with the rod moving more nearly in a horizontal plane, the side-cast is useful when fishing beneath a canopy of trees. It is a means of casting a fly deep under a bush where a trout may be feeding on terrestrial casualties blown in by the wind. There is another important advantage of side casting – with the rod moving just above the surface of the water, it is possible to keep it out of the trout's window of vision.

The principle is essentially the same as for the overhead cast, except that the rod travels almost horizontally. A little extra power and a slight upward lift will be needed on the back cast to clear bank-side weeds, especially when fishing from a river bank well endowed with thistles and the like.

Accurate casting is more difficult to achieve with this technique. Best control of direction is obtained by limiting the angle through which the rod swings so that the line forms a tight loop on the back cast and the fly is less likely to swing to one side or the other before alighting on the water. Watch your line as carefully during the back cast as the forward cast, since the tunnel through which the line must travel may be very narrow.

There will be times when you will want to cast your fly 'round a corner', and the side cast can be used to achieve this effect. To do this you will need to swing the rod through an exaggerated arc, pulling back line slightly with your left hand just before the leader touches down. When you get the timing spot on, the fly will be flicked round to the left in a 'shepherd's crook' form. In practice, accurate casting via this technique is far from easy, but on occasions it can be the means of covering an otherwise unreachable fish.

THE CATAPULT CAST

Through a dense tangle of reeds and branches, you spy a large trout, rising steadily just yards from your bank. You need only get your fly on the water and you *know* it will take it, as long as you keep well back, out of sight. You need a catapult, not a fly rod! Hold the fly in one hand on a very short line, perhaps with little more than the leader projecting from the rod top. Pull back (as with a bow and arrow) so that the spring of the rod is well loaded. Aim towards the required spot on the water and release the fly, which will shoot forward. A fast action rod gives greatest accuracy, but in any case the distance is limited to twice the length of your rod, so you should be able to place your fly close enough to tempt your quarry. One of my very best fish, a six-pounder, fell to this ploy, taking right under the rod tip. Only use this technique if you can see a way of manoeuvring the fish into clear water with enough room for playing and landing.

THE ROLL CAST

Where the only snag-free space is above the water you can put out a line of several rods' length by rolling it across the surface. This technique is ideally suited to wet-fly fishing on rivers whose banks are heavily wooded, but it can also be modified for upstream work with dry fly or for shallow water nymphing.

Assuming you are on the right bank and fishing the wet fly downstream, wait until

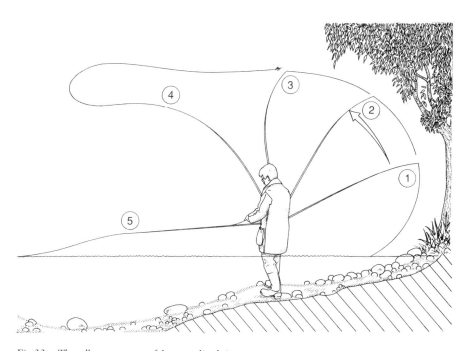

Fig 33   The roll cast – very useful on tree-lined rivers.

the line has come round to the 'dangle'. Steadily lift the rod upstream and then back to the 1 o'clock position. Hold the rod still for a second with the line making a gentle curve down to the surface. Now push the rod down sharply towards the surface of the stream. (This is one technique where plenty of brute force *is* an advantage.) The line should roll out neatly across the water.

You will find that a double-taper floating line works very well when roll casting, although a weight-forward line can be effective over short distances. It is all but impossible to roll out a sinking line any distance with normal trout tackle, so don't even try, or you could end up with a broken rod.

The upstream roll is almost as easy to master. Start by flicking a short length of line upstream. Then strip more line from the reel and, as your fly drifts back towards you, simply roll it forward again in the way I have just described. At first, you may need two or three of these false roll casts to work out a 10-yard line, but you should aim to develop this technique to the point where you can put out all the line you want with as little false casting as possible, since inevitably the line will cause some surface disturbance on each false roll.

SPEY CASTING

A more versatile technique for pushing out a long line across a tree-lined river is the Spey cast. This is a continuous-motion casting technique often associated with the double-handed salmon rod, but Spey casts can also be performed with a single-handed trout or sea trout rod. A right-handed person will generally use the Single Spey when fishing wet fly from the left bank and the Double Spey from the right bank. A left-handed angler will choose the alternative style in each case. Either method can be used when wading in mid-stream.

Let us assume that your fly has swung round to the dangle and that you are on or wading beneath, the left bank. You now want to cast out across the river. With the rod held low and pointing downstream, draw in line, taking coils in your left hand, until you have 10 to 15 yards out beyond the rod tip (depending on the size of rod). Raise the rod towards the vertical, peeling line from the surface before pulling it sharply upstream and then in a loop beside you. Now punch the line out across the river. As the line shoots away, release the coils from the left hand. Aim high in your forward punch and you should be able to cast 15 to 20 yards, even with a trout rod.

Wading beneath the right bank you will need the Double Spey cast. The action is the same as before, but you must precede it by lifting the rod to bring the belly of the line upstream of where you are standing. The traditional way of practising these casts is to call out a waltz time, 1,2,3 . . . 1,2,3 . . . 1,2,3 through each of the stages of the casting action. Of course, if you are ambidextrous, then you have a free choice of Single or Double Spey in most situations.

CASTING A WIGGLY LINE

Conflicting surface currents are the number-one enemy when you fish the dry fly. Natural flies swirl in the surface film, pushed and pulled by these currents. Tethered by a leader, your artificial fly is constrained and so cannot behave naturally. Worse still, if part of your line or leader falls across a run of fast current it will cause the line to bow downstream and your fly will skate across the surface. Small trout *may* find this action irresistible, but older and wiser fish are usually suspicious. Casting directly upstream minimises drag, but this also puts your leader across the fish and may alarm it. In addition, there are many instances in which you *need* to cast across the stream to avoid wading which might send other fish scurrying upstream to forewarn your quarry. Described below is a technique which will allow your fly to float naturally for a little longer before drag sets in.

Using your normal overhead or side-casting technique, wait until the fly is about to alight on the water and then pull back sharply on the line with your left hand. The line and leader should recoil and fall on to the surface in a series of snake-like wiggles. (Once again, the double haul can help achieve the extra line speed necessary for success.) Practise this cast if you intend fishing the dry fly; it is truly invaluable on both chalk and rough streams.

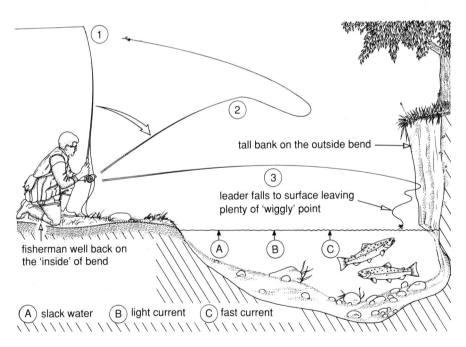

Fig 34   *Bouncing a dry fly against a high bank can create enough slack leader to defeat drag for the second or two necessary to deceive a good trout.*

OTHER CASTING 'TRICKS'

The very best wild trout grow big by eating more than (or more of!) their brethren. They do this by taking up lies which provide plenty of food in a small area, and, on a river, it is the current which brings the food supply. Concentrations of current pose the most extreme problems of drag, however, and need extreme remedies in the form of a very much exaggerated 'wiggly line'.

Bounce casting can achieve this. Where a fish lies in fast current against a high bank, you can cast the fly so that it actually hits the bank before falling back into the water with a slack leader. Another method is to cast too far so that the fly settles on the grass. As the current carries the line downstream the fly should suddenly plop down on to the surface just where you want it! I know that flies do not always do what they are meant to, but when it works, this little trick always leaves me feeling rather smug!

MENDING THE LINE

When the river is high the main problem in fishing the wet fly is that the strong current pulls on the belly of the line. This prevents the fly from sinking and soon

Fig 35 Casting on the river often involves a degree of improvisation. Here the overhead cast is made across the chest to avoid getting caught up in branches.

brings it skating rapidly across at right angles to the flow. These are just the times when there is likely to be a fair bit of colour in the water, and while early season trout and sea trout are noted for their willingness to chase a fly, you do have to give them the opportunity to see it. One answer is to use a long rod and to cast a very long line. Unfortunately, many good fly-fishing rivers are heavily wooded and long-distance casting is rarely feasible in daylight, never mind after dusk.

A second option, and one which is more widely applicable, is to use a 'mended' line. Having cast out, use the rod to lift the belly of the line and flick it upstream by working the rod tip in a circular motion. You may have to mend the line several times as the fly swings across the current.

Using a floating line, this method of mending is quite easily mastered, but not so if a heavy sinker is needed as, for example, when fishing spate rivers early or late in the season. In fact, many sea trout fishermen are unhappy about mending the line in this way, as every time a fly line hits the water, there is the risk that a fish will be spooked by the disturbance. Mending the line must increase this risk.

A better, though admittedly more difficult, technique is the casting of a ready-mended line. If you are right-handed and fishing from the right bank of a stream then this is what to do. Make a side cast, aiming your fly actually at the water (instead of at a point a foot or so above the surface, which is more usual). Use a little more power than necessary for the distance sought, and have more line stripped from the reel than is needed. At the moment your fly touches the water, release the line from the left hand. This spare line will shoot to create an upstream arc on the surface of the stream. You will need lots of practice to get both the aim and timing right, but it is well worth the trouble if you intend fishing for sea trout.

Many anglers are restricted, through lack of casting skills, to trying only for those fish which can be covered by the basic overhead cast. Once you become reasonably competent in the range of casting techniques discussed above, you will enjoy far more opportunities. With practice, casting will become second nature. Then you will be able to concentrate your attention on the more advanced skills of fly fishing – the selection of effective tactics for deceiving your quarry.

5

Fly-Fishing Techniques for River and Stream

Perhaps in some future age, with increased leisure time and improved equipment, a round-in-eighteen will replace a hole-in-one as the golfer's dream; a maximum break in snooker will go unnoticed; darts matches will be but marathon tests of endurance – 180. . .180. . .180. . . And what of fly fishing in such an age? Will there still be confidence-sapping blank days, whether due to wrongly identifying the fly on the water, to failing to spot the dimple of a feeding trout hard against the bank, or to approaching a feeding fish from the wrong direction and so putting it down.

Fishing, and fly fishing in particular, is not a sport for the perfectionist. It may be true that certain items of tackle have already been developed to the verge of perfection; that the most accomplished of us can cast dry fly so that it wafts on to the suface with no more fuss than an egg-laying spinner; and that others win tournaments with heart-stopping casts of great distance or extreme accuracy. It is even conceivable that some prodigy might one day combine these achievements of distance, accuracy and delicacy of presentation in 'the perfect cast'. But, now at least, most of us are a very long way from perfection.

What separates the expert from the tiro is their relative skill and knowledge – the techniques and the rivercraft of fly fishing. In these respects, our most respected experts can only be rated fair, and the average fly fisher, appallingly weak. Long may what remains to be learned outweigh what is understood of the techniques for outwitting a trout with a fly.

WET-FLY FISHING

Shrouded in the mists of time, the origins of fly fishing are obscure. Many believe that wet-fly fishing is the oldest of techniques, and certainly it dates back more than a thousand years, to when materials for making hooks and leaders were crude and ineffective by present-day standards. A heavy iron hook mounted on a trace of horse hair could more readily be concealed in a fly intended to swim submerged in a turbulent race below a weir – ideal wet-fly water. But why do trout take such artificial flies? I have yet to encounter a real fly which can swim against a strong current. There are some aquatic flies which can swim below the surface to lay their eggs amongst plant roots, but even these insects could not cope with the force of current in which wet flies are often successful.

What then does a wet fly represent? Does it imitate an insect or a small fish? And are trout deceived by such crude imitations, or do they take them by some sort of instinctive reaction? I believe we are helped by the opportunism of hungry trout which, seeing something alive and smaller than themselves, assume it is *food*.

As to why a sea trout should take a wet fly, there can be less certainty. Many experienced game fishers believe that the most common reasons are the triggering of an instinct of aggression (since sea trout are predators immediately prior to entering fresh water), or the desire to defend the territory of a temporary lie. I am convinced that there is more to it than this. Neither of these theories can adequately explain why a sea trout which has been resting in a pool for some weeks will follow a fly for several

Fig 36   April on the Yorkshire Nidd at Pately Bridge, where a team of wet flies sweeps across-and-down for brown trout feeding near the river bed.

Fig 37 Wet-fly fishing for sea trout. The loop of line from rod tip to the water's surface allows a fish to turn with the fly in its jaws before feeling any resistance. The size of the loop, and hence the angle of the rod, should match the size of fish anticipated.

yards before cruising back to its deep-water lie. I suggest that both trout and sea trout will, given no reason to suspect the presence of danger, respond to that primeval instinct which brings about the downfall of so many higher mortals – curiosity.

Is it sensible to try and find out the reasons for trout or sea trout taking a wet fly? The angler has several needs in common with a river trout. A trout needs shelter and protection from the dangers of predators; humans need that too. And a trout has a distinct aversion to large amounts of physical exertion. It prefers to avoid fast-water lies. Sea trout are an altogether different proposition. They have no real need of food whilst in the river. (They may begin feeding on flies after they have spent many weeks or months in fresh water, but through most of the season the assumption that they feel no urge to feed appears to be generally valid.)

How strange, then, that this wet-fly method, so successful in deceiving the brown trout, will also tempt its migratory cousin. This is the case not only as the migrant enters the first freshwater pool, when memories of the rich feeding grounds of the estuary must still be fresh, but also after many weeks of fasting in the turgid pools of a river in summer drought.

The Basic 'Across-and-Down' Method

In its simplest form, this technique involves casting a fly, or a team of flies spaced along a leader, across the stream so that it swings through an arc beneath the surface. By gradually lengthening the line or pacing steadily downstream, you can thoroughly search a stretch of river for fish which may be invisible due to the depth or colour of

Fig 38   A team of traditional wet flies tied on gut in the early years of the twentieth century. (Photograph courtesy of Cecil Thomas).

the water. Accurate casting is not essential, as the current will ensure that the fly passes the nose of your quarry. In fast water, fish often hook themselves as they turn after seizing the fly, and for this reason some anglers consider this to be a crude way of catching trout. Certainly, when applied indiscriminately it is a method likely to take a high proportion of undersized fish. But, as we will see in later chapters, there are occasions where wet-fly fishing can be both effective and selective, provided it is applied skilfully.

An important aspect of across-and-down fishing is timing the strike. Tighten too quickly and the fish will feel the hook before turning its head; too late and the trout might be able to eject the hook. Tightening too quickly is a common failing when fishing for large trout or sea trout, which need to be given plenty of time to turn their heads. Unfortunately, there is no simple rule as to how long you should wait before tightening. Length of line in the water, speed and depth of water as well as the size of both fish and fly must figure in the equation. Fortunately, the larger the fish, the less likely it is to eject the fly if you delay tightening beyond the optimum.

Some anglers prefer to rely on the fish hooking themselves, and there is a simple way of achieving this more often than not. All you have to do is leave an arc of line between the top of your rod and the surface of the water. When fishing for small trout a few inches of arc will be enough, but for large sea trout you will need to allow at least a foot of arc.

You may prefer to take some positive action in setting the hook. In this case allow rather more line to arc down on to the surface and watch for the initial tightening of this slack line which is indicative of a take. To set the hook, pull down sharply with your left hand before raising the rod to maintain pressure on the hook hold. This method of striking creates far less surface disturbance than the traditional snatching upwards of the rod. It is also faster and, should you fail to make contact, does not send your fly careering out of control into the trees behind you.

For downstream trout fishing, heavily dressed wet flies such as the Peter Ross and Mallard and Claret are excellent fry representations. Sizes 10 to 14 are effective for both spring and autumn trout. They can be fished on a short line when there is plenty of colour in the water, but in clear conditions you will get better results if you fish 'fine and far off'. This will avoid you or your nylon leader giving the game away to your quarry.

Upstream Wet-Fly Fishing

Here you cast your fly upstream and across. After allowing the fly to sink towards the river bed, retrieve line (either by raising your rod or by pulling in line with your left hand) so that you bring the fly towards you across the current. This behaviour is representative of a hatching insect. The problem now is in spotting the take. Provided that you do so and react reasonably quickly, very few fish will be missed, since you are pulling the hook into the scissors of the jaws of the fish.

Lightly dressed wet flies in sizes 14 to 16 are more imitative of hatching insects. Try the traditional northern spider patterns such as Partridge and Orange or Snipe and Purple.

Both upstream and downstream wet-fly techniques can prove useful to the sea trout fisher, and in later chapters I will give details of some tactics which combine the two wet-fly methods to very good effect.

NYMPH FISHING

Many aquatic flies spend a year or more in nymphal form, as insects, crawling in the mud and gravel of the river bed, or swimming or darting amongst stones or weed. Many of these nymphs are taken by trout which nose them out of their hiding places. Rather fewer fall victim when, ready to hatch into flies, they make the perilous ascent to the suface. Quite the smallest proportion of a trout's diet consists of flies which have left the water and returned either as duns or spinners.

Nymph fishers attempt to imitate both the immature nymphs and, more often, the adult nymph as it prepares for hatching. An artificial nymph can be made to creep slowly along the bottom, or to rise up towards the surface in a manner which many trout find quite irresistible. A reluctant fish will often respond to this 'induced-take' technique. It is rather like a person who, having taken something for granted, suddenly becomes aware of what they could be about to lose when it is almost too late to prevent the loss.

Fig 39   A wild brown trout falls to the induced take on a tiny Hampshire chalk stream.

*Fig 40   Polarised spectacles are invaluable when nymph fishing, as shown in
these two photographs taken (a) without a polarised lens and . . .*

. . . (b) with a polarised lens

Nymph fishing is a three-dimensional challenge. The imitation is usually cast upstream, or upstream and across, so that it sinks towards the river bed as the current carries it downstream. By greasing just part of the leader, the nymph can be made to swim at the required depth. Takes show up as a dipping or a sideways pull of the leader, and these indications may be difficult to spot in rippling water. In clear water, where you are stalking individual fish, you may be able to see the trout react as your nymph passes its head. In deep water, you may not be able to distinguish the outline of the trout clearly, but when it opens its jaws to seize your nymph the white of its tongue should be easily spotted. This is the moment to begin tightening your line to set the hook.

Many successful nymph fishers, including the late Frank Sawyer, a famous Hampshire river keeper, and Arthur Cove, who has devised some very successful tactics for use on stillwaters, have asserted that nymph fishing yields trout of larger average size than any other method. I am inclined to agree with them.

DRY-FLY FISHING

A suitably buoyant artificial fly can be made to represent an insect which alights on, or has recently hatched at, the surface of the water. Dry-fly fishing involves casting a fly, usually, but not always, upstream towards a feeding trout. There is something particularly satisfying about casting to and rising a particular fish, and, for me, this makes dry-fly by far the most exciting style of trout fishing. There are times when fish are determined to remain at the river bed, and it is a case of fish a sunk fly or catch nothing, but if there is any chance of enticing a trout with a floating fly, then I readily foresake all other techniques.

The easiest way to fail with the dry fly is to let the fish see you. So, as you walk to the bottom of the stretch you intend to fish, keep well away from the river's edge. Then, moving slowly back up, listen and watch for rising fish. If you cannot see the trout, watch for a while and try to decide whether it is a sizeable specimen or a juvenile fish. When fishing a rough stream, there may be no sign of rising fish. Then you may choose to 'fish the water', by casting your fly into likely lies. (On chalk streams, fishing the water is frowned upon, and on certain beats it is not allowed.)

When you see a fish rise, note the position and give it time to return to its lie, which will usually be a foot or two upstream of where he took the fly. Position yourself so that the risk of drag on your line is minimised (about which much more in later chapters) and make your first cast a little short of the range you judge to be required. This first tentative cast acts as a 'sighter', and allows you to adjust line length more accurately before putting your fly across the trout. It is important to avoid casting too far, as the splash of your fly line falling in its window will certainly put any self-respecting trout down.

RETRIEVING LINE

When fishing upstream wet fly, nymph or dry fly, you must keep in contact with your fly so that you can react quickly if a trout takes it. As your fly touches down, hook the line over a finger of your rod hand so you can clamp the line tightly if you need to strike. Then, as the fly drifts back towards you, retrieve line with your left hand (if your rod is in your right). Avoid allowing too much slack line to lie on the surface, or you will not be able to tighten quickly enough should a trout take your fly. When you lift off to cast again, avoid snatching. Peel the line smoothly from the water to minimise the surface disturbance.

For short-range fishing (on small streams you rarely have the opportunity for anything else) the retrieve can be made by steadily raising your rod as the fly drifts towards you, and then flicking it back gently and recasting in a single smooth action.

SETTING THE HOOK

If your choice of fly is acceptable, and assuming you present it with the necessary accuracy and delicacy, the trout will take it. Tighten into the fish by drawing in line with your left hand. Now raise the rod steadily towards the vertical to absorb any shock as the trout realises its mistake and dives for the river bed.

There is no need to snatch violently to set a hook. Think of it as merely tightening the line and keeping it in tension so that the fish hooks itself. Speed of reaction can be most valuable sometimes, but being able to control the speed of tightening is much more important. For example, you will find that when a large trout takes your fly in slow or moderately flowing water, you will need to delay the strike for perhaps half a second or more so that the fish has time to turn downwards. Then the hook has something to make contact with, and you are not merely pulling it out of the mouth of the trout. In contrast, if you fish the dry fly or nymph for wild brown trout on a mountain stream it is unlikely that your reactions can ever be too fast. These trout are very quick to eject the fly when they detect the deception. It is as if all aspects of their life are played out at an increased pace compared with their lowland brethren.

When fishing for sea trout in spring a rapid tightening is neither necessary nor conducive to secure hooking. In most cases the fish will have moved quite some distance to take your fly and it is better to give it time to turn back towards its lie. Then it doesn't matter if it does open its jaws, since any slack line trailing downstream will pull the fly deep into the scissors, quite the most secure place for hooking. It takes nerves of steel to do nothing at all when you are convinced that a large sea trout has hold of your fly, and perhaps nothing but a few bitter disappointments can convince you that the fish will more often hook itself than be hooked by a hasty strike on your part.

Summer sea trout resting in quiet pools are an altogether different proposition. When the river is very low the sea trout become stale and lazy, only taking a fly if it moves tantalisingly close to their noses. As an indication of the take, all that may register on the line is a tiny vibration, a momentary tightening or slackening. To hook the sea trout you must tighten the line immediately and firmly, keeping it really tight so that as the fish shakes its head the hook is not allowed to come free. Hold the rod high to absorb the impact of that first lunge, for all his lethargy will have been shaken off and your sea trout will use every trick in the book before surrendering to your rod. You must try to avoid letting the line fall slack if the fish runs towards you. You will lose very few trout with a tight line even when fishing with flies tied on barbless hooks.

PLAYING AND LANDING A FISH

There must be more riverside stories exchanged on the subject of the one that got away than just about any other fishing topic. And yet, as you may have noticed, some people do seem to be much 'luckier' than others. While there must always be an element of luck in fishing, averaged over the season I believe luck is but a small contributor to results. Good (appropriate) tackle can make a difference, but there is no dismissing the importance of technique – using the tackle to its fullest potential to present the fly adequately. More good fish are lost within a yard of the net than at any other point during the fight.

It is possible to plan the playing and landing your catch and in so doing ensure that you come off the victor more often. What generally happens the moment you tighten or strike depends on what sort of fish and of what size, and on the nature of the fishery itself. If the fishery holds a variety of species then one thing that will help you decide on tactics is being able to identify your catch early in the fight. Brown trout generally try to bore down to the bed of the river very soon after hooking. The larger specimens are usually solitary fish which will head for the safety of whatever cover they can find. On shallow streams, weed beds and snaggy bank-side holes act as magnets for these trout, while on larger rivers, trout hooked in shallow water invariably head towards the deeper trenches. Their runs follow the contours of the bed of the river, sometimes leaving the line snagged around boulders, submerged tree trunks or other hazards. Keeping the fish up in the water away from these snags must be your top priority on weedy or rocky fisheries.

Playing a Trout in Weedy Glides

On chalk streams it is usually best to play a brown trout on the surface despite the risk of sudden strain on the leader as the fish leaps clear of the surface. I suggest you avoid using very fast action rods for just this reason. A softer action absorbs the transient shocks and allows you to apply a higher average strain with safety. This makes it easier to turn a fighting fish without the leader breaking or the hook pulling free. Rainbow trout, unless hooked in deep water, tend to leap for the first few seconds of the fight, and display less tendency to dive for weed. Large rainbows can be quite determined fighters, however, and may very quickly strip the line to the backing. Their initial runs are often relatively straight, either upstream or down, away from the pull exerted by the line. The traditional advice is to lower the rod tip when you see the fish leap, and at short range this can be an effective method of reducing leader strain. When you have many yards of line in the water, drag prevents the shock transients being transmitted to the rod, so the strain must be borne by the hook-hold and the leader.

Sea Trout in Deep Pools

Sea trout usually leap both at the instant of hooking and also repeatedly during the fight. A tail-walking five-pounder is an awe-inspiring sight and quite enough to strike fear into the most implacable of fly fishers. When hooked in deep water, a sea trout is usually reluctant to leave the pool, and if you play it carefully it can be encouraged to fight in a restricted area, leaving the rest of the shoal relatively undisturbed. You can then increase the pressure as the fish is tiring. A firm tightening is needed to set the hook in the bony jaws of a sea trout. Thereafter, try to keep the line tight without exceeding the strain used during striking. The important thing is not to bully a large sea trout or it will be off into fast water where you will have much more difficulty in keeping the upper hand.

NETTING YOUR CATCH

Fish which are to be returned should neither be played to exhaustion nor netted if they can be brought to hand and released while still in the water. It is better to risk the fish escaping than to return it in a condition from which it cannot recover.

Fig 41   When fully played out, a fish turns on to its side. This two-pounder is brought over the waiting net . . .

A fish can 'let go' at any time, but it does seem that far too many are lost at the net. It is not uncommon to find that the fly has come loose during netting – a fish 'almost lost'! There is a right way to net a large fish. Play the fish until it turns on its side, when it is ready for netting, then raise your rod to the vertical and bring the fish, head-first, across the surface towards you. Keep the net submerged so that the fish is unaware of its presence until it is over the net. Finally, lift the net and lower your rod to let the line go slack. If the fish is to be killed for eating then dispatch it immediately, while it is still in the net. It is not good to see an angler fumbling with a gasping trout which could be cleanly killed if a proper implement were to hand. Never go fishing without your priest. Stones, fixed fence posts, handles of landing nets and the like are *not* effective substitutes. Below are some of the more common ways in which fish are lost at the net.

Chasing

Here the fish is brought in the general region of the net and then the angler or an 'accomplice' scoops wildly with the net hoping to catch the trout rather as if it were a butterfly. What better way to encourage the fish to make a final desperate lunge for freedom?

Gill Netting

Here the net is kept well up so that the fish has to jump over the rim to get in. Instead, of course, he dives below the rim getting tangled by the gills in the meshing. A quick

. . . and the net is raised.

lift of the net and the fish is pulled a foot or more clear of the surface before crashing back, with injuries to its gill cover, causing an almost certain leader break.

Snagged Droppers

There are times when using a team of flies is appropriate, but fish can easily be lost by hooking the net with a dropper fly while the fish on the point is free to swim away. If a trout has taken the point fly, holding the rod well up should help keep the droppers clear of the net. Ensure that the head of the fish is kept above surface as it is brought towards you. Then it cannot dive beneath the net leaving your leader attached thereto by the dropper.

Just as serious a threat occurs if the trout has taken your dropper. Now the point fly is trailing behind and could easily catch on bank-side weeds, leaving the fish dangling and you quite helpless to control it. If the trout makes a dash for such an obstruction, push the rod tip out across the water to turn your fish away from the snag.

I once had an unpleasant experience when fishing at night for sea trout. A two-pounder took my dropper fly at the same instant that a smaller sea trout snatched the point. Both were well hooked but at no time did I feel at all in control of the fight. At first, I thought I had at last met up with that elusive double-figure sea trout. Fortunately, I saw what the problem was when both fish leapt at the same time, and eventually I managed to draw the larger fish into the net before releasing the smaller one by grasping the shank of the fly. When fishing with a team of flies, keep the net well clear until you are certain the fish is ready for netting.

PART II
SPRING TACTICS

6

Spring Trouting on Lowland Rough Streams

There can be few prospects less inspiring for a fly fisher than that of the opening day on a major spate river. After a mild, wet winter, the river runs bank-high and deeply coloured. All sensible trout are tucked safely into bank-side scour holes or rest in the lea of obstructions, away from the full force of the current. Rarely will they be tempted by a fly. A cold, dry winter allows but a trickle of melt water from the mountains. Upper reaches of the main river may freeze over completely and the trout lie torpid in the deeper pools. There is little or no fly life. Nymphs will not hatch until triggered by a rise in temperature. Again, the chances of tempting a trout with fly or nymph are quite remote.

Not so on the myriad smaller lowland streams and brooks which rise in the foothills and converge like leaf-veins on to the stalk of the main river. They offer quite a different, and more worthwhile, proposition. Many of these gentler brooks and streams are at their best for just a few weeks at the beginning, and again at the end, of the trouting season. In high summer they may be reduced to mere trickles linking near-stagnant pools, offering poor sport save, perhaps, for a brief flurry around dusk. But in springtime, as the trout drop back downstream after spawning in the head-waters, they take up temporary lies, in places which may be high and dry in a month or two. Now is your chance to sample some of the most challenging fly fishing, to seek a wary and worthy adversary, but one which nevertheless feeds avidly throughout the day. Concealment will be vital, and the casting will rarely be easy, in an environment which favours the hunted rather than the hunter. The key to success will be spotting your quarry before it sees you, and that means knowing where to look and what to look for.

SPRING TROUT LIES

One of the nice things about spring trouting is that the fish are well distributed along the river, and not all crowded into a few 'hot spots'. Later in the year, long stretches of water may be devoid of anything but tiny fingerling trout. Now, however, the fish range widely in search of food, still in short supply following the scouring winter floods which carry many small creatures away to the estuary.

Spring trout are widespread but they are not to be found everywhere. The challenge is not simply to catch a few fish (for it must be admitted that, in spring, trout are at quite their most co-operative), but to catch the 'big bullies' of the stream. They seem to know the best places for a growing trout to live, and we need to learn to find these favoured lies.

What Makes a Lie Attractive to a Trout?

The most obvious factor is food; all other considerations *must* be secondary. Having recovered from the stress of spawning and survived the rigours of winter, food is now their top priority so much so that in early spring trout will even take risks with safety in order to recharge their muscle larders. Later in the year other considerations weigh more heavily, and may even dominate. Even now the wiser old trout will give preference to lies which offer security from predators, or, at least, a quick escape route. They also try to avoid lying directly in the main current, preferring to rest in a pocket of quiet water alongside the food channel. There they lie in wait, ready to seize any passing morsel.

With these requirements in mind, search the water for likely food supplies. If there are no aquatic flies hatching, look first for places where insects, spiders and so on will fall or be blown onto or into the water. Then try to work out where the current will carry this food. Wherever the current becomes concentrated, you may find a mouth waiting to be fed.

DRY-FLY TACTICS

Adult trout are infrequent risers in the cold waters of spring. Only a steady surface food supply will tempt them to lie in mid-water where the current is stronger and where they are more vulnerable to heron and cormorant. Surface fly life is generally scarce until April or early May. Possible exceptions are the Large Dark Olive and the March Brown. Prolific hatches of duns of both species are the portent of great dry-fly fishing. Generally preferring the faster boulder-strewn stretches, Large Dark Olives emerge from late morning to mid-afternoon throughout the winter months on all but the coldest of days. The March Brown is a later arrival, again preferring faster water, and generally putting in an appearance towards the end of the month. Unfortunately, not all rough streams are favoured by the presence of this invaluable insect.

Close imitation of either of these species is unnecessary, and any dun imitation cast into the right spot seems to be acceptable. However, the right spot is not always easy to find. Simply casting a dry fly into the midst of a hatch is rarely productive, for two reasons. Firstly, the rough and tumble of the stream can easily swamp a dry fly before it has drifted a yard downstream, and, secondly, there is the dry-fly fisherman's arch-enemy – drag. It is possible to tie buoyant flies with ethafoam bodies to give greater resistance to swamping, but I know of only one way to defeat drag when surface currents are very turbulent – cast your fly very close to the nose of the trout.

Rises in rough water can be quite difficult to spot. Your chances are much improved, of course, if you know where to expect them, and below are a few suggestions.

Nature's Food Funnels

These are places where the surface current narrows so that the flotsam is concentrated into a thin stream. When the river is high following rain, branches of bank-side bushes and leaning trees may be submerged, deflecting the surface currents. Deeper down, the current is largely unaffected, while up above any insects or other floating food morsels are swept around the obstruction. You can expect a trout to take up residence in the safety of the sunken branches ready to slide out and seize any food which drifts past.

If you see a trout rising steadily in such a lie, it is important to time your cast correctly. On seeing a suitable meal, the trout will leave his lie and drop downstream

Fig 42 Trout often take up lies near 'food funnels'. Here the current is constrained into a narrow channel at the entrance to a pool on the River Nadder in Wiltshire.

while swimming up towards the surface. Then, seizing the fly, the fish will settle down beneath the surface before swimming back under the bush and upstream to take up position in its lie. You must try to estimate how long all this will take, otherwise your fly will pass unnoticed. It is better to wait too long than to cast too quickly after a rise. In very fast water the taking spot can be several feet downstream of the lie itself. Then there is always the danger that the trout will see your line as it falls onto the surface. This is an argument in favour of longer leaders and delicate casting (not always practicable in the windy conditions so common at the beginning of the season). If the trout rises as you are casting, 'feather back' by pulling back line with your reel hand, so that the fly falls short of the target zone. It takes a bit of practice to do this without creating line splash, but it is well worth taking the trouble to learn.

In breezy weather these food funnels are difficult lies to cover because you need to cast accurately. As the surface current is changing direction around the obstruction, your fly will have to fall no more than a foot or so upstream of the lie. But that is not all! An inch or two to one side and your fly will be caught up; too far the other way and it may pass by unnoticed. You may find it best to aim short and wide with a 'sighting shot', adjusting distance and direction before making the final cast.

If your fly is ignored, do not leave it on the water to drift back too far or drag will set in. Wise old trout studiously ignore dragging flies, but the tiddlers, which invariably line up below the prime lie, will find them an irresistible temptation. The commotion as you tighten into one of these small fish may disturb your intended quarry, thereby depriving you of a second chance. You must judge when the fly has passed well beyond the trout's window of vision, and peel the line gently from the surface before recasting.

Other places where you may find food funnels are where the current flows between large boulders, sunken trees or collapsed banks. Also, try the run into any pool sited on a sharp bend in the river. These are nearly always places where the river bed slopes from shallow to deep towards the outside of the bend, and this results in a concentration of surface current through a narrow neck at the head of the pool. Fishing from the shallow side, the main problem is avoiding drag. If the trout takes your fly immediately it reaches the head of the pool, you have a fair chance of success. If, on the other hand, it follows the fly down into quieter water the fish will probably be put off as your fly begins skating across towards you.

The problems multiply if you try to cover the lie from the other bank. Almost invariably, on the outside of a bend, the bank will be high with a sheer drop to the water. Casting from a standing or even a kneeling position will be unsatisfactory, because you will need to see over the bank to position the fly accurately. Sometimes you can get away with crawling slowly to the edge and peering over, but watch the position of the sun. Either your shadow falling on the water or the glint of reflected light from your rod can be enough to send your quarry darting for cover. If the water is not too deep, the best plan would be to wade very slowly up from the tail of the pool to a position from which you can reach the lie with an upstream cast. With the line and leader lying almost directly along the flow of the current, drag will be at a minimum, so your main concern will be accuracy of direction and distance. Here, you may be able to use the sheer bank as an ally, bouncing your fly against it a few

Trouting on a mountain stream in County Kerry, Eire. The trout lie in tiny pools between crashing waterfalls, and feed almost exclusively on terrestrial insects blown onto the water.

Light dancing on the ripples of a stream: not the best of circumstances for fish detection. Polarised sunglasses make it easier to spot the rise to a fly.

Wet-fly fishing on the River Glaslyn in North Wales.

An overcast day on a lonely moorland stream; but the fishing is far from dull.

Dry flies: Top row: *Daddy-Long-Legs; G & H Sedge; Silver Sedge.* Middle row: *BWO Dun; Grannom; Iron Blue Dun; Ginger Quill.* Bottom row: *Yellow Sally; Sherry Spinner; Gold-Ribbed Hare's Ear.*

Wet flies and nymphs: Top row: *Pheasant Tail Nymph; Mayfly Nymph; Gold-Ribbed Hare's Ear.* Middle row: *Mallard & Claret; Black & Peacock Spider; Coch-y-Bonddu; March Brown Spider.* Bottom row: *Longhorn Sedge Pupa; Nightshift Nymph; Plummet Nymph; Partridge & Orange.*

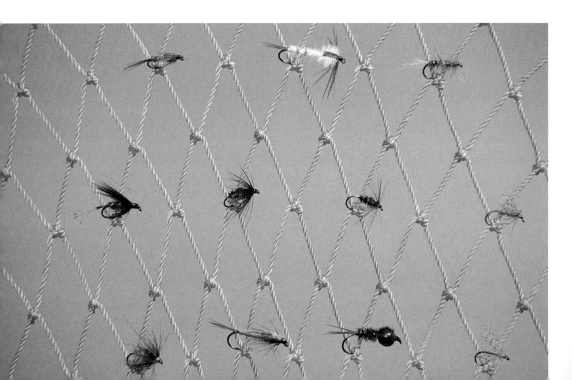

Sea trout lures: Top row: *Hairy Mary*; *Stoat's Tail*. Middle row: *Dyffryn Demon*; *Sweeney Todd*; *Connemara Black*. Bottom row: *Butcher*; *Tandem Alexandra*; *Teal, Silver & Blue*.

A side cast places a dry Black Gnat deep beneath an overhanging alder on the Glaslyn. Trout in these types of lies are often the easiest to deceive if only you can get a fly to them.

An autumn evening on the Teifi, and a team of wet flies search the tail of a pool for sea trout.

Deceived by a dry fly, a hill stream trout makes a determined attempt to escape downstream.

An undercut bank provides shade for sea trout during the day. A weighted fly cast upstream and brought back slightly faster than the current often provokes a response.

A sea trout at dusk from the junction of Lough Leane and the River Laune, Killarney.

The author with a fine evening's catch of sea trout from the Teifi.

inches above the water-line so that the fly drops back on to the surface nice and gently. This is a very satisfying tactic when it is rewarded by an enthusiastic take!

Nature's Larders

All trout are lazy, but some are particularly so, preferring to collect their food when it suits *them*. They lie against the bank hardly moving a fin as a conveyor-belt of food and other floating debris circulates above their heads. I call these circulating eddies 'insect graveyards'. In reality, they accumulate both flotsam and food in various degrees of decay and distress. Often concealed in the scum created by a waterfall are numerous creatures, aquatic and terrestrial, which have become trapped in the foam. Casting a bushy dry fly to the edge of the scum can prove very effective.

Rocky gorges are ideal places for this style of fishing, as they usually contain outcrops beside which whirlpools are formed. These whirls spin on downstream collecting debris as they go until they find a quiet eddy. There the flotsam settles, circulating gently. And there, too, you can enjoy some of the best spring trouting. Do not expect the splashy rise form of the opportunist trout; these will be quiet sipping rises detectable only as a momentary parting of the scum as two or three insects are scooped down at once. You need to watch your fly very carefully indeed or you will miss the signal to tighten. Let representation take second place to visibility. You may

Fig 43   The daddy-long-legs is not just an autumn fly. They can be found in the meadows throughout the season, and are well worth a try on windy days.

well get results with a bright orange Soldier Palmer or a G and H sedge, both of which should show up well.

Terrestrial Visitors

Most of the land-based insects likely to find their way on to the water do not appear until at least April. One exception is the crane-fly or daddy-long-legs. The larger species are flies of later summer and autumn, but there are hundreds of species of crane-fly, and some of the smaller ones can be found in rough grassland very early in the year. On a breezy day you may see one or two struggling on the surface of a pool. They do not usually suffer for long as trout are very partial to crane-flies. A few imitations on size 12 hooks are worthy of a place in your fly box.

I have yet to see beetles on the water as early as March, but spiders are definitely at work all through the winter in the bushes overhanging the stream. Hawthorns provide ideal habitat for these particular *arachnids* which, despite their acrobatic skills, do occasionally take an unplanned dip. A small hackled Black Gnat cast gently under any low-hanging hawthorn bush is always worth a try if there is a stiff breeze to disturb the equilibrium of the web builders. A Black and Peacock Spider fished just sub-surface and brought downstream a little faster than the current does the trick better on a calm day, I find.

Sedges in Springtime

Caddis flies are often referred to by anglers as sedges, and with good reason. Many species inhabit the slower glides and pools bordered by reeds and sedges. Early in the season the new growth will barely be visible above the brown of the previous year's foliage. Flattened by the winter floodwater, this matted carpet of decaying leaves harbours vast quantities of sedge or caddis nymphs. Several kinds of sedge flies emerge during daytime in the spring. They are generally the smaller species and all can be copied adequately by a representation of one early fly – the Grannom.

Trout feeding on sedges are best located by ear. Walk along the bank behind the reed beds and listen for a swirl and a plop as a hatching sedge is scooped from the surface. Sometimes trout will forage right in amongst the reeds, and to tempt one of these intrepid explorers you will have to risk losing a fly or two.

If the water is of safe wading depth, then the fishing is not at all difficult. From a position well away from the bank, cast diagonally so that your fly falls hard against the reeds. As it drifts gently downstream you will have to mend your line to prevent the faster surface current in mid-stream dragging the fly away from the reeds. The slight movement of your fly as you mend the line is no disadvantage at all. In fact, you may find it useful to give your fly a twitch or two by pulling sharply on the line now and then to simulate the antics of a hatching sedge fly.

You will need to give the trout time to turn down after taking the fly, but once you have tightened up, be ready to bully the fish quickly away from the reeds, or you may well get snagged. A sideways strike is ideal if there are no overhanging trees in the way. In any case, try to play the fish on the surface where it has little chance of

Fig 44 Dapping for sedge feeders on a small stream. A long rod is ideal for this tactic, which is most effective as dusk descends.

knowing which way to turn for safety. (Because of the shock forces involved, 4lb nylon is the minimum I use for this style of fishing.)

Another tactic for these sedge feeders is a form of dapping. On hearing the rise of a trout, simply lower your fly over the reeds until the fly touches the surface. (Look for the tell-tale rings as a sign that you have the right amount of line beyond the rod tip.) Then lift the fly a couple of inches and lower it again, all the while swinging your rod round to follow the downstream flow of the current. You will need a short leader – 3–4ft will do nicely – otherwise the weight of your line will pull the leader back through the rod rings when you raise your rod. (Alternatively, use a leader much longer than your rod, so that all of the main line remains on the reel.)

Takes can come as something of a surprise – both to you *and* to the fish. The rod does the striking as the trout turns down, so all you need do is apply pressure via the rod tip to make sure your trout heads for open water. Do not try this technique unless you have a landing net with a long handle, or you may leave a tired trout stranded in the middle of dense weed from which it may never escape.

Traditional sedge imitations can be used for this style of fishing, but I prefer a pattern with lots of buoyancy. The brown and orange G and H Sedge – one of the many innovations in which the creative mind of John Goddard was involved – seems purpose-built for dapping. Tied with hollow fibres of deep hair (Nature's equivalent of double glazing), the G and H Sedge can take any amount of dapping and remain

Fig 45   Wet-fly fishing on the River Usk. The 'dead drift' was used to carry the fly below the tiddlers in the shallows. Now the rod is raised to work the fly through the lie of a larger trout beneath the overhanging branch.

steadfastly afloat. When tied properly, this also happens to be one of the most durable of the artificial flies.

WET-FLY TACTICS

Some fly fishers despise this style of fishing, condemning it as an indiscriminate method in which both large and small trout hook themselves with little or no skill required on the part of the angler. It is true that when a trout will rise, the dry fly offers the added excitement of a visible take, but, if you care to accept it, there is a special challenge in fishing the wet fly – selective fishing.

If you can distinguish between the rise of a large and a small trout (with reasonable eyesight and after some practice, this is usually feasible), then selective fishing with the dry fly is not all that difficult. You simply avoid casting to the tiddlers. It requires a lot more skill to fish selectively with a team of wet flies. However, it *can* be done, and I will describe one tactic which works well.

Remember that you will be upstream of your quarry and casting across so that your flies swing round in an arc towards your bank. The trout you are after will be lying in any sort of depression to avoid the full force of the current. Places to look out for are beside large boulders, rocky outcrops jutting from the bank, gulleys and ledges, and beneath undercut banks where the course of the river turns sharply. A recce when the water is clear helps locate these lies, but if the water is brown on your first visit to a new fishery you will have to look for clues at the surface. For example, quiet patches of water in an otherwise choppy run usually indicate a depression just upstream of the calm water.

Assuming that you have located what you suspect to be the lie of a large trout, the problem is that a wet fly cannot be cast straight into the lie; it takes time for your fly to sink to the required depth. (In spring this usually means right down to the river bed.) While it is sinking, your fly will probably be visible to many small trout which are not sufficiently dominant to secure one of the better lies in the stream. If your wet fly swims across the current it will be seen as 'alive' and fair game for any of these undersized fish. You won't want to hook these tiddlers as it is quite likely that your intended quarry will take off at the first hint of something wrong and, far more important, the small fry have a nasty habit of launching themselves head-long at a fly. The resultant foul-hooking causes a wound from which the young trout may not recover. This need rarely happen if you allow your fly to drift like inert debris as it passes the tiddlers, and bring it to life as it nears the lie of a larger trout. This behaviour is not unlike that of a hatching fly, and is very likely to induce a take if the lie is occupied.

I have had best results with drab flies (those which look like bits of weed or sticks drifting with the current). If the water is reasonably clear try a Mallard and Claret or a

Fig 46   The author fishing the Plummet Nymph, an ideal pattern for searching the deep undertow of a waterfall.

March Brown. Less effective in terms of avoiding the small fry are attractor flies such as the Silver Doctor and Dunkeld, although you may need a bit of flash in coloured water to tempt a trout at all. Whatever fly pattern you choose, you will find that small fry will more often ignore a fly moving on a dead drift with the current.

A CASE FOR NYMPHING

Rarely in spring is the water clear and slow enough for trout to be visible on the bed of a rough stream. More often the water will be both high *and* coloured. These are not ideal conditions in which to fish the artificial nymph, but there is one tactic which works extremely well at such times. It will tempt the trout which refuses to take surface food and cannot be covered properly with a wet fly. This is 'sink-and-draw' fishing with a heavily weighted nymph.

The water immediately below a waterfall is a maelstrom of conflicting currents. Any ordinary nymph would be swept along, indistinguishable from the twigs and other debris which come down river following rain. Here I bring out my secret weapon, the Plummet nymph. As a general nymph representation it is as unimpressive as Sawyer's Pheasant Tail nymph, of which it is a derivative. A split shot forms the thorax, while peacock herl, copper wire and a few pheasant tail fibres complete the deception. Tying silk is an unnecessary luxury. Indeed, I am quite happy to carry a few hooks, shot, wire and feathers and tie up these nymphs by the waterside without tools of any sort.

The secret is in the method of fishing. The Plummet nymph is projected (I hesitate to call it casting, as these heavily weighted flies are awkward in the air, to say the least) at the vertical face of a waterfall, and it has sufficient weight to penetrate the surface. The nymph is carried by the force of the water deep down under the falls. You must judge when the nymph is near the bottom (the usual way is 'a bit less than last time' if you got snagged on your previous cast!) and then raise your rod, pulling back line with your reel hand so that the nymph swims up through the undertow and back towards you.

There is no need to watch your leader for evidence of a take. When a trout seizes a Plummet nymph there is usually no doubt at all about it. The line tightens in a flash as the trout dives back to the safety of the quiet water deep beneath the falls. The rod tip can easily be pulled down to the horizontal if you are taken unawares. I always keep a small loop of line held loosely in my reel hand. This loop slips smoothly through my fingers to prevent a leader break if I get a really strong take.

INFLUENCE OF THE WEATHER

Spring fishing is at its best during settled spells of high pressure. If there is an early morning frost then fish the deeper water with wet fly and nymph. As the sun clears away the frost the first fly hatches may appear, and it is worth changing over to dry fly, especially if you see good fish rising. Three or four hours around midday are quite

Fig 47   Classic wet-fly water – the upper reaches of the River Cych.

enough fishing for me at the beginning of the season, particularly as Nature has arranged most of the fly hatches to occur around that period.

During prolonged periods of rain or drizzle, which can last days in some regions, the rivers find a new equilibrium, fining down to a good colour for fly fishing, albeit flowing faster than you might like. With this warmer weather come longer fishing hours, as flies will now hatch through most of the day. These are ideal conditions for the wet-fly tactics discussed above.

The poorest of fishing usually coincides with a break in fine weather. After a long dry spell, heavy rain brings all sorts of flotsam down river, and as the level begins to rise you may be able to take a good trout or two on the dry fly. A variety of bank-side creatures fall casualty to a flash flood, and for a while the trout do not waste the opportunity of feeding both on the surface and below. However, having eaten their fill of worms, slugs, etc., the fish tuck themselves hard against the banks or the bed of the river, digest their feast and conserve the energy it provides. First to need food again will be the smaller trout which, like all children, require small amounts of food often. While the water is still brown you may see these tiny trout avidly tackling food morsels larger even than themselves. It will be a day or two before the adult fish take more than a passing interest in flies.

Fig 48   Inevitably, some immature trout will be caught. This half-pounder is being returned carefully with its head upstream.

WHERE TO START?

When fishing in familiar territory, you will naturally try the places which have proved successful in the past. But what about spring fishing on waters totally new to you? Suppose it is a blustery March morning. The water is high and slightly coloured from recent rain. You walk the whole beat looking for a rising trout and draw a blank. Do not despair. Fish may well show after an hour or so.

For the moment, keep an eye out for any of the trout-holding features described above. Shun those long, straight, canal-like sections where the casting is easy, as they hold little attraction for adult trout. You might like to start with a weighted nymph in the deeper lies, and you can always switch to the dry fly if a hatch brings trout to the top around midday. Later, perhaps, you could try a team of wet flies fished on a dead drift through the shallow run down into some deeper mid-streams lies. That is one of the really nice things about spring fishing on lowland rough streams – it affords the opportunity for variety in techniques and tactics.

7

Late Spring on Hill and Mountain Streams

Impatiently we await the start of the new season, but when opening day arrives, our eagerness is rarely shared by the trout! Following a cold winter it can be well into April before the fish move readily to surface flies. In no time at all the Mayfly is with us and trout feed furiously during what used to be called 'duffer's fortnight'. Then, almost overnight, the feast is over and surface activity becomes confined to a few precious hours around dawn and dusk. During the day the trout rest on the river bed, interested in nothing but the occasional nymph until the sun dips toward the horizon. It can be a frustrating time for the fly fisher, and particularly for those keen on fishing the dry fly.

However, it need not be so. Spring lasts much longer for the hill and mountain stream fisher. All he needs do is follow Spring as she creeps slowly up into the hills. The lowland snowdrops of February have mountain cousins which bloom in April. The trout of these highland waters also lose all track of time. Much of the countryside is liberally painted with tiny brooks and streams falling from the hills through narrow rocky gorges and steep wooded vales, eventually converging on the fertile valleys of the lowland rivers. What may be overgrown, unfishable trickles in late summer can offer superb trouting in surroundings of beauty and solitude for two or three months of the year. It is a wonderful thought that, you can be fishing for wild trout, high in the hills, where an artificial fly has never been cast before.

THERE'S GOLD IN THEM THERE RILLS!

While the main rivers are often heavily coloured and uninviting during the first few weeks of the season, spring extends a warmer welcome for the fly fisher on the tributaries, offering superb trout fishing in surroundings of beauty and solitude.

Those who can master the somewhat unusual techniques of fishing these rills enjoy spring fishing *par excellence*, and often for remarkably sporting trout. I have taken a brown trout of 1¼lb from a stream which would barely have filled one bucket per minute in summertime. I have seen plenty of bigger fish there, too, though not before they have seen me, unfortunately! The largest rough-stream trout that I have ever seen was at the bottom of the Bishopston River, a steep hill stream on the Gower Peninsula. This tiny torrent pours out into a small marsh to form a serpentine pool before seeping through a tall bank of stones which normally prevents entry by sea trout or salmon. The solitary cruising monster I sighted there was about two feet long and must have topped three pounds. It may have been a sea trout, marooned after a storm, but I prefer to believe that it was a wild brown trout. Of course, fish of this size are exceptional trout for acid streams, and even a half-pounder on light tackle in a very confined space is a tough adversary, and will leave you with a real sense of achievement at the end of a successful battle.

Fig 49 In late summer the upper reaches of the River Senny in mid-Wales are little more than overgrown, unfishable trickles. In spring, such hill streams offer superb trouting in surroundings of beauty and solitude.

COPING IN CONFINED SPACES

Tackle for this sort of rugged terrain need not be expensive or bulky. For years I used a 7ft built-cane rod which was many years my senior. Miraculously, it survived the ordeal, for rough stream work can be very hard on a fly rod. More recently, I obtained a pair of 7ft carbon brook rods – a number 4 and a number 5 (AFTM ratings). The lighter of the two had a softer action which I much prefer for this sort of fishing, for two reasons. Firstly, I still catch more trees than trout when pursuing these wilderness fish, and a soft rod rarely sets the hook deeply. With a little jiggling, the fly can usually be dislodged. A fast-action rod would be more likely to snap the leader or at least set the hook hard, and while retrieving a fly is rarely hazardous on small streams, it is a good way to encourage the trout to leave the dinner table! My second reason for choosing a softer action rod is that casting is never a textbook technique in confined spaces, and a soft-action rod is much more versatile when casting. The side cast, roll cast and, sometimes, the catapult cast are used in preference to the overhead cast in brook fishing.

Two things a fast-action rod definitely wins at (at least, used the way I handle them) are 'casting round corners' and striking into a fish. I discussed casting techniques in Chapter 4, but below is one solution to the problem of how to tighten quickly into a fish when using a soft rod in a confined place.

Fig 50 Late June, but it's still spring on this moorland stream, where trout rise throughout the day.

Fig 51   Side-casting keeps the line below the bank and minimises the effects of a gusting wind.

Assuming that you are holding the rod in your right hand with the line passing between forefinger and rod butt, keep the left hand holding the fly line and near to the rod. When a fish takes, pull down quickly with the left hand. If the rod is not pointing straight at the fish (which of course it should never be), the hook will be set very quickly and the spring of the rod will absorb any excess shock. Now raise the rod *in the direction in which you made the cast.* Should you fail to make contact with the fish, the fly is unlikely to catch anything else, as can so easily happen with a more conventional technique.

The mouths of these slow-growing wild trout are bony and hard, so it is essential to keep the fish on a tight line even if you are not using barbless flies. In any case, given slack line for just a moment, the trout will invariably head for the cover of rocks or roots from which its extraction will be difficult, if not impossible.

Occasionally, you will get your fly stuck in trees or bushes. This is especially likely at the beginning of the season when, in the absence of foliage, you may not notice a projecting twig until too late. The first golden rule for safely recovering a fly from a tree is not to snatch. A very gentle lift of the rod is often enough to ease the fly over the branch. If that fails, try pulling from the opposite direction. A few sharp jerks may snap the twig where a steady pull would only result in the nylon leader parting. Of course, if you are fishing a single fly (I rarely fish more than one fly on small streams), you can try winding in all of your line until you can use the rod tip to unhook the fly.

This rod tip release trick is very satisfying when it works, but do be careful not to damage the top section of your rod.

On moorland streams there are usually few trees, and you might expect the casting to be much easier. This is rarely the case as strong winds often make accurate casting extremely difficult, and the absence of cover means you have to keep well back from the trout to avoid being seen. Side casting in the lea of the bank of the stream is often the only way of combatting a gusting wind. (This has the secondary advantage of keeping any glint of sunlight on the rod well away from the trout's window.) Even when you have skilfully cast your fly to drift over a feeding trout, the wind has one more weapon. It can be quite difficult to spot the fast rise of a trout to your fly in the rippled surface. Polarised sunglasses help a great deal in this respect, as they reduce the glare due to reflections from the surface. (In any case, some form of eye protection is strongly advisable when trying to cope with gusting winds, even for the most expert of casters.)

Moorland streams invariably take the most direct routes between the hills. This means that when the wind is against you (blowing downstream) on one section, you may have to walk several miles to find a more sheltered stretch. Wind bothers the trout rather less. They are quite used to seeing flies skitter across the surface, blown by the wind, so you need not worry unduly about what will happen to your fly after you have cast it onto the stream. Most moorland streams are shallow, and so demand accurate casting. Unfortunately, this is made doubly difficult on windy days by the

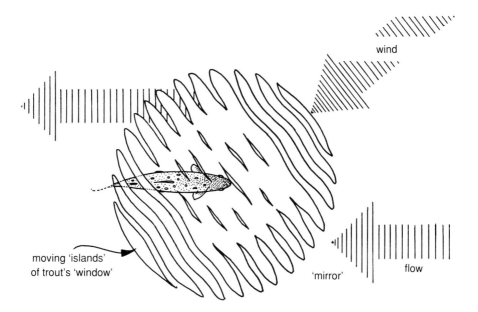

Fig 52   Wind rippling the surface distorts the edges of the trout's window, creating a moving pattern of islands of window.

surface ripple, which distorts the edges of the trout's window, creating a dancing pattern of light through detached 'islands' of window.

The few bits of spare tackle you need with you will fit easily into your pockets, so a shoulder bag is a luxury to be carried only when personal refreshments exceed pocket capacity. If somebody could design a landing net which packs down to almost nothing, is not magnetically attracted to thorns and barbed wire, and does not insist on opening up with the netting stretched tight like a tennis racket, then I would recommend it for brook and mountain stream work. Until then, I suggest you stick to the technique of carefully bringing the fish to hand. I have lost one or two really good trout when attempting this, but perhaps just as many would have escaped at the net.

Conservation-minded fishermen cool their hands in the water before touching the fish, and only provide sufficient restraint to aid removal of the hook. This is so much easier if barbless flies are used. As an alternative, flies can be tied on barbed hooks which have had the barb folded back with a small pair of pliers. This provides slightly better holding power than a smooth hook point, but makes removal very much easier than when using a conventional hook.

FLIES FOR UPLAND STREAMS

A few of the trout of these tiny hill streams grow quickly, but not the fussy feeders amongst them. Natural selection appears to have resulted in hill and mountain stream trout having very catholic tastes, so a modest selection of flies will do, certainly for the first couple of months of the season. Of course, the offering must resemble *something* which the fish recognise as a food form (a fly), or it must behave like something trying hard to avoid being eaten up (a lure). In the latter category, there are days when scaled-down Dog Nobblers will attract trout, and other days when they will scare them half to death. For many years I have used weighted, streamer-style flashy flies as a spate is fining down and have fished them 'sink-and-draw' style through the slower pockets of water. Little more than miniature, unglorified mackerel lures they have, surprisingly, caught trout; but put one into a clear water pool and you might as well be fishing on the moon.

Dry Flies

To represent the few upwinged flies found at high altitudes, useful dry-fly patterns include the March Brown and that universal solution for 'don't knows', Greenwell's Glory. These in sizes 14 and 16, with a few small sedge imitations, would be useful spring patterns to try. Terrestrial flies are more important than aquatic flies on mountain streams. The Coch-y-Bonddu (a 'beetle' fly), grasshopper imitations, and a selection of daddy-long-legs patterns of various sizes, would complete my menu for surface feeders.

Nymphs

There is very little scope for conventional across-and-down wet-fly fishing, but Greenwell's Nymphs, Pheasant Tails, and my Night Shift Nymphs comprise a formidable armoury with which to attack hill and mountain stream trout.

TACTICS

As if to compensate for their being easily deceived by an artificial fly, these wild brown trout are readily frightened by a heavy footfall or rapid movement. Add to that the virtual impossibility of casting at them from long range, and it soon becomes apparent where the greatest skill is needed – not so much in the fishing as in the approach. Once startled, the trout disappear. They don't necessarily swim off into deep water, for there may be none around. They rarely fade slowly down to lie on the river bed as I have seen many a chalk-stream fish do on my incautious approach. But disappear they certainly do, into crevices or under boulders, from whence they are slow to return.

Slow, careful movements and casting from cover are essential. When re-casting, drift the fly to the edge of the pool rather than risk the disturbance of lifting the line

Fig 53   Concealment and presentation are the keys to success on hill streams. Here, the author uses the steep gradient of a hill stream to advantage, casting to trout which are almost at eye-level.

off the surface of the water. It will rarely be possible to take more than one trout from a pool, so this is a very mobile style of fly fishing. In a typical day, I might easily cover several miles of water, making just a cast or two here and there on the way, with plenty of walking (or climbing!) in between.

Avoiding Drag

Despite the small scale involved, it can be surprisingly difficult to present a fly well when fishing these small upland waters. The stream fisher's ubiquitous problem of 'drag' (where varying speeds of the surface currents across the brook cause the fly to skate across the surface) still has to be overcome. On a larger river the technique of aiming the fly at a point a foot or two above the surface, pulling back sharply just as the line straightens out, is well known. The effect is to produce a 'wiggly' line on the surface which behaves a bit like weak elastic, allowing different parts of the line to travel at different speeds. This reduces drag on the fly, at least for the few moments during which we hope to deceive a fish. This principle can be applied to any flowing watercourse, but on really small brooks it is nearly always possible to cast your line so that it lies on the water from whichever direction will minimise drag. To achieve this you must first study the surface currents, betrayed by floating particles or current ripples, before choosing your method of casting.

Casting Tricks

The position from which to cast is invariably dictated by considerations of personal concealment, and the direction from which any sunlight is streaming. The skills of the reservoir fly fisher who can cover a cruising rainbow at 30 yards' range will not be called upon here, but they will be replaced by new demands. It may be difficult, at first, to accept that the challenge is not in placing a fly on the nose of a feeding fish, but in getting the fly into the water at all! There are all sorts of 'wrinkles' you can try, like floating a dry fly downstream on a dead leaf and jerking it free just in front of a good fish, thereby avoiding a shoal of smaller fry ahead of it; like casting your fly across a boulder and listening for a splash as it is seized by a trout lying in the hollow depression ahead of the boulder, and many more.

FINDING THE LIES

Mountain stream trout are like any other trout – they are nervous creatures. They know that moving shadows spell danger, and that safety is in concealment. The problem on upland streams is that there are precious few places for trout to hide. One feature which always gives trout a sense of security is depth, and deep holes are carved by falling water. I readily confess that the myriad little waterfalls on a mountain stream are just as much an attraction for me.

Wherever water tumbles over a ledge or pours through a narrow gorge, I expect to find trout of above average size. And usually I do. Trout get used to collecting the

Fig 54   A landing net is an unnecessary encumbrance on most hill streams. Here a fighting lightweight is brought to hand; it will be released from the barbless fly without being lifted from the water.

Fig 55   A battling quarter-pounder is deceived by a dry fly on the upper reaches of a drought stricken River Tawe.

Fig 56   The take! A hill stream trout takes a dry fly on the lip of a pool . . .

. . . and is hooked! Note the use of the 'left-hand strike' technique, which is much faster than, and should precede, the raising of the rod.

drowned casualties which drop from the pool or glide above, so offer them something from your fly box via the same route. Dry flies are rarely as successful as nymphs in these types of places. It is not that a dry fly would be rejected by the fish, but rather that you would have great difficulty in detecting the take.

Try a weighted nymph cast at the face of the waterfall. If the drop is just a couple of feet or less, you may be able to cast your nymph on to the lip of the waterfall so that it sinks into the surface before being swept over. Once your nymph has sunk in the undertow below the fall, lift your rod and watch or feel for an induced take. You should be able to tempt a few half-pounders from below falls on streams where the average adult fish reach less than half that weight.

Occasionally, you may make contact with a real monster, especially at the beginning and again towards the end of the season, so don't fish *too* fine. A 4lb point will not spook trout in turbulent water, and you may need to use a bit of pressure to keep a fighting fish clear of obstructions.

As you continue to develop your awareness of what makes a lie attractive to brown trout, you will concern yourself less with how to cast to the trout – that will come automatically. More and more you will find yourself working out how to get into a suitable casting position without being seen by your adversary. Then you will be thinking like a hunter.

8

Spring Tactics for Spate River Trout

Spate river trout offer a unique challenge. They are not particularly difficult to catch, and, unlike the brown trout of the fertile chalk streams, they do not have a superabundance of food to choose from. Selective feeding is rarely a problem. But there is still a problem of selectivity for the fly fisher. The majority of spate river fish are immature Salmonids, parr and fry of salmon and sea trout, as well as young brown trout. For every adult trout there will be hundreds of juvenile fish, all competing for the sparse food supply of early spring.

Young Salmonids seem to be programmed to feed and survive on impulse: 'If it moves and is smaller than me, I must give chase, catch it and eat it; if it is bigger than me, I must run and hide or I will be eaten', and in a spate river this simple philosophy seems quite appropriate. If you simply want to catch fish, a spate river would be the ideal place to maximise your success. A wet fly fished across-and-down on a long line could search half a mile of river in an hour, and great slaughter would be virtually assured. But to fish selectively, to tempt the big bullies of the stream whilst leaving the tiddlers unmolested — that is the real challenge of trouting on a spate river.

REDUCING THE RISKS TO SMALL FRY

Avoiding injury to immature brown trout is difficult. Quite often they attack a fly with such ineptitude that, having failed to find their target, they roll across the fly and become foul hooked. Many anglers now use barbless hooks to minimise the risk of harming these small trout. My experience certainly supports the view that few sizeable brown trout will be lost as a result of adopting this practice. For many years I have made a point of returning *all* my native river trout (and small sea trout), and I would happily fish barbless even if I believed it did carry a small penalty in terms of lost fish. For those who cannot dress their own flies, however, it may be difficult to obtain them tied on barbless hooks. The simple solution to this problem is to fold back the barb, using a pair of round-nosed pliers to avoid cutting the fine wire of the hook.

The real problem remains, of course. Hooking undersized trout is a bad thing, and should be avoided wherever possible. Each small fish I catch is a cause of concern and regret, and for that reason I try to use tackle, techniques and tactics which will reduce the likelihood of hooking small fry. As a bonus, many of these ideas increase the chances of catching the bigger trout, so there is a selfish motive in adopting them.

SELECTIVE FISHING WITH THE WET FLY

It might be thought that using a larger than normal wet fly would deter the smaller fish, but brown trout are rarely put off by the size of their prey, and they will readily

Fig 57   This natural weir on the River Nidd has a special attraction for both trout and fishermen.

Fig 58   A boulder-strewn spate river affords ample lies where trout can escape the full force of the current while surveying the food channels.

launch themselves at a lure as big as (and sometimes bigger than) themselves. I have, on occasion, hooked 2in trout when fishing with a high-water salmon fly.

Although by far the majority of my trouting is by dry-fly or nymph techniques, there are times when wet-fly methods are the only practicable way of fishing. Then I like to fish the water selectively, choosing to work the fly through pockets of water likely to hold better quality fish. Places to look for are where sub-surface features provide shelter from the full force of the current. There a trout can lie near to the main food channel.

The problem is that a wet fly needs time to sink to the required depth. Quite often this means getting the fly to swim near to the river bed where the trout will be lying. Casting directly into such lies does not provide the required results. Traditional wet-fly tactics involve casting across the river so that the fly (or a team of flies) travels across and down the river. As it does so, it sinks towards the bed before rising again when the line straightens out with the fly directly downstream. Shallow water upstream of the prime lie is likely to hold fry. These small trout will often chase and seize the fly as it swims across their path. It is these juvenile fish that we really need to avoid hooking, and there is something which can help achieve this.

When the water level is high (for example as it falls following a spate, a time when wet-fly fishing might be preferred), there is likely to be a lot of debris drifting down with the current. Trout swallow quite a lot of this rubbish in any case, but eventually they learn to differentiate between inert matter and real food such as nymphs, small fishes and drowning insects. I believe they differentiate between edible and inedible morsels not so much by their form – which might be difficult to distinguish in coloured or broken water – but by their behaviour. Swimming or struggling particles are selected for preference. So, if you can ensure that your fly behaves like drifting debris while it is sinking, and like a living creature when it approaches your chosen lie, then the chances of it being taken by small fry should be greatly reduced. And you should also increase your prospects of deceiving one of the bigger trout in the lie further downstream.

Your fly should be cast with an upstream mend. If you have not yet mastered the technique, it is well worth putting in some practice at side-casting to achieve this effect. Alternatively, you will have to mend the line immediately it has fallen onto the surface. Allow your fly to drift down to the lie you intend to fish. You may have to let out extra line to maintain a dead drift over shallow water where the small fry are feeding. If you are successful, takes from small trout will be far less frequent than in traditional across-and-down fishing. When your fly arrives at its intended destination, hold back its progress by raising your rod. The fly will begin to rise towards the surface and it will swim slowly across the river towards your bank. This behaviour normally proves irresistible to brown trout and is, in essence, the principle behind the 'induced take' or Netheravon style, developed by Frank Sawyer and Oliver Kite.

SELECTIVITY WITH THE DRY FLY

It is, of course, very satisfying to stalk a wild trout, observing the rise form and only casting to the fish when you are sure it is of a respectable size. On spate rivers, particularly when the water-level is high, many anglers find it necessary to 'fish the water'. In summer it is not too difficult to sort out the 'wheat from the chaff' before casting to a rising fish, and I would most strongly recommend this approach to all conservation minded anglers. But what about when the water is flowing fast, perhaps with the surface broken so that it is almost impossible to predict the size of a trout from its rise form? The truth is that fishing the water at random *must* result in immature fish being hooked. After a heavy spate it is the smaller fish which begin taking surface food first. While all trout will gorge themselves on terrestrial casualties as the water rises up the banks, small fish need feeding 'little and often', and so begin looking for food soon after the spate has subsided.

The only tactic I know of which consistently reduces the chances of catching small trout in these conditions is to fish places where there are few, if any, small fry. This, in turn, means fishing either where there are no trout at all (and most of us do quite enough of that!) or, more constructively, seeking out spots which hold the better quality fish, the ones which deter (or devour) the small fry. Thus, when fishing your favourite spate river in heavy water, it will pay you to cast your dry fly into the better lies. Provided the rise in water level is not substantial, these will be the places where you have seen good fish rise under more normal water conditions.

READING THE WATER

The idea discussed above, for locating fish in coloured water, is no help, of course, when fishing stretches of water which are new to you. Then you will have to learn to read the water. The keys to success are locating the trout and devising a means of presenting a suitable offering without forewarning the fish. Once you have hooked a trout, it is a relatively simple matter to play it away from snags and draw it into calm water for netting or release. Below are some places to look out for when surveying a new stretch of river.

Below stretches of broken water   Favourite haunts of large trout are the narrow funnels at the tail of a run of broken water, where the bed shelves into a pool. The fish lie in the quiet eddies beside these funnels, enjoying the concentration of food which the current provides.

Weir pools   The deeper, quieter water beside weirs and other waterfalls will also hold quality trout. These kinds of places are usually best fished with a nymph, as the trout in such lies get used to feeding on submerged insects as they drift out from the undertow.

Fig 59   Spring trouting on the swollen River Teifi.

The head of a pool Fish queue up in pecking order, with the small fry confined to the shallow tail of a pool. A dry fly cast into the glide at the head of a pool will often be taken by trout of above average size for the river. They are more easily deceived when a ripple disturbs the surface, so if the wind is gusting, do not rush to cast during a calm spell. Wait a few moments, if necessary, and time your casting to coincide with maximum surface disturbance.

To minimise drag, you may have to approach some lies by wading up the pool. Wade slowly, and the shoals of small fry will be shepherded along in front of your feet. Stumble and splash, and they will flee, setting up a chain reaction until harbingers of doom forewarn the large trout at the head of the pool. Then your only chance is to come back at another time and wade more carefully.

It may take several minutes to get into a good position for casting, but this is time well spent. You now have a chance of casting to an undisturbed fish, perhaps in an eddy beside the run into a pool. You will know that if your fly drags badly on your

Fig 60 A dry fly is quickly swamped in turbulent water. Here, a wet-fly cast upstream and across elicits a response from trout used to making split-second decisions on dietary matters.

122

first cast, the chances of raising a trout on this and subsequent attempts will be much reduced, so it is vital to plan your approach and the lie of your line on the water. Try casting a dry fly on to the back of the stickle above the pool, so that it swirls down the last yard before drifting into the calmer water. This will put a snake in your leader and allow you to fish the eddies longer before drag sets in. Expect a take as the fly enters the calm water. If nothing rises, tie on a weighted nymph and cast again. This time, retrieve line slowly to draw the nymph up through the eddy. If a trout takes a nymph on the retrieve it will, most likely, hook itself.

Swirls around obstructions Look out for features on the river bed which could provide a trout with some respite from the current. Submerged or partly submerged boulders create turbulence and constrict the current, forcing food through narrow channels. Trout lie in the slack water in the lea of a boulder, ready to dart out and intercept any passing morsels. Where the boulder breaks the surface, the dry fly is a good bet. Nymphs are usually more effective where the water is deep and the boulders are covered.

In coloured water you may not be able to see the boulders on the river bed. Look for up-wellings at the surface. Every irregularity on the bed is reflected as turbulence at the surface. The water doesn't well up directly over the obstruction, but some distance downstream. How far downstream depends on the depth and speed of the water, but if you fish a team of three wet flies spaced 18in apart you do not have to be particularly accurate in your estimate.

Fig 61   A plump pounder from beneath a hawthorn bush on the River Teifi.

123

Cast upstream and to one side of the turbulence and allow your flies to sink and drift across the lie. If the flies get caught up, let out more line and the current will often pull them free. An alternative approach is to fish a shorter line upstream and across. When fishing the upstream wet fly in fast water, you should find it easier to get your flies down to where the trout are lying. Lift the rod tip steadily as the team of flies crosses the boulder. If your flies sink too deeply they are likely to get snagged, and you may have to disturb the trout by wading upstream to free your tackle.

Rock gulleys and leaning trees often cause necks in the river where the water swirls and tumbles. This surface turbulence overwhelms hatching insects, and trout learn that these places mean food. A dry fly would soon be drowned in the 'boil'. This in itself is not a problem, since the natural insects suffer a similar fate, but bite detection would be almost impossible. A wet fly, cast from upstream, can be worked across and into the turbulent water. Fish which inhabit such lies get used to making split-second decisions on dietary matters, so be prepared for some crashing takes!

Overhanging bushes   Hawthorn trees are second only to willows in their determination to hang on to a fly if you give them half a chance. Even so, what fly fisher can resist a few casts beneath an overhanging hawthorn, for they are home to so many

Fig 62   Where it runs over a gravel bed, a spate river is constantly changing. A wading stick not only provides extra support, but it also allows the angler to probe the depth before stepping into the unknown.

terrestrial creatures. On a breezy day, and most specially if the wind is gusting, numerous small creatures suffer climbing accidents, to the evident delight of the trout waiting beneath. Occasionally, you may be able to create an 'artificial hatch' by shaking a bush at the head of a pool and waiting for the trout in the pool to rise. This trick doesn't always work, and I believe it depends how much breeze there has been in the recent past.

Dry Black Gnats or spider pattern wet flies are the armaments you will need. Approach slowly from downstream and across, casting short in the first instance as a 'sighter'. Too long a cast and either the fish will be lined or your fly will hit the bank. (In either case it will cost you your chance on that lie.) Extend the necessary line, wait for a lull in the wind, and cast your fly right under the bush, so that it alights on the surface like an insect dropping in from the branches above. If a trout rises to your fly, tighten up and apply side strain at once, before he can dart for the sanctuary of the roots, for a hawthorn's roots are as unyielding as its branches.

Tactics are the key to selective fishing on a spate river. Fish in the right sorts of places, using appropriate techniques, and you will greatly reduce the likelihood of hooking juvenile fish. Selective fishing need not reduce, and can on occasion increase, your chances of catching quality fish. On spate rivers, even in difficult post-food conditions, fly fishing should not and need not mean 'fry fishing'.

9

Early Days on a Chalk Stream

It was late April on the Test, the weather cloudy with a damp wind gusting to force 5 (downstream, of course!). I had learned from my host that, although the river had not yet been stocked, some nice over-wintered brown trout had been showing. 'They'll do nicely', I thought!

I arrived at the fishing hut around 5.30 p.m. and walked the length of both beats. Nothing! Back down again, and still no sign of a rising trout until, just before the hut, I heard a faint flop near a coppiced alder. Dropping on to all fours I skirted the alder to approach the bush from downstream. Another good plop, and this time I saw tell-tale rings radiating from a point less than a foot from the bank, beneath the alder.

There was a gap of just a few inches between the branches and the surface of the stream. In a flat calm it would have been worth a try, but in this wind? Oh well, perhaps just one shot. On went a small dark sedge. Side-casting into the wind, I placed my fly delicately onto the water several yards from the trout. Impatiently, I waited for the wind to abate. In the first lull I cast again, this time straight into the bush. Annoyed at my incompetence, I broke free at the point, tied on a second sedge and cast it with unerring precision into the bush, as company for the first.

Apart from a few flies, which I knew I could recover later, what was there to lose? So, aiming high above the top of the alder, I let out more line. The fly landed upstream of the bush, drifted under it, and was sucked down into the depths. Wow! It really works!

I tightened, and there was a mighty splash under the alder. I scrambled to untangle my line from the branches as the trout, discovering its mistake, tore out into mid-stream. After a brief but spectacular battle, in which the trout spent as much time above the surface as below, my net engulfed a 2½lb cock brown trout. It being rather a dark fish, I returned the trout to fight another day.

EDUCATED TROUT

Some chalk streams open for trouting on 1 April. Others wait until May when the fish have recovered from spawning and there is more fly life about. (With so many chalk streams being stocked from fish farms, the former reason must be academic now.) Certainly, April can be a difficult month, with water clarity poor and hatches of flies confined to limited periods. On the other hand, it can be a good month for tempting large wild or over-wintered brown trout. Many of these are fish which had become wise to the anglers' ways a winter ago. Some may have been pricked and lost; others will have taken up lies passed every day by numerous anglers.

'Car-park' trout are notorious for acquiring a cunning which defies all comers. These Aunt Sally fish are covered by each angler on arrival and again before departure. At first they may stop feeding and 'fade' or sink to the river bed. After a few weeks of this sort of treatment they ignore all artificial flies, but continue to take the real thing. Only the heaviest of splashy casts will cause them to seek temporary shelter until the 'air raid' is over.

Several angling writers have suggested that if you cast repeatedly in rapid succession to an educated trout it will, on occasion lose its resolve and take your fly. It is difficult to imagine a better way of educating trout! The late Richard Walker reported casting the same fly to a trout more than forty times before tempting and catching it. Certainly, in my experience, changing the fly for another pattern seems to do little to enhance one's chances with these wily old fish. I try, of course, for what angler can

Fig 63   The first sea pool on the Hampshire Avon at Mudeford, a productive spot for sea trout fishing.

resist the sight of a large trout feeding on surface fly, but I do so with little reason for optimism.

Things are quite different in spring, at least initially. After a winter's rest from bombardment, these educated trout are once again catchable. But they are still a great challenge. A careless footfall, a clumsy cast, a rod raised too high and all is lost, for they quickly regain their guile.

EARLY HATCHES

The Large Dark Olive hatches around midday throughout winter on many chalk streams, particularly near to the source where water temperature is less influenced by weather above ground. By April, when the first of the chalk stream fisheries open, hatches of this fly can be quite prolific, although they rarely last more than one or two hours. The March Brown, another early upwinged fly of importance to river anglers, occurs on many rough streams. This fly is not often seen on chalk streams. Apart from size (the March Brown is bigger than the Large Dark Olive), these two species have a somewhat similar appearance. Consequently, experienced rough stream fishermen mistake the chalk stream hatch from time to time.

The dun of the Large Dark Olive can be imitated well enough with either a Greenwell's Glory or a Gold Ribbed Hare's Ear. Whatever pattern you choose, make sure it is well oiled. Grease all but the last few inches of your leader, too, as the turbulent waters of spring quickly pull an ungreased fly and leader below the surface. This, in itself, is not so serious a problem, for trout will readily take the hatching dun (unlike the spinner, few of which return to the water after egg-laying). The difficulty is in seeing the take, especially on a bright spring day. Indeed, it is not always an easy matter to spot a rising trout at this time of the year. The water is fast and turbulent, and sometimes the trout make very little disturbance as they suck flies from the surface.

AUDIBLE RISE FORMS

On arriving at your beat, stand still for a minute or two and scan the surface for signs of a rising fish. The lies of last autumn may well be occupied, but it is likely that the trout will now be more widely distributed throughout the fishery. On very breezy days, it is almost impossible to see a trout rising twenty yards away, so you must walk very slowly upstream, looking *and listening* all the time. You can often locate spring risers, not by sight but by the sounds they make as they break the surface. These audible rise forms not only help you to find the trout, they also contain clues to what the fish are feeding on. A trout sipping spent spinners from the surface makes a gulping sound, the pitch of which is related to the size of its mouth cavity. Another rise which gives a guide to the size of the trout is the slashing rise of a trout to a hatching sedge. As the sedge fly skitters across the surface in its attempt to become airborne, the trout has to change direction to intercept the fly. The swirling rise is

Fig 64   A sunny day on the Itchen, where trailing 'onion' beds break the surface periodically, and can be mistaken for rising trout.

Fig 65   A trout takes an early-season sedge fly from the surface in a slashing rise which is accompanied by a distinct 'splosh'.

accompanied by a sound which I categorise as a 'splish', a 'splash' or a 'splosh' according to the size of the trout. These sounds are, in my case, accompanied by a release of adrenalin, the volume thereof also variable!

MAYFLY TIME

In late April or early May, well before the main hatch begins, the first intrepid Mayfly nymphs emerge from the silt of the river bed and drift lazily to the surface. There they rest, seemingly oblivious to any danger, as they part and flutter their wings before that vital test flight. Surprisingly, the majority of these early risers do reach the safety of the bank-side bushes. (Perhaps the trout cannot believe their eyes!) Later, when the hatch is properly under way, the first brave trout pokes an exploratory nose at an emerging Mayfly dun. Satisfied that it is not a mirage, it casts off its reticence and downs the fly . . . and another . . . and another.

As if the other trout had been waiting for such a signal from their food taster, in no time at all the stream is aboil with rising fish. A large trout, lying just beneath the surface, sips Mayflies from a streamy run between two wracks of weed. A smaller, less experienced fish launches itself clear of the water – far too late – in an attempt to intercept a dun during take-off. Seemingly unaware of danger, a grand old trout who has remained in the deepest of lies since last June, now joins in the feast, taking up its feeding station in a shallow backwater where the hatch is at its most dense.

The Mayflies hatch in their thousands for several hours each day. The trout seem to have unlimited appetites for them, gorging themselves and generally paying little attention to hatches of other flies. There is little wonder, then, that fly fishers feel drawn to the river during these precious few weeks. At times things can get very hectic with so many rising trout to choose from. Yet rarely can the fishing be described as easy (save when a prolonged downpour brings a run-off from the roads to colour the water) – certainly not easy enough to justify the traditional label of 'Duffer's Fortnight'. The real challenge of Mayfly time, of course, is to tempt with a dry fly one of those wise old leviathans which only a Mayfly party will bring to the surface.

The artificial Mayfly is not an easy fly to cast. It is large, and offers considerable air resistance. The secret is not to use too fine a leader point. With big fish on the feed in weedy water, a fine point could result in breakage. This is made all the more likely by the tendency of the Mayfly to hinge at the knot and, particularly when winged patterns are used, to spin during casting. As a result, after half an hour's fishing the strength of the nylon may be considerably reduced. It takes more skill to deceive a trout when fishing with 6lb rather than 3lb nylon as your leader point. But is it not better to lose a few chances than to leave a fly in the jaws of a trout?

Fig 66   A genuine Mayfly dun. The hackled imitation is more robust and has better hooking properties.

Winged Mayfly imitations are best reserved for short-range work. When casting more than ten or twelve yards, you will need perfect timing, otherwise the wings are likely to be damaged in a very short time. My preference for hackled Mayfly dun patterns is only partly based on this, as hackled patterns also tend to have better hooking properties. One other problem with winged Mayflies is their annoying tendency to alight with the wings in anything but the upright attitude. Mayfly spinners, or 'spent gnats' as they are sometimes called, lie on the surface with their wings outstretched. A hackled fly would not be a very effective representation of the spent fly, and you should use a winged pattern. Again, this is a fly best fished at short range whenever possible.

During the early part of a Mayfly hatch, trout rise to the duns with great gusto, and they are likely to forgive the occasional clumsy cast. Later, as the hatch provides a superabundance of food, the fish become less tolerant of imperfections both in presentation and in representation. When your Mayfly is just one of many drifting over a trout, it is not surprising that a steel hook bedecked with fur and feather is rejected. This is when the Mayfly nymph comes into its own. Grease your leader to within an inch of the nymph and cast it to drift inert over a rising trout. With the nymph just below the surface, the rise form will look and sound very similar to that when a floating fly is taken. You will have to watch your leader for a sign that the trout has indeed taken your offering in preference to one of the many natural insects drifting overhead.

When both duns and spinners are equally abundant, trout generally take more spinners than duns. Of least effort to intercept are the spent gnats, of course, for they take no evasive action at all. When a nymph doesn't do the trick and you can see both duns and spinners on the water, tie on a spent gnat. This will usually tempt a fish or two provided you cast a wiggly line to minimise drag. (Actually, drag is somewhat less of a problem when you fish with large dry flies, because they tend to cling to the surface and act like a 'sea anchor' to resist the pull of the leader.)

When a trout takes your Mayfly, do not be in too much of a hurry to strike. A Mayfly is a substantial mouthful and trout will need to take their time over it. (They also find it a difficult fly to eject quickly.) Give the trout time to turn down before tightening. Bigger fish take longer to turn and are slower to spit out an artificial once they discover the deception, so you should have plenty of time to tighten.

DAPPING THE MAYFLY

In southern Ireland, Mayfly time is dapping time. Anglers go out in boats on the great lakes to fish for trout with long rods. Silk floss is attached to a nylon leader to help the wind carry the fly in front of the drifting boat. The Mayfly is made to skip and dance on the waves, and some mighty trout are taken by this means. In contrast, dapping on a chalk stream is a short-range tactic. Once again, it is at its most effective on breezy days. First, you must find a trout which is feeding within one rod's distance of your bank. Allow for the wind as you cast, and try to get just the fly and no more than an inch or two of leader on the surface, a foot or two upstream of the trout. The wind

*Fig 67   Dapping a Mayfly on the Alre. Where a stream is heavily overgrown,
dapping may be the only practicable tactic.*

can make casting very difficult, but on the other hand a good ripple does help you
remain concealed from your quarry.

If you get the chance to fish any of the tiny feeder streams at Mayfly time, do not be
put off by the difficulty (or impossibility in many cases) of casting your fly there.
Dapping is a means of presenting a fly through an almost impenetrable tangle of
undergrowth. One useful tactic involves pinching a split shot on to the leader 2in
above the Mayfly. Wind in your line until the shot reaches the top ring. Then, when
you see or hear a rising trout, you can pass your rod through any gap larger than 2in.
Once your Mayfly is over the water, let out line (the shot will carry your leader
through the rod rings) until the fly alights on the surface. Trout in these tiny feeders
are easy to catch provided you move very slowly to avoid forewarning them. You
should only use this tactic when you are confident that you will be able to pull your
rod clear to play and net the trout.

If you ask a farmer for permission to fish in an overgrown stream just a yard or two
in width, you may get a very funny look indeed. And if he sees you fishing with your
reel in your pocket and using just the top joint of your rod, his suspicions would seem
to be confirmed!

One blustery April afternoon on a Hampshire stream, I came across a steady riser in a
little bay between two grey alders. I had seen no hatch of upwinged flies, and I
guessed that it had taken up that bank-side lie to benefit from the wind-borne spring
harvest from the meadows. There I had seen a few crane-flies and rather more sedges.

Despite much waving of my cap in the air, I had failed to catch a sedge fly, but was pretty sure they were Grannom. I tied on a small deer hair sedge and crept, on all fours, to within 6 yards of the feeding trout. Using the side-cast to get below the worst of the wind I offered my fly. Up came a neb in a splashing rise which I could hardly miss. 'God save the Queen . . . tighten!' (Any such phrase will do to help you delay the strike until the trout has turned his head down; otherwise you are likely to pull the fly from his jaws.)

The line went tight, the rod was pulled down in a sweeping curve, and I was into my first chalk stream trout of the season. The excitement was short-lived, however, for the trout made but one short run before floating to the surface on its side. I brought a 2lb over-wintered hen brown trout over my net and lifted her on to the bank for a photograph. She was a beautiful fish with red and black spots on golden flanks, marred only by a long vertical scar (probably a heron strike) behind the dorsal fin.

With the evidence in emulsion, I returned the trout carefully to the river, holding her head upstream until she slithered from my hand. A flick of her tail sent her cruising towards mid-stream and out of sight.

I walked the length of my allotted beat, searching in vain for another rising trout. On returning to the little bay between the alders, I found a steady riser in the place of my earlier success. The grannom had dried out well in the intervening half hour, and when I cast it a yard above the rise it floated down gently and was taken with a good splash. My prayer for Her Majesty's longevity preceded a great commotion. On tightening into the fish, it thrashed the surface to foam before getting its head down and making a surging run, first towards my bank and then across the river. I managed to turn it before it gained the sanctuary of a wrack of *Ranunculus*, and my reel sang again as the trout tore off upstream. It gained about 15 yards against the maximum pressure I dared apply. Then it pulled a very nasty trick. It turned about and raced towards me. Before I could gather in the slack line, the trout used the pull of the current to help it towards the safety of another weed bed downstream, below the bottom alder. Side-strain had no effect. I could neither turn nor stop that fish, and inevitably, I was weeded.

Hand-lining will sometimes free a weeded fish. On this occasion it didn't, but I could feel that the trout was still on. I let the line go slack, peeled off another couple of yards from the reel, and waited. After a while the line began to tighten. The trout had extricated itself from the weed and was swimming upstream, no doubt prompted by the pull of the current on the slack line. I reeled in and pulled my line clear of the weed. A few detached fronds of *Ranunculus* slid down the leader and across the nose of the trout. All resistance ceased instantly as the fish gave up the fight, blinded by a blanket of weed. From a wild, uncontrollable demon it was transformed to a meek and passive creature. I led it gently to my waiting net and lifted out *the same trout I had caught less than an hour earlier*. Like some people, some trout never learn!

10
The Early Runners

Long before what should have been sunset, day gave up the unequal struggle, beating a hasty retreat as if sulking from the angry threats of dark scudding clouds. Like the clouds themselves, those threats had been far from empty. Having risen for several hours, the river now held steady, its waters a dull greenish grey – the portent of prime sea trout fishing on many spate rivers.

The rain had given way to a fitful drizzle as I made my first tentative cast across the run-off from a long, deep pool above a stretch of broken water. From the right bank, casting with an upstream mend in the line, I released line from the reel allowing the fly to sink as it was swept towards the rocky ledge. Spring sea trout often lie beside this ledge, resting awhile after running the fast, broken stretch below.

My fly swam slowly in front of the ledge. It should swing nice and smoothly all the way round to my bank, unless . . . Yes! The fly had stopped, and the current was now putting a downstream belly into the line, drawing it towards the bank. A steady lift, a firm strike and the rod was wrenched down in an arc. Contact! A silver, tail-walking sea trout churned the surface to foam before beginning its first high-speed traverse of the pool. Giving line, retrieving line, keeping in contact as best I could, now, in the battle for supremacy, my nerves were firmly under control; the shakes would come later, whatever the outcome.

Several times the sea trout erupted from the depths, high into the air, before crashing down onto its side – or would it be onto my leader? But the hook-hold was good and a few minutes later the prize – a fresh-run fish of almost four pounds – lay gleaming in my net. Not such a big sea trout for springtime, but the hour brought two more from the same lie, neither under three pounds and each a shining model of perfection. This is spring sea trouting, and for me it is the very cream of game angling.

SPRING SEA TROUT

Springers! These streamlined torpedoes are more aggressive than any other game fish I know. Splashing through the foam of a rocky gorge or carving a 'v' across the surface of a quiet pool, an early-run sea trout will lunge furiously at any little thing which approaches too close to its chosen lie. All you need do is run your fly at the right depth across an occupied lie and battle will be joined. It sounds easy. So why have these migratory trout got such a reputation for being difficult to catch?

I can think of three very good reasons why you might fail to make contact with sea trout: you may be visible or audible to the fish, your fly may go undetected by the fish, or you may be fishing where there are no sea trout present. Taking the first of these points, the eyesight of a sea trout is acutely sensitive. In clear water, even on the darkest of nights, sea trout can see a distance of several feet, and very much further by day. This is why fly fishing at night is so productive, but it also causes real problems when you try to catch sea trout during the daytime. These shy fish will hide them-selves away under ledges or tree roots at the slightest hint of danger. The sight of flailing arms and rod or the sound of stumbling boots on rock or shingle can be enough to clear a pool of any taking sea trout instantly. These fish will not usually leave the pool, but they will ignore your flies, leaving you puzzled and frustrated.

When fishing in clear water at dusk, I have discovered that sea trout can see me when I can't see them . . . and vice versa! (This second finding is obviously useful, and I will come back to it again shortly.) Many times, when sitting beside a pool waiting for the light to fade, I have raised my arm to make the first cast of the evening only to send a sea trout careering away from under my feet. I have learned that it pays to sit well back from the water's edge and to make the first cast onto the water beside my own bank.

It is always worth a few moments' thought, as you approach a sea trout pool, to decide how you can avoid appearing as a silhouette on the skyline. Open, treeless banks are ideal places for casting, but they rarely provide the best fishing. As you gain experience of casting in the dark, tuck in close beside or beneath any trees or bushes which can help provide better concealment. This is especially important when there is a bright moon.

When dark descends on a quiet pool, sea trout can be taken right under your rod tip. You still need to avoid making a noise with your boots, but by wearing drab clothing you should be invisible to the fish even at close range. I mentioned that it is still possible to see them if the water is clear and not too deep. You need to get into a position where the surface reflects the dark of the bank or of trees rather than the silver of the sky. Sea trout show up as vague golden flashes (I call them 'winks') which are visible for just a brief moment as the fish turn and reflect the light of the night sky. These cruising sea trout will take a fly if you work it through the water at points where you see them turning. As sea trout are shoal fish, it is quite common for a long spell of inactivity to be broken for just a few minutes as three or four spring fish cruise around in front of you. (In summer you may encounter several dozen fish in a shoal, and the water can flash and shimmer like a fireworks display.) Fish hard at such times, for they are precious in spring, and skilful fishing can bring great returns.

Fig 68   Evening fishing for sea trout on the River Laune, Eire.

*Fig 69   Open, treeless stretches make for easy casting but difficult fishing.
Tucking in close beside a bush affords better concealment on calm water in early
evening.*

The second cause of failure is the fly going undetected by your quarry. In clear
water, spring sea trout will move to a fly several yards away provided it is presented at
the right depth. By some means – maybe detection of vibrations as the fly swims
through the water – sea trout can sense the presence of a fly moving through a quiet
pool. They can do this in what, to us, may appear to be almost total darkness, even
when the water is brown after a spate. But I find that they only have this amazing
homing ability in quiet pools and gentle glides. In the rough and tumble, the noise of
the water confuses this long-range auditory sensing system. Sight then becomes the
most important means by which a fish locates the fly. If I am right, this could explain
why pitch blackness rarely provides good night fishing conditions early in the season
when high water levels are usually encountered.

Sea trout do not rest in mid-water for any length of time. You may see them erupt
periodically from the depths, but most of the time they hug the bed of the river where
they can hold station with the minimum of effort. For best results, therefore, your fly
should swim at the same depth as the fish, near the bottom. Failing to get right down
to the river bed is, I am convinced, the single most significant cause of poor results
with spring sea trout.

The third reason for failure with spring sea trout is the most difficult to put right.
No amount of skill can compensate for fishing where there are no sea trout! You must
find a sea trout lie which is occupied; only then will your expertise count for anything. In spring, the river will certainly not be teeming with fish, and some spots will

be far more attractive to sea trout than others. So how do you find these hot spots? There is no substitute for experience on a river, but very often when you find a productive lie, similar spots elsewhere will prove equally good. By making a careful note of productive lies, you can build up a 'library' of likely sea trout lies to help you when you visit new fisheries. Below are some suggestions for promising features to look out for, and some tactics for tempting their occupants.

RUNNING FISH AND RESTING FISH

Most of the fish you see breaking the surface will be intent on running up river; they will rarely, if ever, take a fly. You will soon come to recognise the humping rise of a running sea trout, for invariably the head breaks the surface facing upstream and the motion is usually more horizontal than vertical. There is little point in casting across the path of a running sea trout. Indeed, many would consider it rather unsporting since in fast water there is a distinct risk of foul-hooking. Leave the runners to their running; look, instead, for resting fish. Rising fish which swirl on the surface are sometimes takers. Fish which leap vertically a foot or two into the air before crashing on to their sides are also worth noting. They rarely take while so unsettled, but some time later you may well be able to induce an offer to your fly.

The best takers are often the quiet cruisers. Not totally static, they have chosen a temporary lie from which they make occasional forays, perhaps patrolling and protecting their 'territory'. They may take a fly while cruising, and are even more likely to do so if your fly disturbs them while they are in residence.

THE LOWER REACHES

From the last sea pool on a river, through to the top of the tidal influence, spring sea trout tend to run straight through. The estuarial waters may be worth a little more of your time in summer, but if you have the choice go a mile or more above the top of the tidal reach for your early-season sea trouting. The larger spring fish do tend to run quite a long way upstream before settling with any permanence into lies. After the effort of forging up through rough water they will rest, albeit briefly, in temporary lies beside gulleys, ledges, undercut banks or sunken trees. These are not the easiest of places in which to present a fly.

The tail of a pool, either above a waterfall or after a long run of broken water, can often serve as a temporary respite. Here is a tactic for such spots. I came across this idea one afternoon when walking the river bank, surveying a pool I intended to fish that evening. A fair-sized sea trout surged up through the run below the pool, keeping to the main current in water less than a foot deep. Every now and then its progress was marked by a shower of spray as its thrashing tail broke the surface. On arrival at the lip of the pool, where the current slackened into deeper water, the sea trout paused as if confused. I watched the fish swim from left to right and back again as if seeking the main channel. Three times that sea trout crossed the lip of the pool before pushing on into the deep water – three times – and if my fly had been drifting across the tail of the pool that fish would have seen it not once, but three times. This, I thought, must surely improve the odds.

Early in the evening settle into a position where you can drift your fly across the tail of the pool. A sunk line, or at the very least heavily weighted flies, will be necessary to avoid your lure skimming across the surface. Keep the rod tip held high (it helps reduce drag), and hold a coil of line loosely in your hand so that you can give slack on the take. This is vital, otherwise you will simply pull the fly away from the jaws of your quarry. Ideally, you want to hook your fish in the scissors, and to do this you need slack line downstream of it before you tighten.

To be on the safe side, I aim to apply minimum tightening force until the fish has run upstream. Then I can strike again to set the hook firmly. This works well most times, but on occasion it has backfired and I have been left with a tight line running down over a waterfall. Then what? Usually, something has to part – either the line or the hook-hold. I have tried just slackening off and waiting to see if anything happens, and once the fish swam back up the falls. I retrieved my line and landed my prize!

There is good logic behind this suggestion that you should not try to fight both the fish and the current. Give slack line to a fish which runs downstream. What causes its retreat is the pull of your line. When you peel off slack line from the reel the current will carry it downstream, and, as soon as the fish hesitates in its head-long surge, a loop of line will be drawn below it. The current acting on this loop of line will apply a

Fig 70   Weighty tube flies are called for when fishing the deep channels below this natural waterfall on the upper Towy.

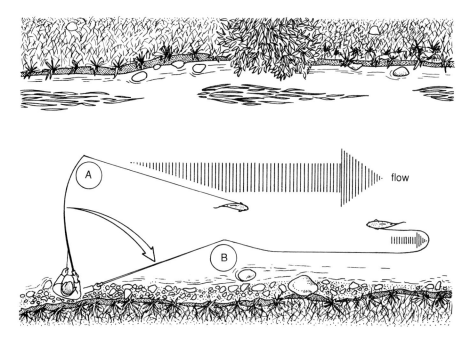

Fig 71   When a sea trout runs downstream in fast water, swing the rod from A to B and let out slack line. The fish will usually turn upstream to fight the pull of current on the belly of the line.

downstream force, and in turning to resist this pull, the sea trout will play right into your hands (or net). Once you have the fish upstream of your position, it is you and the current versus the sea trout, and the odds are turned much more in your favour. At the same time, the force on the fly drives the hook more firmly into the scissors instead of tending to pull the hook out from the jaws – altogether a more encouraging thought.

FEEDER STREAMS

Very occasionally, a localised cloudburst may cause a tributary to burst its banks, pouring coloured water into an otherwise clear main river. Sea trout then leave the main river and pack the lower pools of the feeder. As the tributary fines down you can enjoy some quite spectacular fly fishing for a few days. Gradually, the sea trout will drop back towards the main river, but I believe that many of those which will eventually run the tributary in autumn settle into residence in the slack water of the confluence pool. I observed such a resident shoal for several weeks and watched their backs darken gradually as the season advanced. At first the fishing was easy – perhaps too easy. But a fortnight after the spate those sea trout were much less inclined to move to a fly.

Fig 72   A spring sea trout from the River Cych, a tributary of the Teifi.

In the absence of a tributary flood, I suggest you persevere with the main river when seeking spring sea trout. Fish the tributaries for trout, of course, but wait until summer or early autumn before getting too serious about sea trouting on the smaller streams, unless local knowledge suggests they differ from the general pattern I have described.

THE MIDDLE REACHES

Further up river the shoals split up. Fish rest for days at a time before moving on slowly at night (or by day when a spate colours the water). Permanent residents – 'potted fish' as they are sometimes called – take up deep-water lies. Many of these can only be reached with wet lines cast upstream and allowed to sink on the drift down towards the lie. Large flies fished after dark can sometimes tempt these difficult fish, but do not expect too much co-operation from your quarry. You will have to get your fly quite close to the place where you think a sea trout is resting, then lift the rod tip to pull the fly away from the fish. If all goes well there should be a crashing take, enough to set the hook firmly and your reel screaming as a well-rested fish puts its muscle to good use.

I know from observation that sea trout will also rest up in those pockets of quiet water in front of large boulders in areas of heavy current. (On shingle beds a depression forms ahead of boulders, rather than behind as you might perhaps expect.) Rarely have I managed to tempt fish from such lies, and then only during the hours of daylight. Large bright lures have been most successful, again suggesting that visibility is more important when fishing these 'noisy' stretches of water.

Heavily-shaded areas of otherwise open water provide cover much sought after by sea trout fresh up from the estuary. On bright days you will have more success fishing under the trees than in the open water, and this seems to be the case even when the river is running coloured. Conventional across-and-down techniques can be used, but you will probably find that the sea trout are tucked firmly against the bank and will stay there unless you drop your fly very close to the edge. This is difficult fishing, especially if you have to side-cast to get beneath a canopy of foliage.

I first discovered the importance of accurate casting in this type of situation on the

Fig 73   Derek Hoskin plays a lively spring fish on the Teifi.

River Conwy near Llanrwst in north Wales. On a wide and deep section of the river I was struggling to reach the far bank from a mid-stream casting position. Standing knee-high in water I was, at best, able to cast 20 yards with my 9ft number 7 rod and double-taper line. I managed to drop my line out where I wanted it on about one cast in four. Each time I did so, sea trout would follow the fly across to mid-stream before snatching at it and careering back towards safety. When the fly fell short by a yard or two, it elicited not the slightest response from the sea trout. Two fine spring fish fell victim to my rod that day, but had I been using more powerful tackle to give me just another few yards, I might well have enjoyed a red-letter day.

THE UPPER REACHES

You might begin your spring fishing in April on the lower reaches of a spate river, while on the upstream fishery it is often mid-May or early June before fly fishing becomes anything more than an excuse for fresh air and exercise. Just how long it takes the sea trout to reach the head-waters depends on the length and nature of the river, on how fast the fish run, and how much rest they take on the way up. Rainfall in the river catchment has a very big influence, of course. Most years I am happy to begin fishing in April or early May on the lower beats of my local rivers, moving to the middle reaches in early June and following the large spring fish upstream through the month. I have found no special tactics necessary on these upstream fisheries, but the fish are certainly more difficult to tempt the longer they have been away from the sea. (Award yourself double credit for catching a sea trout from the headwaters or from tiny feeder streams!)

DEEP-WATER POOLS AND GORGES

Using a floating line you cannot present a fly deeper than the length of your leader, and in a pool with a strong current your fly will inevitably settle at a depth much less than this. Sinking lines are, therefore, essential for some spring fishing, but they have the disadvantage of taking the fly right down to the river bed in slack water. In contrast, with a floating line and suitably weighted fly you can arrange for your fly to swim just above the bottom, clear of rocks and other snags. Provided that the wind is not gusting (which makes casting large flies on long leaders a dangerous pursuit), I will use up to 15ft of leader at night rather than change to a sunk line. Assuming you are standing on the shallower side of a pool and casting across and down, the ideal path of your fly is illustrated in Fig 74.

You want your fly to sink almost to the river bed as it moves from position A to position B, to hold that depth across the middle region B to C, and then to rise towards the surface while fishing from C to D. Provided that you cast with (or make after casting) an upstream mend and then slowly retrieve line during the drift between C and D, this is precisely what you get when fishing with a floating line.

There is a way of achieving the same effect with a sunk line, and that is to use a

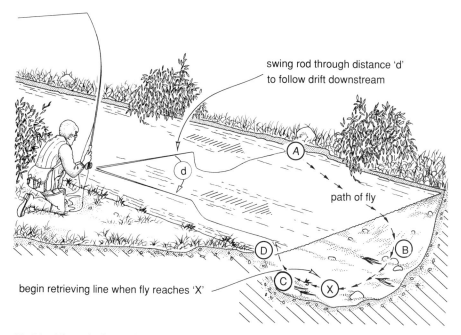

swing rod through distance 'd'
to follow drift downstream

path of fly

begin retrieving line when fly reaches 'X'

Fig 74   The path of a weighted fly fished on a floating line. Ideally, when sea trout are lying on the river bed, the fly should swim a few inches above the bed. Leader length or fly weight can be altered to achieve this.

buoyant fly. An under-dressing of ethafoam can be used for this purpose. Provided the line itself does not get snagged, this idea works a treat, and you do not then need a long leader to fish a very deep pool.

Even with a fast-sinking line, drag may prevent your fly from getting down to the required fishing depth in fast-water gorges. A solution to this problem is to cast upstream and allow the line to sink as it returns to you. There will be very little drag, because line and water will be travelling at more or less the same speed. When the fly reaches you, raise your rod to bring the line round in an arc, and watch the bend in the line for any sign of a take. Gradually, lengthen the distance you cast upstream. If you cast too far you may feel your fly drag or even snag on the bottom. (Gorges are notorious for collecting wedged trees and the like.) Next time, do not cast quite so far, and your fly should swim just above the obstruction.

CHOOSING YOUR CASTING POSITION

Spring sea trout generally run large (sometimes into double figures) so you will want to ensure that any fish you hook can be played out and landed safely. For example, if you cast a long line from position A in Fig 75, it is doubtful whether you will be able to prevent a hooked fish snagging you in the tangle of roots and branches under the

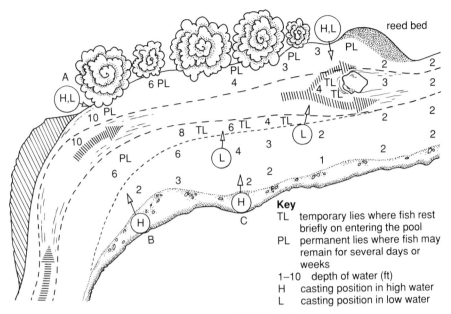

Fig 75   A typical spate river pool showing temporary lies (TL) and permanent lies (PL). The shallower temporary lies lose their attraction once the heavy waters of spring have subsided.

bank. Surely it is best not to hook a sea trout when there is a reasonable prospect of a breakage and the fish being left ensnared? Most of the other lies under the trees on the left bank are only fishable when the river is low enough to allow wading. Even then, your rod will have to be held high to avoid the drag of mid-stream currents. If it is unsafe to wade, then fish from positions B and C, concentrating on the temporary lies to the right of the main current.

By day you will have to consider where your shadow will fall and where the water will be shaded by trees, bushes or large boulders. Sea trout lying in natural shade are less likely to be spooked by your movements, so you should be able to approach them more closely, cast more accurately and, perhaps, avoid drag from surface currents. Boulders beneath the surface can provide shade in daytime. Upwelling currents betray the presence of these sunken obstructions, but remember that the surface boil will be some distance downstream of the boulder. You will have to allow for this when casting and working your fly towards a boulder lie.

TO RETRIEVE OR NOT TO RETRIEVE?

Stillwater fly fishers who visit sea trout rivers often ask whether or not to retrieve. My standard answer is, 'Maybe, but more slowly than you are used to!' In fact, it is rarely necessary to retrieve line at all while your fly is swinging across the current. Retrieving a floating line draws the fly up towards the surface and reduces your chance of taking a sea trout. Even with a sinking line, if your fly will swing right round to the 'dangle' without snagging the bottom then let it do so. Hold the fly on the dangle for a few seconds before beginning a slow retrieve or lift-off, as it is quite common for a sea trout to follow the fly from deep water into shallow and to pause before snatching the fly and darting back towards its lie.

DETECTING THE TAKE

In totally slack water (something of an unusual situation in spring), it may be necessary to work the fly by retrieving line. Make this movement as slow as possible, and watch the bend in the line as it falls away from the rod tip. At the slightest suggestion of a take (the line tightening, falling slack or pulling to one side), no matter how small the movement, strike. Strike hard, do not just tighten up. These sea trout have bony jaws. On feeling the hook your fish will probably leap high into the air, shaking its head violently. This is quite enough to release a partially set hook. But worse is to follow. The shock as the fish crashes to the surface, followed by several more on subsequent leaps, will test the hook hold more than in any other branch of angling.

If anything, the problem is reversed when fishing for sea trout by conventional across-and-down techniques in fast water. Delaying the strike until the fish has turned requires courage. If you hold your rod low the fish *might* hook itself, albeit only momentarily, or your leader might break with the shock of the take!

Fast-water takes are rarely difficult to detect. Intuitively you might expect quite a few slack-line takes but, in practice, they rarely occur. There must be times when a sea trout takes hold of the fly and swims directly upstream, but this still leaves a loop of leader trailing down behind the fish, and the pull of the current registers as a tightening of the line. The only exception I have found is when fishing with a mended line (a loop of line intentionally cast or flicked upstream on to the surface to slow down the rate at which the fly swings across the current). Then, nothing registers at the rod tip until the line has been pulled into a downstream loop.

Some time ago I discovered that, even though I hesitated, uncertain about that first slight twitch as the sea trout took hold of the fly, it was still worth striking, as, even a second or more later, the fish was still there. Spring sea trout will hang on to a fly for quite some time as long as they do not feel too much drag. This again is further justification for keeping the rod held really high. The first pull the sea trout feels is when you set the hook.

FLIES FOR SPRING SEA TROUT

The most important feature of a sea trout fly is its behaviour in the water – how it moves and, in particular, how quickly and at what depth it swims. If you get this right then choice of pattern is, I am convinced, of secondary importance.

In coloured or turbulent water, high visibility is needed, so bright colours and

Fig 76   Sea trout flies for spring fishing. Top: single-hook flies can be weighted with lead foil under-dressing. Middle: double hooks give a more secure hook-hold and may not require additional weight. Bottom: tube flies can be tied on plastic, aluminium or brass tubing in various lengths. They are used with treble hooks.

plenty of silver or gold flash are called for. Teal Silver and Blue, Medecine, Silver Doctor and Dunkeld have all served me well. Start off with smaller flies by day (size 10 or 8), and change to something bigger as dusk descends. Tube flies can be tied in a range of weights in each size simply by changing the tube material. Use plastic tubes for surface or near-surface fishing, then you can add wire under-dressing to get below the surface more quickly. For fishing in really fast currents you may need to tie your flies on brass tubes. These are far from easy to cast, and for safety's sake, beginners are advised to avoid them. An alternative is to use a less weighty fly with a sink-tip or a sinking line.

When fishing slowly drifting pools, I get better results with darker flies. Silver is still important, but I blend it with red and black. The Butcher, Zulu and Sweeney Todd are all good patterns for spring as well as summer. Hooks as small as size 12 may be necessary in bright conditions, but do not hesitate to go up as large as size 6 or even 4 when darkness falls.

Conventional flies swim with the hook point downwards, and so are prone to snagging on ledges or other sunken obstructions. A pattern which Derek Hoskin and I devised some years ago to overcome this uses a keel hook. The dressing is a hybrid, combining features of both the Butcher and the Sweeney Todd; we call it the Dyffryn Demon, and it has proven itself over many seasons. One practical tip is to dress this fly in a range of weights, using the heavy foil from the top of wine bottles as under-dressing. Use a range of tying silk colours as a guide to selection – black for un-weighted, green for medium-sinking and red for the 'plummet' version.

SPRING NIGHTS

All-night fishing on British rivers in April is strictly for masochists. It really is not necessary or worthwhile to suffer the cold for so little return. In the chill waters of spring, start your fishing an hour or so before dusk (earlier, of course, if the water is coloured) and try for sea trout as they enter the tail of a pool. After dark, move up to cover any known or suspected lies on the pool. By 9 o'clock, the activity will almost certainly be over. Come the middle of May it is worth persevering until about 11 o'clock extending this to an hour or so after midnight a month later. Keep your all-night stamina in reserve for July and August when the nights are less chilly and sea trout really can be taken right through until dawn.

THE VALUE OF RECORDING

Where the river bed is rocky and, therefore, very stable, knowledge of the location of productive lies should be valuable for life. Sea trout find some lies attractive throughout the season, in flood and in drought. Other lies only hold sea trout over a narrow range of water levels. It pays to note not only the location but also the water level when recording your spring fishing results. Where the river runs over gravel, huge disturbances in the contour of the bed occur from one year to another as material shifts progressively downstream with each flood. One season's deep pool may become a shallow riffle just a few months later, and the business of learning the river must begin all over again. For this reason, fish the more stable sections of the river in spring, when high and coloured water conditions make daytime reconnaisance impossible.

I still refer to the river below my cottage as 'home pool', because when I first came to live on the banks of the River Cych it held good salmon and sea trout lies. Now, it is a cascade of tumbling white water in spring, and a rippling shallow in high summer.

Demonstrations of fishing technique can be unmitigated flops, and so it is nice to be able to recount an instance when one of the above ideas worked spectacularly on the day. I was to demonstrate for a visitor the tactic for fishing the lip of a pool. I pointed out a spot just ahead of the lip where a submerged rock caused a noticeable upwelling of the surface. (The rock actually breaks the surface at low water.) I explained to my guest that I had previously seen sea trout saw backwards and forwards across the lip of the pool and then rest briefly beside the rock before running on into the deep water. I cast across the tail of the pool and immediately a fish slashed at my fly and was hooked. It was a good fight with a fine sea trout of just over three pounds.

'Fluke!' taunted my guest. 'Now do it again!'

I did as instructed, already more than delighted with my good fortune. The fly swung across the lie again. Immediately, a second sea trout was on – and a better fish, too. Five minutes later, the spring balance registered 4¼lb. My guest was convinced. I was amazed, but pre-empted any suggestion that we should try again. (I once caught six sea trout in successive casts, but these were the plentiful fish of summer-time.)

Waiting for the first of the spring run can be frustrating and trying on the nerves – so much tense anticipation and often so very little action. But when, at last, your line goes tight and your reel sings out stridently, shattering the peace of an April evening, you will need all your nerve. The battle has only just begun, and you could so easily be into the fish of a lifetime – a leaping, tail-walking super-trout, worth every waiting minute.

PART III
SUMMER TACTICS

11

High Season on a Rough Stream

The heavy waters of March and April which scoured the bedrock and cut savagely into the bank sides have fallen back. The stream quietly licks its wounds as the season of warmth and growth stimulates all forms of river life. The trout, too, have shaken off their winter lethargy and feed avidly on the spring harvest. As the river level falls so the path of the main current changes and the dominant trout migrate to their summer lies. If our attempts at deception are successful, the lies will be more permanent than their occupants!

Sub-surface life emerges with the increase in water temperature, presenting the nymph fisherman with his three-dimensional challenge. Terrestrials drop in and encourage snacks between meals, and it is usually possible to find a rising fish in some lie or other throughout the lengthening days.

TACTICS FOR THE MAYFLY MADNESS

On rain-fed streams, hatches of Mayfly are even less predictable than on the chalk streams. One year you might see prolific hatches in the first week in May, while in the following season you might have to wait until the beginning of June before the first greendrakes (Mayfly duns) emerge. The emergence of the Mayfly is largely dependent upon water temperature, and in spring this can vary from a few degrees above freezing to approaching 20 °C, the danger point for most Salmonids.

Not all rough streams have Mayfly hatches, and, on those that do, rarely are they so abundant that trout become gorged and sulky. There is, perhaps, some justification for the title 'duffer's fortnight' being applied to Mayfly time on rough streams rather than chalk streams. It is the one time when many of the trout cast off their shyness. The small proportion of very large trout, which through the rest of the year feed close to the river bed, are induced to rise during a hatch of Mayfly duns or, more often, to a fall of spinners in the evening. But these wise old trout retain their shyness, and will retire from the scene at your first heavy footfall or splashy cast.

The Beginning of the Hatch

Once the first few Mayflies emerge, rough stream trout seem to lose interest in other upwinged flies during the day. In the evening, spinners and sedge flies would seem equally acceptable, but in the cold light of day, other duns usually escape unmolested

Fig 77 Few rough streams have a greater variety of fly life than the River Usk, which provides outstanding trout fishing.

while the fish fight over the greendrakes. I have seen trout collide on the surface, so anxious have they been to secure a hatching Mayfly. The fishing is simplicity itself. Just cast your artificial wherever you see a good trout rise. You even get more time to tighten into it, as it will hang on to a Mayfly rather longer than it would a smaller artificial fly before ejecting it.

Stony stretches of river may be almost devoid of Mayfly nymphs, so concentrate your efforts where the hatch is likely to be most dense. Muddy backwaters, eddies beside weir pools and silted feeder stream junctions are favourite haunts of the Mayfly nymph. Do not worry too much if the water is shallow, for, provided they do not get disturbed, trout will swim with their dorsals out of the water in order to secure a *Danica* dinner. (I once watched a brown trout beach itself by lunging towards a mud-flat in an attempt to take a skittering Mayfly dun.)

In Times of Plenty

When the Mayfly hatch is at its peak, you might have difficulty getting a trout to accept your imitation, even though it may be taking every natural Mayfly it sees. This must be a sign of some inadequacy of the artificial, for we are nowhere near having devised a pattern which trout *prefer* to the real thing. The key to success at times like this is variation or even exaggeration. Try a Mayfly much larger or much smaller than those on the water. If you dress your own flies, make some up with bodies both lighter and darker than the natural Mayfly. In my experience, artificial Mayflies rather smaller and *considerably darker* than the genuine fly are most often successful.

After the Carnival

For a week or more after the last Mayfly hatch, trout can be tempted up with an artificial. The spinner is particularly effective whenever there is an evening rise. In early July I have made some fine catches on the greydrake when trout seemed to be preoccupied with Sherry Spinners (spinners of the Blue Winged Olive) during the evening rise.

POST-MAYFLY NYMPH FISHING TACTICS

On all but the barest of rough streams, the fishing gets more difficult as July advances. Hot sunny days inhibit fly hatches, and those few which do emerge are often ignored by the torpid trout. To tempt trout in the heat of the day you need tactics for fishing below the surface.

Nymph Fishing in Fast Water

In all but the swiftest of runs it is only necessary for a fish to hug the bed of the stream while waiting to intercept its next helping, for here the current is much weaker than at the surface. You can easily verify this when wading. A slight shuffling of the feet

*Fig 78   A bright summer day on the River Usk, and no sign of a rising trout.
But hard against the bank, something stirs, and a dry fly is cast accurately to cover
the spot.*

disturbs waterlogged debris which drifts downstream more slowly than the surface
flotsam. This effect causes a problem for the nymph fisherman, as the more rapidly
moving surface layer applies a force via the floating section of the leader pulling the
nymph upwards. As a result, the rate of sinking is significantly slower than for the
same nymph cast into still water.

For many years I puzzled as to why my nymphs were less successful in a current
than in near-static pools. After all, a trout in flowing water gets a more distorted image
of the nymph and far less time to choose from the 'menu'. Having realised that the
variation in current between surface and river bed is the source of this problem, a
solution was not hard to find. It is simply a matter of increasing the length of the non-
greased section of the leader. Generally, I select a length of about one and a third times
the depth of the stream, and then vary the weight of the nymph to suit the strength of
the current. This approach to setting the fishing depth has a significant advantage
compared with adding or removing floatant from the leader. That is, the distance
above the lie which the nymph should be cast remains more or less constant. Anima-
tion of the artificial nymph is provided via the leader due to the fluctuations in flow in
the surface layers – the equivalent in three dimensions of 'surface drag' when you fish
the dry fly.

Detecting the take when fast water nymphing can be difficult. A small piece of

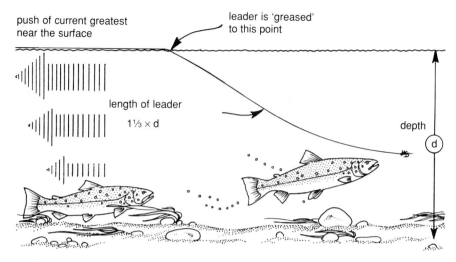

push of current greatest
near the surface

leader is 'greased'
to this point

length of leader
1⅓ × d

depth

d

Fig 79   A strong current at the surface and a weaker current near the river bed cause an upward thrust, countering the weight of the nymph and reducing its rate of sinking.

orange silk tied in at the end of the floating section of the leader can be a great help when the water is turbulent. Watch the floating leader for a pull downwards or to one side. You will need to react swiftly to set the hook before the trout realises the deception.

In calmer waters, the tantalising spectre of an escaping nymph may be suggested by raising your rod tip as the nymph nears its quarry. The resulting 'induced take' rarely needs a strike to set the hook. Sawyer's Pheasant Tail Nymphs tied on heavy forged hooks of sizes 10 or even 8 may be needed to get down well in fast runs. Smaller nymphs, down to size 16, are useful in near-static pools and slow eddies. Larger nymphs can also be used, provided that they are tied on fine wire hooks so that they sink slowly and, more importantly, rise up like a hatching nymph when you retrieve line.

The larger rough stream trout are infrequent risers and take most of their meals 'in bed'. Not surprisingly, then, an analysis at the end of the season usually shows that nymph fishing has accounted for trout of a better average size than other techniques.

DRY-FLY TACTICS

For many fly fishers, summer and the dry fly are inextricably intertwined. It is a time when skill is amply rewarded and incompetence mercilessly punished. But to catch trout consistently, perseverance with a single tactic is far from a virtue. What you need is a range of dry-fly tactics to suit the wide variety of opportunities a rough stream presents to the summer angler.

Fig 80   The evening rise does not always materialise, but it is still worth persevering as darkness falls. This beautiful 3lb hen fish was deceived by a large G and H Sedge as the glow in the western sky was fading.

Downstream Dry Fly

Where access to a rough stream lie is not possible from below, try floating a dry fly downstream. Considerable stealth is needed to get into position above a fish without putting it down. Cast sideways and as close to the surface of the stream as possible or the trout will see the rod flash in its window of vision and it will be off like a rocket. In some instances you will be able to use the current to present your fly, simply by letting out line from your reel. More often this will cause too much drag, and you may need to cast a wiggly line so that your fly alights just upstream of a feeding trout and drifts over the lie without dragging.

Trout weighing a pound or more are no more difficult to hook on a dry fly fished downstream than they are with conventional upstream fishing. Smaller trout, which you must expect on most rough streams, detect the deception and open their jaws more quickly. If you strike when the trout's mouth is open you will pull your fly away and miss your fish. If your reactions are not fast enough, there is a way of gaining a little more time: use flies which the trout do not eject so readily. A trout will quickly spit out a bare hook, but will hold on longer if the hook is well concealed within the dressing. For fishing the dry fly downstream, tie size 12 flies on size 14 or even size 16 hooks. You will have to strike more firmly, of course, because the bulky dressing masks the hook.

When no Flies Hatch

On the warmest and calmest of summer days it is very disappointing (but quite common) to arrive at the river only to find no sign of a rising fish. My advice would be to *take a walk!* Look for places different from the norm; there fish behaviour may also differ. A heavily shaded stretch of an otherwise open stream may well hold a rising trout or two. Where a feeder provides an inflow of cooler water could also be productive. Cattle drinks – whether occupied by cattle or not – seem busy places for surface-feeding trout when other reaches are devoid of activity. (Perhaps hatching times are altered by all the disturbance of the silt on the bed of the stream.)

The Evening Rise

June usually heralds the first real evening rise, which from now on assumes increased importance as daytime hatches wane. The impending close of the day finds both the trout and the angler cramming their last frantic efforts into the period of dying light. You may be tempted to cast your fly at every rise, but the fish are generally at their most selective around dusk. It is common to find that only one or two patterns of imitation provide any success at all. The maxim to adopt is, 'If at first you don't succeed, pack it in and try something else!' Certainly, there are times when the trout seem only to be interested in tiny buzzers and gnats the size of a wind knot in 2lb nylon. When your smallest artificial is ignored there is just one last chance – shock tactics! A big daddy-long-legs imitation added to the soup will occasionally be met with open jaws.

A WET-FLY TACTIC

For the dog days what more suitable quarry than the dog trout? It is the bully of the stream, and it relies on hit-and-run tactics to secure its meals. Long gone are the days when it was prepared to exert itself to surface for floating morsels or to chase small fry through the shallow margins. Its feeding pattern now consists of brief forays into the current to snap up the victims of its ambush, thence to return to the security of its lair under a sunken log, a deep undercut or a jungle of tree roots.

The whereabouts of these old dog trout (they are often real whoppers compared with the average for the stream) can be discovered by lying full-length and peering, through polarised sunglasses, over the high banks. The sudden appearance of your head and shoulders projecting over the water will cause instant panic amongst the inhabitants below, so you must ease your way slowly to a suitable vantage point. You may have to spend ten or fifteen minutes watching as first the fry and then the better fish resume their feeding stations. Suddenly, a large black shape darts out as if from nowhere, seizes its prey and, just as quickly, disappears. A dog trout! So far, so good! Now to nobble him . . . with a Dog Nobbler; what else?

You will find it preferable for this style of fishing to use a longer rod than is normal for small stream trouting. (I use a 9ft carbon rod matched to an AFTM7 line.) This

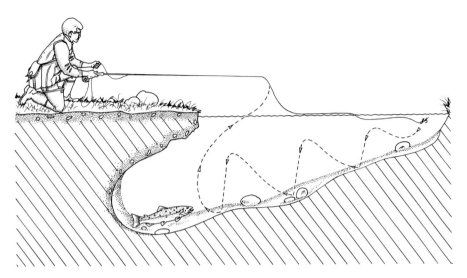

Fig 81   A Dog Nobbler (a lure heavily weighted at the head) can be fished 'sink-and-draw' style to tempt old 'dog trout' out from the security of an undercut bank.

will enable you to keep well back from the edge of the bank, out of sight of those wary old trout. A 2½lb leader about six feet long is ideal when fishing at short range. A longer leader results in insufficient line beyond the rod tip and the annoying problem of line falling back through the rod rings whenever the rod is raised.

Crouching well back from the stream, make a gentle cast so that the rod tip finishes up just about level with the edge of the bank and the lure enters the water a yard or so upstream and to the outside of the suspected lie. Allow your weighted lure to sink to the river bed before repeatedly raising and lowering the rod tip just a few inches. This will cause the lure to swim downstream and across in a 'sink-and-draw' motion. Progressively, draw in line to continue this style of fishing as you bring the lure upstream of the lie, finally withdrawing your lure from the water to recast.

If the first two or three casts do not result in a sharp snatch it is as well to rest the water for a few minutes before trying again with a smaller lure or one of a different colour. In coloured water, brightly coloured lures may work, but when the stream runs low and clear you will probably get better results with small black or brown Dog Nobblers. When you feel a fish snatch at your lure, strike firmly to set the hook and to turn the fish out into the main current where it can be played and landed. Pushing the rod forward to apply side strain will prevent the trout returning to its lair where the line could become snagged.

For several seasons I had fished a tiny Sussex stream, never taking a trout of more than six ounces. There is one particular pool no more than three yards wide and perhaps six yards long fed via a narrow gulley which acts as a food funnel. I suspected that an old dog trout had its hideout in an undercut where the current had scooped a deep hollow. The pool held shoals of small dace and grayling, none apparently bigger than a couple of ounces. Flicking my line from behind a pair of large alder trunks, my fly had not had time to sink more than a few inches when there was a splash. Down went my rod tip until it touched the surface, automatically applying enough side strain to hold the trout away from the safety of its lair. The fight which followed in that confined space was one which I will always remember, but eventually it was mine. It topped the pound mark by just an ounce – truly a specimen fish for this tiny fishery.

12

Small Stream Nymph Fishing by Night and by Day

Summertime! The pressure is high and the river, low and clear, drifts lazily through silent meadows. Unruffled by breeze, undinted by rising fish, the mirror-like pools mock any suggestion of life beneath the leaden surface. Dawn's sparse hatch of olives is but a dim memory in the midday haze – no trickle of terrestrials to further tempt leviathan. Few insects are akin to mad dogs and Englishmen, and any which do sally forth hold steadfast to their terrestrial pathways. To fish a dry fly in these conditions is pointless. Any trout not enjoying a siesta will be feeding well below the surface, foraging amongst the trailing weed as much in search of shade, perhaps, as in any real hope of dislodging nymphs from their verdant sanctuary. This is a time for fishing the nymph – not some imitation of the adolescent struggling to break its ties with the surface film, but a scavenging infant creeping along the bed of a dark deep pool.

Shadows lengthen and fade as the sun rolls over the horizon. Colour drains from the landscape and dusk's dark stain steals onto the stage, prompting the hatch of evening sedge flies. The wise old trout hold back, resolute in their fast, until some skittering sedge proves irresistible to an immature fish which slashes wildly, hopelessly wide of its target. This is the signal. Within minutes, the surface is alive with splashing trout fry. Two small fish collide at the surface as they compete for the same morsel. Adults soon lose their resolve and move into their feeding stations. There they hover, just below the surface, ready to intercept the emerging sedges.

Against the glowing embers of the evening sky I tie on a large sedge and grease my leader. A good fish rises and I cast to it, trying to guess which way the trout will cruise. Emerging sedge pupae make for restless, roving trout. In the excitement of the hatch both angler and trout discard order and discipline; my line crashes heavily onto the surface and the fly is ignored. The trout continues to cruise back and forth, swirling at the hatching flies. I cast again. I guess wrong and the trout rises a yard ahead of my offering. Then, in no more than the time it takes to replace a tangled leader, the hatch is over. Peace and tranquillity return. The stillness does not last, of course. Later, the female sedge flies, having mated, begin returning to deposit their eggs. Many species settle onto the water – often none too gently – and inject their eggs through the surface film. On all but the darkest of nights, these returning sedges provide an opportunity for sport through to midnight and beyond. If you are blessed with good night vision, a dry fly can be effective. However, there is another method, a most deadly nymphing tactic, which works wonders on the night shift.

DAYTIME TACTICS

Many of the trout which are visible in their surface-feeding lies during a hatch of fly will move to areas of gentler flow to rest through the heat of the day. For some this means settling on to the river bed; for others it involves moving to new lies altogether. Some common resting places from which a nymph may tempt a trout are listed below.

Undercuts As the day advances, a trout seen earlier in a surface-feeding lie beside the bank will often withdraw beneath an undercut near the river bed. If you have marked the spot accurately then try drifting a nymph past the lie. With the trout beneath the bank on which you are standing, it is a simple matter to cast a weighted nymph so that it drops close to the edge a few yards upstream of the lie. Provided your line falls gently onto the surface there is no need to worry about the trout seeing your fly line ('lining' the fish), so a very long leader is unnecessary.

If a nymph fished on a dead drift is ignored, cast again, this time raising the rod tip as your nymph approaches the suspected lie beneath the undercut. It is a good idea to move the rod outwards from the bank as you try to induce a take, as the trout will invariably dart back towards its sanctuary where your leader could become snagged on a root. If at first you don't succeed, let the nymph drift further downstream before trying for the induced take. Then try a little further upstream. The undercut may not be directly alongside the surface-feeding lie.

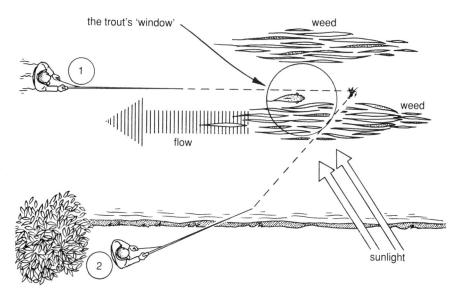

Fig 82   A trout lies in the shade of a wrack of emerging weed. The shadow of the line cast by the angler at 1 may put the trout down. Casting from position 2, the shadow of the line lies across the weed bed.

Behind weed beds Close inspection (with polarised spectacles) of the tail of a wrack of streamer weed may reveal that the longest 'frond' is actually the tail of a trout, sheltering its head and back from the glare of the sun. Occasionally, the trout will push forwards into the weed before drifting downstream to take any food dislodged by the disturbance. A weighted nymph cast to drift between weed beds and given a little life as it comes alongside the trout will sometimes result in that tell-tale movement of the jaw which is visible from above. As soon as the trout moves, begin tightening. There is a temptation to delay until you are quite sure that the fish has seen and been deceived by your offering. This delay is unaffordable! Strike first and check afterwards, or you will miss most of the opportunities.

If strong sunlight streams from the left bank (looking downstream), a trout will often lie on the right-hand edge of a weed bed, resting its right eye from the surface glare while surveying the food channel with its left. If you were to cast to the left of the weed bed the shadow of your line might startle the trout, so cast to the right. In taking this approach, your nymph is more likely to be seen and taken than one presented nearer the left bank where it might be obscured by the weed.

There is another difficulty to overcome. When you cast from a position directly below, the trout may see your line on the surface. Using a long leader or a fast-sinking

Fig 83 When the river is low, trout feed beside the wracks of emerging weed. Here, on Ireland's River Flesk, there is more weed than water, so accurate casting is called for.

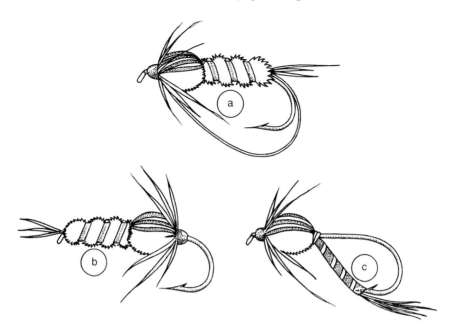

*Fig 84   Three ways of making a fly with a weed guard: (a) with a loop of 20lb
nylon; (b) reverse tied and dambuster-style flies and nymphs; (c) the Tube
Nymph.*

nymph pattern could provide a solution, but a better approach is to cast at an angle to
the current so that your line falls across the weed bed. This is certainly practical if the
weed does not break the surface; however, with the river low and weed growth
strong many of the best lies will be between wracks of emerging weeds. Of course, the
tactic of casting across the weed beds can still be used on a 'one shot' basis, but if you
hook the weed the ensuing disturbance is likely to put down your quarry.

The problem of surface weed is not insurmountable – you could try a nymph tied
with a weed guard. There are various methods for achieving this end, such as tying a
length of 20lb breaking strain nylon to the hook shank before dressing the nymph and
then looping it back and tying it in with the head. Another solution involves using
reverse-tied nymph patterns (called 'dambusters') which have stiff hackles tied at the
bend of the hook to fend off weed.

There is an interesting alternative which I call the 'Tube Nymph'. Here the nymph
pattern is tied on to a piece of thin PVC tubing of the type used to insulate electrical
conductors. The head end of the tube is tied just behind the eye of the hook. The free
end of the tube is then trimmed to length so that it just clips over the point of the
hook. The idea behind all of these methods is that the weed guard will quickly
collapse once the nymph is grasped by the jaws of a trout. The tube nymph has the
advantage that the tail, abdomen and thorax can be dressed on to the tube before
fitting it to the hook. This makes it one of the easiest styles of artificial flies to tie.

When you hook a trout from a lie between weed beds its first reaction, and one you
must resist at all costs, is to dive for the safety of the weed. Either bring the trout

quickly to the top and keep its head above the surface, or apply force to turn its head downstream to fight in a weed-free area. In either case, you will not succeed if you use a fine nylon point. For this style of nymphing I recommend at least 4lb breaking strain as the point of your leader.

Fast-water lies　Fast, shallow water has little attraction for trout if it is not shaded, either by trees and bushes on the banks or by virtue of weeds growing in the river bed. But on rain-fed rivers these rapid stretches often harbour the most abundant source of food for trout – stone-fly nymphs – and in shallow well-shaded runs trout will feed throughout the day with their backs barely covered by water. Even here the basic requirements of food, nearby shelter and an easy lie away from the full force of the current should be your guide to locating trout. Very often a sub-surface feature such as a large boulder or sunken tree can be the provider of all three. Food is channelled around the obstruction, passing a quiet eddy in its lea and, upstream or alongside, a deep depression into which the trout can bolt at the slightest hint of danger.

Cast a weighted nymph upstream and across on a greased leader and allow it to drift back with the current. Surface turbulence will pull your leader from side to side and ensure that the nymph rises and falls – a sort of 'reluctant debutante' – on its journey downstream. A dip or a sharp sideways pull on your leader is the signal to tighten smartly. To simulate a stone-fly nymph dislodged from its resting place your nymph *must* trip along the river bed, so, to avoid false indications from stones and sunken debris, I recommend that you use a well-guarded pattern such as the Tube Nymph.

Fig 85　Derek Hoskin casts a weighted nymph into a deep water lie on the River Cych.

Slow-water pools Bright sunlight is attenuated as it filters to the bed of pools, the deepest of which are often the daytime haunts of the very largest trout in the stream. These fish rarely, if ever, take flies from the surface. Small insects barely feature in their diets, but should a nymph offer itself at close range there is always a chance it will be seized. The nymphs you will find there, carrying their shelters with them as they crawl through the detritus, are caddis grubs, the nymphs of sedge flies. During a prolonged spell of sunny weather, a blanket of fine algae grows on everything on the river bed. The caddis grubs carry their share of this green cotton wool, but trout soon learn that these green and hairy creepers are easy food. They scoop them up, complete with their houses of sticks and stones and their algal overcoats.

An excellent imitation of this insect is Tom's Green Nymph. Tom Chapman, who devised this simple pattern made from olive seal's fur, used it for fishing the margins of the clear chalk-spring lakes at Peckham's Copse in West Sussex. The pattern works well on most rain-fed rivers and on the slower of the chalk streams. This nymph is at its most deadly when fished very slowly through static pools and deep-water eddies.

Cast across the pool and allow time for the nymph to sink to the river bed before beginning a slow 'figure-of-eight' retrieve. Takes in deep water can be difficult to detect, so avoid jerking the line during the retrieve and watch for the slightest irregularity in the progress of your leader across the surface.

NYMPHS AT NIGHT

During periods of settled high pressure the evening rise is at its most predictable. There will *usually* be one; it should start a little before or after sunset. Its duration may be just a few minutes or several hours! Occasionally, for no apparent reason, the evening rise is a complete non-event. It is often something of a disappointment, particularly if you restrict yourself to surface fishing. At the start of the rise, by all means fish a dry fly to match the hatch (e.g. of duns), or the fall (of egg-laying spinners or spent flies). But as dusk descends and the flurry of surface activity ceases, nymph fishing can increase your chances of catching specimen fish whose life-styles have become almost entirely nocturnal.

The Emerging Sedge Pupa

Some types of sedge flies which hatch at the surface (as opposed to those which crawl out of the water to pupate), make quite a song and dance of the process. They scutter across the surface before struggling into the air. The familiar slashing rise of a trout taking an emerging sedge is possibly the result of a last-moment change in direction which the trout finds necessary to intercept the escaping insect.

Traditional dry flies are a poor means of representing this scuttering action. A better match is obtained with a suitable imitation fished just sub-surface. A good general representation is Richard Walker's Sedge Pupa. The key to successful sedge fishing is accurate representation of the *behaviour* of the insect. Casting a fly from air to water is not an effective means of imitating the transition from pupa to fly, but you *can* copy

Fig 86 The Pheasant Tail Nymph, probably the most successful general representation ever devised.

the scuttering movements of a sedge struggling to escape its pupal case and break through the surface film.

It is normal, when dry-fly fishing, to grease your leader to within six to ten inches of the fly. I cannot recommend this practice when fishing the emerging sedge, as a buoyant leader will send out ripples whenever you twitch the fly. Instead, grease the two or three inches of leader nearest to the fly, then leave at least a yard of nylon free of floatant. Degrease this section thoroughly after handling the leader as even a small amount of the natural oils from your hands could prevent it sinking below the surface. Once your fly alights on (and sinks *into*) the surface, twitch it periodically as it drifts through a suspected lie. This movement serves three purposes – it attracts attention, it creates the illusion of life and it reduces the opportunity for the trout to examine in detail your imperfect imitation.

The Night-Shift Nymph

The final stage of the evening rise often brings trout to the surface to take female sedges as they return to lay their eggs. Here again, a nymph pattern can be as effective as a traditional dry sedge. Some sedge flies do lay their eggs on the bed of the river, generally after alighting on vegetation and crawling down amongst the roots and stones near the bank of the river. I am not aware of any species which dives through the surface to swim down, but a heavy nymph cast into slow-moving water is sometimes taken 'on the drop'.

Most takes come, however, once the nymph has sunk to the bed of a pool and is made to swim up again by retrieving line. With a long, smooth retrieve the nymph will imitate an exhausted sedge drifting back to the surface after completing its egg laying. The surprising thing about this tactic is that it continues to catch trout long after the splashing of surface feeders has ceased. Provided there is enough moonlight you can take trout well into the small hours of the morning.

There are some serious problems to be overcome when fishing heavily wooded streams in near-darkness, the most obvious being how to get your fly into the water at all! Daytime reconnaissance of each pool is vital, particularly if you intend wading. You must decide not only where to cast your nymph, but also *how* you will cast. Is there room for conventional overhead or side-casting, or will you have to improvise? (Darkness is not an ideal environment for trying out techniques with which you are unfamiliar!) Check the flow through the pool, since you will have to retrieve line somewhat faster than the current to get your nymph to rise towards the surface. Finally, if you cannot fish from the banks, find a safe point of access and note some distinctive landmark, as things can look very different at night.

Fig 87   Trout fishing after sunset on the River Usk. When the surface rise has ceased, trout continue to feed on hatching sedge flies. This is an ideal time to use a fast-sinking pattern such as the Night-Shift Nymph.

The nymph I use at night is a very simple dressing consisting of a torpedo-shaped body and thorax made from orange baling twine (raffia is a suitable substitute). I add a short tail of pheasant wing fibres and a black hackle, but I readily confess that these are mainly to avoid embarrassment should another angler catch a glimpse of these Night-Shift Nymphs in my fly box. I am convinced that neither the colour nor the shape of these nymphs is of any great significance. Size is important – they should represent a substantial mouthful for a trout. I tie the Night-Shift Nymph on long-shank hooks in sizes 8 and 10.

The most important feature of this pattern is the distinct plop with which it enters the water. With no bushy dubbed body to cushion the impact or delay the sinking, the Night-Shift Nymph dives straight down. The audible splash as it enters the water may attract the attention of a trout, but it also confirms the accuracy of your cast. Without this signal you can be sure of catching no trout, as your fly is high and dry somewhere on the bank or in a bush.

This tactic has the added virtue of selective fishing. Very rarely do I hook under-sized trout when nymphing at night. More often it is a way of tempting larger, wiser old fish who have long since ceased rising to surface flies. And, of course, on many streams there is the distinct chance of encountering the occasional sea trout, so do not fish too fine. Takes are far from gentle, so be warned. A 4lb point is the minimum I recommend for night fishing, and if large sea trout are a possibility then 6lb nylon is safer, especially in the intimate surroundings of a heavily wooded small stream.

Search the water methodically, paying particular attention to the region where the depth shelves at the head of the pool. If you have adequate casting space, a good process is to cover the pool in a series of casts fanning across from one bank to the other. Then lengthen your line a little and repeat the process. Often the best fish lie in deep water near the head of the pool and, on being hooked, quickly dart towards the shallows of the pool tail where submerged debris can present a special hazard in the dark.

While fishing from the bank of a small Hampshire stream one evening, I made a temporary connection with the 23.15 from Waterloo! With a tortured screech from my reel a fish surged upstream and I stumbled after it for some fifteen yards before a regiment of grey alders made further overland progress impossible. I knew the pool was at least four feet deep, but in the moonlight it looked decidedly menacing. Discretion overtook indecision and, holding my rod well up to absorb shocks as much as possible, I applied rim pressure as backing quickly followed the main line. My luck and backing ran out together and, with a distant thrashing of the surface which I will never forget, the leviathan returned to its domain while I was left to ponder what might have been.

13

The 'Dog Days' on a Chalk Stream

There are days when I really believe that I'm beginning to understand rough stream trout – not fully, of course, but enough to predict their behaviour reasonably well when stalking them with a fly. After all, their lives are not unlike ours – times of plenty, perhaps, but also periods of struggle for survival, and the occasional disaster or set-back just when things seem to be going well. For them, food gathering is the top priority and they cannot afford to be too choosy.

As for brown trout on chalk streams, they are an entirely different matter. Take, for example, a day in 1987 when I visited the River Test between Stockbridge and Romsey. Nothing much was showing, except a shoal of miniature rainbow trout (escapees, no doubt, from one of the numerous hatcheries with which this most famous of chalk valleys is now afflicted). Resting awhile beside a small bay between tall alders, I noticed a disturbance on the edge of the current. Was it a rise? I watched several olives sail by unmolested, and I was about to turn away when there it was again – a very good neb. It had taken something from just below the surface, possibly a hatching olive.

A careful scan through polaroids revealed a nice trout finning steadily near the bed in 3ft of water. I slithered back from the edge, tied on a Greenwells and I drifted the fly over its lie a dozen times, with no response. Yet, it was still rising to the occasional natural fly. Very puzzling! I tried a couple of other olive patterns before tying on a sedge pupa. This it took first cast. Instinctively, I raised my rod – much too fast. The line went tight, the trout splashed on the surface and my fly was catapulted vertically, fixing the leader to the rod like a child's first attempt at knitting.

A good chance wasted . . . but no! The fish was livid. No longer selective in its diet, it now slashed at everything that drifted near. The surface churned furiously every few seconds. I had never seen anything like it before.

Finally, my leader untangled, I wafted a fly in the direction of the aggressor. Splash . . . two . . . three, tighten, and the fight was on. The trout lunged, first for the near-side bank and then downstream, where it could use the pull of the current. Within two minutes I was really on the defensive as it surged up through a weed bed. Luck was on my side and the weed parted leaving a few crowfoot fronds across the leader. Its vision obscured, the trout, a beautifully marked two-pounder, came meekly to the net. I puzzled then, as I do now, why that trout, feeding so selectively before feeling my hook, should have thrown all caution to the wind. Surely, by any logic, it should have gone down and stayed down.

SUMMER TROUT

The chalk stream trout are now fat and lazy after the spring harvest. With so much sub-surface food to choose from, they rarely take floating flies during the day, and when they do rise it is often selectively, to one species of insect. It is said they will, on occasion, take one sex of upwinged dun and reject the other, but I have never noticed this, and probably never will, for to spot the difference between a male and a female fly at any distance you would need to have very good eyesight. When stationary and at close range they are easily distinguished. There are often slight colour differences, the males tend to be smaller and thinner in the body and they have a pair of claspers behind the tail. The most obvious distinction is in the eyes, which extend above the head in the males only.

This, above all, is the time and the place to find trout – and brown trout in particular – feeding selectively. The usual rules of concealment, careful approach and delicate casting may no longer be enough to fill your basket. You will need to observe the rise form, to deduce whether the trout are nymphing or taking surface flies. At times, your artificial will have to match the hatching insect closely if you are to deceive the most fastidious of these summer feeders.

MORNING TACTICS

There may be an early rise before the sun gets on to the water. Usually the trout will be taking midges, so a small black gnat or a midge pupa imitation might tempt a fish

Fig 88   A beautifully marked two-pounder from the River Test.

or two. The rise becomes sporadic as the morning shadows shorten. *Caenis* and Small Dark Olives hatch throughout the day on many chalk streams. Both are very small flies, and a size 16 imitation is quite adequate. With such tiny dry flies, a fine leader is essential, otherwise the fly does not cast well and rides badly on the surface. Three-pound nylon is what I generally use, although the extra fineness of the recently introduced double-strength nylon could provide valuable insurance should a good fish make a dash towards weed.

I have spent many a summer day casting dry flies to nymphing trout. That was before I learned to read the rise forms. Then, a surface disturbance was a rise; now it is a feeding fish, and the form of the rise is a clue to *what* it is feeding on.

Reading the Rise

Where a steady trickle of food drifts over a feeding trout, it lies about half its body length beneath the surface so that it can raise its head and intercept the food by sipping it from the surface. As the trout tilts upwards, the current carries it downstream so, on taking the fly, it levels out, gives a slight kick of the tail and returns to its lie. At the surface all you see is a neb (the mouth and nose of the trout) breaking the surface for a fraction of a second. Reed smuts and spent spinners are often taken in this way. Concentric rings spread out from the rise. In general, the bigger the fish, the bigger its

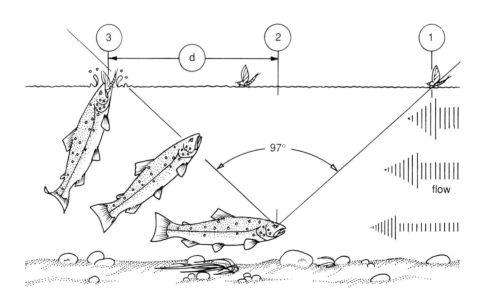

Fig 89 The centre of the rise occurs at a distance, d, downstream from the lie of a trout, depending upon the depth at which the trout lies and the strength of the current. A dry fly should be cast so that it enters the trout's window naturally, at position 1.

neb and the greater the surface disturbance. The whole pattern of rings drifts downstream with the current, and it is important to wait a second or two for the trout to regain its lie before casting *a little ahead* of where the fish broke the surface.

In a sparse hatch or fall of flies, trout often display more anxiety, splashing at the fly, sometimes leaving the water to snap at an escaping dun. Terrestrial flies, such as the daddy-long-legs, are often snatched from the surface with great gusto and commotion and it is rarely possible to judge the size of the trout from the size of the splash unless you are able to watch it rise several times. The trout will have powered up from near the river bed and, depending on the strength of the current and depth of water, its lie may be several feet upstream of the rise itself. Position yourself so that you can place your fly on the surface well above the point of the rise without lining the fish. A line cast at an angle to the current is much better than one cast from directly behind the fish.

Flies which skitter across the surface (hatching sedges and Mayflies have this habit) cause the trout to change direction at the last moment. The surge of displaced water as the fish turns rapidly creates a slashing rise form and a lovely sound to the ears of a fly

Fig 90   A difficult day on the River Alre. With the sun almost directly overhead it is essential to make use of any available cover.

fisher. These walloping rises are a good indication as to the size of the trout – the deeper the sound, the larger the fish.

During the day, trout shun the bright surface layers, restricting their feeding to nymphs and other small creatures of the depths. It can be very difficult to tempt a trout which is feeding by evicting nymphs from their weedy sanctuaries. A sparse hatch of *Caenis* or Small Dark Olives may elicit no surface reaction, but you may see the water bulge up towards the surface. This upwelling is caused by trout rising to mid-water to seize the nymphs on their way to the surface. A small Pheasant Tail Nymph fished Netheravon-style (induced take) is the tactic to try when trout are 'bulging'.

Swamped terrestrials or stillborn flies, and emerging pupae or nymphs just below the surface are taken with a head and tail rise. The only part of the trout which breaks the surface is its back, and the dorsal fin is an excellent guide to the size of the trout. The fish have plenty of time to inspect these morsels, so your imitation has got to be a very good one or you will find this the most frustrating rise form of all.

IN THE HEAT OF THE DAY

With the late-summer sun beating down, the scent and sounds of harvest across the countryside and the clear stream ambling gently through the valley who could wish for anything more? Well, the chalk stream trout fisher, for one! While the sun is almost directly overhead there will be little or no sign of a rising fish. Occasionally a nonconformist trout, lying in a shaded backwater, will decide on an afternoon snack, and with the water gin-clear great stealth is needed to get within 20 yards without putting it down. At this distance, I can cast a dry fly to fall two feet ahead and not more than six inches to the side of a trout quite readily . . . on perhaps one cast in ten. (No wind, of course. There would *have to be* a flat calm!) Well, that is the challenge. It's either that or try nymphing with the (no less demanding) induced-take method, at least until the evening rise.

Nymphing Tactics

I have found no better general nymph representation than Frank Sawyer's Pheasant Tail Nymph. The pattern is so simple that it can be tied at the riverside, if necessary, without a vice. The secret of nymphing, I am convinced, lies in the working of the nymph through the water. The late Oliver Kite could induce a take with just a bare hook, cast above and to the side of a trout, and given a couple of upward jerks as it came alongside its quarry. Behaviour is the key. If you want to imitate a caddis, do not tie on a caddis imitation and then fish it at high speed. Draw it slowly along the river bed in the deepest, slowest of pools. (There is some surprisingly deep water on the outer bends of many chalk streams.)

The Netheravon tactic, or induced take, is a way of imitating hatching olives as they swim towards the surface while drifting downstream. Most of these nymphs are poor swimmers, so it makes sense not to bring your imitation to the surface too quickly. A few small lifts of the rod tip, enough to raise the nymph a couple of inches

Fig 91   Nymph fishing on the River Test during a sporadic evening rise.

at a time, should be quite sufficient. Sedge pupae, on the other hand, swim more quickly to the surface, and I have had more success with sedge pupa imitations by pulling them steadily upwards without a pause. Very few sedges hatch before tea-time in high summer, however.

The Itchen, the Test and the Hampshire Avon are just three examples of fast-flowing chalk streams on which it is particularly difficult to detect the take when nymph fishing. The traditional method is to grease the leader to within a foot or so of the nymph (according to the depth you want it to fish), and to watch for the floating section of nylon to dip down or pull to one side. At short range this is not too difficult, but the streamy nature of the surface makes it a more difficult proposition above about 10 yards. (Frank Sawyer, an outstanding exponent of the art of chalk stream nymph fishing, used to reckon 20 yards was his limit, but he was an exceptional fly fisher.)

Water abstraction – not always directly from the river, but more often from boreholes which drain the chalk sponge, or aquifer – lowers the water-table and has left some chalk streams with very little flow. There it is easy to spot the dipping of your leader. But on the larger, faster rivers you may find it better to watch the fish for some response as you lift your nymph, and to judge the all-important moment of tightening accordingly. If the trout turns and darts downstream, assume that it has gone after your nymph, and tighten as it turns its head back upstream. If the nymph passes very close to the trout, and you see the white of its open jaws, begin tightening. Its jaws will have closed on the nymph by the time your reaction has been transmitted down the leader.

Provided that you tighten steadily, without snatching, it is quite likely that a missed fish will allow you another chance – a luxury rarely afforded to the dry-fly fisherman. Rest the fish a minute or two to let it get back to its lie before casting again. If you get no response after two or three tries, wait a minute or two and then try drifting your nymph past its other flank. It is surprising how many trout seem to have better eyesight on one side than the other.

THE ENIGMA OF THE EVENING RISE

Who could fish the evening rise on a chalk stream in high summer and ever forget it? The wildly unrealistic aspirations; the anticipation; the excitement as the first neb breaks the surface; the mounting tension and growing sense of urgency as time creeps on, light drains from the sky and mocking trout take flies galore – nymphs, duns, spinners, midges and sedges (in fact, anything but your artificial) – these are the phases of an evening on a chalk stream. With luck, a trout or two will make a mistake, and, if you don't, your reward will be the freshest supper dish imaginable.

One night the evening rise may last two hours or more while the next it might be over in minutes, or it might not materialise at all. Weather has everything to do with it, of course, and no doubt it affects both flies and trout. I have seen good evening hatches and falls of spinners with barely a fish moving, and at other times trout would seem to be queueing up for sparse rations as a drop in pressure holds back the transposition from nymph to dun and from dun to spinner.

Sedges are reliable creatures, and there are usually a few trout waiting for their emergence even on those mysterious evenings when the sun's glow fades over a glassy river undinted by fish or fly. Beside the reeds lie, unseen, the brown trout of an earlier generation. No longer prepared to fight it out with shoals of stocked rainbow trout, these pensionable fish await the emergence of the great sedges of summer – the Caperer, Silver Sedge and Large Cinnamon. If you have failed to tempt a trout during the evening rise, use the last of the light to tie on a G and H or a Silver Sedge, and walk beside the reed beds *listening, not looking.*

Listen for the splosh of a swirling trout taking a hatching sedge; it is a distinctive sound. Without peering over the reeds, judge the position of the 'epicentre' from the pattern of rings spreading out into the stream. Gently cast your fly so that only the leader rests on the water, keep your sedge on a fairly tight line (a little drag is no bad thing), and wait for the splash which tells you to tighten. Push the rod tip outwards to keep the trout away from the reeds, and good luck in the ensuing battle!

I recall an evening on a Hampshire chalk stream. I had fished badly during the evening rise, tempting three nice fish (two on a Sherry Spinner during a fall of Blue Winged Olive spinners, and one on a Greenwell's). The two larger fish, both brown trout, had weeded me and I was left with a lowly rainbow of about three pounds. I vowed to play the next fish on the surface, and increased my point from 3lb to 5lb in

Fig 92   The Hampshire Avon at Amesbury.

preparation. The result – no more takes! So I walked, watched, listened and waited for the sedge rise.

At last, a good fish moved, hard against a tall bank of reeds on my side of the stream. 'Ideal,' I thought, and got into position. I wafted my orange G and H Sedge in its direction. Once . . . twice . . . a dozen times or more it ignored my passing fly. I rested it. Splosh! Another short-lived sedge! This time I had its position marked well, and I cast again . . . and again . . . There had to be an answer. In near darkness I bit off the G and H and tied on a Silver Sedge. One last try! Splosh, and I was into him. 'Keep him on the top,' I said to myself as the trout bore ever deeper toward imagined but unseen wracks of water crowfoot.

The curve in my rod told me that any more strain would surely part my leader. Upstream it powered, and I stumbled after it, line still screaming from my reel. Then it turned across and down, and I began reeling in, desperately trying to get back in touch with the fish. I did, with a bang. Over went the rod tip, the reel gave a brief screech of anguish and the line fell slack. Defeated, no, totally humiliated, I knew it was time to pack up. As I wound in, my trembling fingers felt the smoothness of the line, the leader, miraculously free from wind knots, and the point, with *a curly piglet's tail* where the fly should have been. A double indignity – I had lost control of the fish *and* my knot had failed! I crept off to bed in disgrace.

14

Things that go Bump in the Night

My team of flies searched the pool in a sweeping arc. Steadily, I retrieved line, rod held high, white line barely visible against the backdrop of trees. It was a warm moonless night with just the odd star piercing the light cloud covering.

Was that a slight holding back of the line, or had I imagined it? Another pull, this time more definite. I tightened firmly. Away went a sea trout, off into the night, leaping and splashing, shattering the dull mirror of the pool as it surged downstream. I turned its head before it caught the pull of the race into the falls below, and slowly it returned, all the time straining for the deeper water beneath the far bank. A minute later the silver flank of a shining two-pounder slid over my waiting net.

Having administered the last rites, I released my dropper fly from the scissors of its jaw, set the fish down on a boulder and raised my rod to cast again. The deceased vacated its rocky perch and slithered to a halt beside me. My line refused to cast. 'There must be some connection,' I thought. And there was! My point fly was firmly embedded in the tongue of the fish. It seemed as if, not content with one fly, that sea trout had been determined to ambush the whole of my team.

PLANNING THE CAMPAIGN

By the time many of us can get away for a few days' holiday we are into July and August – the dog days of trout fishing – with the very best of river and stillwater trouting behind us. But at least one type of fly fishing is at its peak during the school holidays – sea trout fishing. In Chapter 10, early-season sea trout which run up river in the heavier waters of spring were considered. The summer sea trout is an altogether different animal, and for best results it requires a change in both tactics and fishing technique. Before discussing some of the fishing methods which have proved effective for this most temperamental of migratory fish, it is important to recognise what (normally) has been happening to the river, and how this will affect our quarry.

Throughout most of the summer, the water level in a spate river varies between *low* and *very low*. The river becomes a series of pools of almost static water interconnected by shallow broken runs. Yet sea trout do manage to work their way upstream. At dusk, they can be seen energetically coursing up the shallows, cutting a foaming wake as their powerful caudals send spray (and maybe gravel too!) into the air.

Pools form wherever the course of the stream is other than a straight and featureless canal. Usually, they are shallow on the concave side, shelving to deeper water against

Fig 93 Killarney's Lough Leane where it drains into the River Laune. Dusk is the time to intercept sea trout as they enter the lough.

181

Fig 94   A good catch of summer sea trout averaging over 2lb.

the outer bank. Good holding water for summer sea trout is often heavily shaded by overhanging trees on the deepest side of the pool. However, sea trout are opportunists and will happily settle in the shade of any submerged obstruction, or beneath undercut meadow-banks. It seems that their main considerations when selecting a daytime lie are to avoid a strong current and to get out of the sunlight.

In the warm low-water conditions, a heavy growth of algae builds up on rocks and weeds alike unless a flash flood should occur to clear it. This green 'cotton wool' creates problems for the fly fisher, and is certainly not liked by the resident trout which avoid it by day, preferring the faster channels for their feeding. It may be annoyance at the build-up of a coat of silt and algae through the day that prompts sea trout to leap and splash on the surface as darkness descends.

The Summer Migrants

While the spring run of sea trout move through the river at an amazing speed, the summer migration is an altogether more leisurely affair. Shoals of sea trout, which have remained concealed throughout the day, form up at the head of a pool as light fades. Peering over a high bank into the top of a clear pool on a summer evening can be quite a heart-stopping experience. Dozens, and sometimes hundreds of sea trout can be seen lying almost stationary, waiting to continue their ascent of the river by night. Some may move up through just one pool, while others will travel many miles before finding a resting place which takes their fancy. One of the worst things you can do is to cast a line across the head of a pool before it is really dark. This can throw the

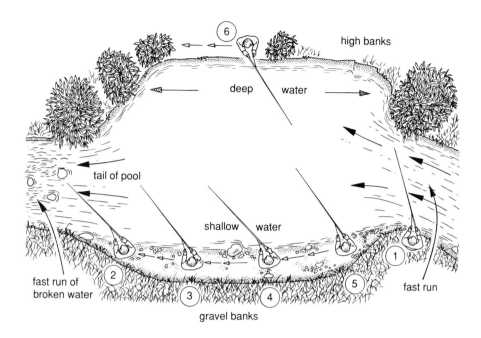

high banks

deep water

tail of pool

shallow water

fast run of
broken water

gravel banks

fast run

Fig 95   A strategy for summer sea trout fishing. A fish can sometimes be taken from fast, broken water in the early evening. Strong tackle is advised, as grilse will also take the fly at this time of day.

fish into total confusion, in which state they may do just about anything – except take a fly.

Identifying the Holding Features

Of prime importance in selecting where to fish is that there should be features which make the water attractive to sea trout. The first criterion is that suitable daytime lies should be within easy access. This generally means deep water or very well sheltered and shaded shallower water. The second consideration is comfort. Sea trout will not accept battling against a strong current except when they are running up river. Obstructions which provide some respite from the current are essential before sea trout will rest in fast broken water. Since most sea trout feed very little in fresh water in summer, a plentiful food supply is not vital.

A REVISED STRATEGY FOR FISHING SEA TROUT POOLS

The occasional fish or two may be seen moving up into a pool throughout the night, but once the main shoal has passed it is generally more productive to concentrate fishing the main pool itself. A popular method is to move to the head of the pool to

Fig 96   This summer sea trout from the River Cych is ready for the net.

begin casting, covering a sector of water thoroughly before moving downstream two or three paces and repeating the process. In this way, the whole of a 50-yard pool can be covered in perhaps an hour or two before returning upstream to repeat the 'slow march'. This is certainly a good way of searching out the taking lies, but it does not take account of what I, at least, observe to be the normal behaviour of sea trout.

On entering the pool, they may take up temporary lies just a few yards up from the lip and hold there for a brief period before, it seems, deciding whether to run on up river or to seek a resting place in the pool. Some do keep on running, and choose to follow the main channel of deeper water. These fish are not generally interested in taking a fly. Others move into the shallower water on either side of the main stream, and swim in small shoals, up from the tail through the middle of the pool, as the night progresses. For this reason I prefer to begin fishing the lower third of the pool, moving next to the middle and finally the top section. (Of course it is not sensible to do a reverse 'slow march' process, since each cast would be lining any fish to be covered by subsequent casts.)

TACTICS FOR EARLY EVENING

It is possible to take a fish or two well before dark – although generally these will be the smaller 'school' sea trout in the one to two pound region – and the best places are the stretches of broken water between pools. Start fishing just below the tail of a pool, casting a long line across-and-down from shallow water into deep so that the fly runs close to the far bank before swinging round and into the shallows. Using this technique early in the evening you should not disturb the fish waiting in the pool.

There is a way of taking one or more of the leading fish – sometimes quite big ones – from the shoal at the head of a pool before darkness descends, but it requires nerves of steel! Move down the run until you are about twenty yards above the next pool. Cast a long line as before, if necessary feeding out extra line and allowing the current to carry it downstream, until your fly is about to enter the top of the pool on the far side. Now let the fly swing gently across, taking up a yard or two of line so that only the fly and the leader enter the pool. Slowly work the fly up from the pool once it reaches the shallow side.

With luck you will entice a take, and a vicious one at that! Now you must hold it. The sea trout will almost certainly try to bolt back into the pool, and if you let it go, the shoal will follow in disarray. Keep the rod tip high and on no account allow the fish to turn. (The immense power of a sea trout comes from the use of its tail, which, of course, cannot be used for swimming backwards!) If prevented from making progress downstream, the sea trout will usually surge across to the deeper side of the run, and by keeping a steady pressure on the fish, you will be able to guide it upstream of your own position. Now you can get the current working for you to tire your fish. Even in the low-water conditions of summer use nothing less than a 6lb leader for sea trout fishing – level breaking strain throughout, so the only knots are to the loop on the fly line and to the fly itself – and check the leader regularly throughout the night for signs of chafing or wind knots. A fresh leader each night should be your golden rule.

Many newcomers to sea trout fishing make two serious mistakes and as a result they miss much of the best sport. Perhaps they find it hard to believe that such big fish will move in so close.

1. Avoid wading if at all possible, especially if the night is really dark with no moon or with heavy cloud cover. Fish driven from the shallows by heavy splashing boots are unlikely to settle for quite some time.
2. Do not start by casting a long line. In all probability you will put your fly line on top of one or more sea trout cruising right under your feet. A very high proportion of the sea trout I catch are taken with only the leader in contact with the water, and quite the minority require a cast of more than 5 or 6 yards.

TACTICS FOR THE DEAD OF NIGHT

As night wears on, the sea trout will eventually move back into deeper water. After midnight, many fly fishers switch to a sinking line to get down to the fish. I find a sinking line awkward to handle in the dark, and prefer to use a sink-tip line for my deep-water fishing. According to the depth of water and the strength of current I vary the leader length from about 6ft up to 15ft, which I can still manage better in the dark than I can a sinking line. When fishing slow deep pools, a very slow retrieve is most attractive to sea trout. Strike at the slightest hint of a take. Indeed, strike even if you are convinced that you have just missed a take. In many cases the line falling slack is simply an indication that the fish is swimming towards you, and has not let go at all.

By 2 o'clock in the morning the sea trout will have moved back into deeper water and you must present the fly at depth in order to tempt them. If you cannot fish deep enough using a floating line or sink-top with long leader and heavy fly, then a sinking line must be used. This causes real problems where the shallows are thickly coated in algae. As the fly is retrieved, it too gets covered and must be cleaned before each fresh cast is made – not much fun! When using a floating line there is no real problem. All you have to do is speed up the retrieve as the fly enters the shallows and it will swim up towards the surface.

With a sinking line I have only found one real solution – fish from the other bank. You may have to move to a different pool where the river course bends away, or it may be safe to cross at the run between two pools; but beware! Every year lives are lost by people wading in spate rivers. Do not wade at night unless you have carefully checked the river out in daylight. It is easy to lose one's footing in low-water conditions where the rocks have become slippery and pot-holes are concealed by weed growth. Waders are not the impediment to swimming which some people believe, but when full of water they can make it doubly difficult to haul oneself up a sheer bank, especially when further encumbered with a tackle bag and landing net.

A sinking line is ideal when casting into the shallows and allowing the fly to swing across into deeper water, as the fly follows the contour of the river bed. However, you must make sure that the handle of your landing net can extend sufficiently to reach the water, before fishing from such a spot. While I rarely take many fish after about 1 o'clock in the morning, some of my best sea trout have come to the fly fished in deep gulleys far into the night.

Downstream Fishing

When fishing downstream, cast across and down the pool so that the line falls with a mend upstream of the fly. (This technique is outlined in Chapter 4.) If you find casting a ready-mended line difficult, then make a normal overhead cast and mend the line by quickly moving the rod tip in a circular motion so that the portion of line nearest to you lifts from the surface of the water to fall again further upstream. If there is sufficient light, concentrate on the bend in the line where it touches the water; if not, you will have to fish by feel. Allow the fly to swing right round until it reaches the side. Allow it to rest for a few seconds before retrieving line steadily. At the slightest hint of movement of the line, strike, and strike hard! A fish may be following the fly towards you, so the indication of a take may be almost imperceptible. In due course you will develop a sort of sixth sense as to when to strike.

The difficult part of this technique is in detecting the gentle takes of fish which would otherwise not bother to snatch at a fly passing more quickly in front of their noses. It is a method of fishing which calls for intense concentration. A white or fluorescent cream line aids visibility. These are readily available in floating form, but less readily as sinkers. The best sinking line I have found is mid-grey, which shows up surprisingly well in moonlight.

DAWN TACTICS

Fishing right through the night can be productive (sometimes!). More often, there is intense activity for two or three hours after dusk followed by a lull of an hour or two when very little surface activity is matched by inactivity on the part of the sea trout in the depths. Later, as dawn begins to break, sea trout return from the deep water to leap and splash in the shallows, mainly at the tail of a pool. Conventional across-and-down fishing can be used to good effect, but as the sky lightens the fish become jittery. This is the time to revert to a floating line and upstream tactics.

THE PRACTICALITIES OF NIGHT FISHING

Choose your casting position carefully, so that you can cover the water you intend to fish without overstretching your casting capability. Long-distance casting can usually be avoided; many sea trout are taken when only the leader is in contact with the water. Few anglers feel as confident of their casting in the dark as in daylight, and the splash of a badly cast fly line only serves to put fish down. Where the bank is free of casting obstructions it is often feasible to fish without wading. If possible, cast from a sitting position so that you do not disturb the fish as they come in close.

Another important consideration is that it must be feasible to play and land a sea trout from the spot selected. There is no justification for hooking a fish if, for example, it is clearly impossible to prevent it from careering down a waterfall. (I know of one good fish which was lost after escaping *up* a waterfall!)

Torchlight

Sea trout do not like lights shone onto the water at night, so to avoid disturbing the fish, and any other fishermen in the vicinity, make any tackle adjustments with a very low-power, localised light directed away from the water.

Judging Distance in the Dark

It can be difficult to judge distances in the dark, and fly fishing very heavily over-grown water at night is for the very expert (or the very patient) only. Ironically, these stretches of the stream can be the most productive, especially on otherwise heavily fished waters, because the fish are so rarely disturbed there. If you are able to make a daytime survey, your chances will be very much improved. Make a mental note of any overhanging branches and decide on the best technique for casting the fly. Try out a few casts and make sure that your fly does not get caught on obstructions behind you. If so, can you solve the problem with a Spey cast or a roll cast?

A colleague of mine puts a touch of nail varnish on his line every 5 yards. He can feel the varnish marks as he lengthens line at night, and so gets a reasonably accurate idea of how far he is casting.

Wading

There are stretches of water where sea trout rarely move far from the main channel of current. This is particularly so where there is little or no current on the shallow side of the pool. Once the shallows have been well tried it may help to wade carefully to a position from which more of the water can be covered easily without using an excessively long line. On such stretches I take up a position in mid-stream from which I can cover the water to either side. On hooking a fish I prefer to play it out and net it *in situ* so as to minimise disturbance. This is impracticable if one connects with a really big sea trout, of course, when both feet will be needed on *terra firma* as quickly as possible in order to follow any long hard run the fish may make.

If wading is necessary, always survey the water by daylight to check depths, current strengths and to look out for hazards such as ledges. Remember too, that the beds of spate rivers are changing all the time, so a pool which you have fished before may need another daylight survey if a spate has intervened.

Playing and Landing Sea Trout at Night

On first feeling the hook, a sea trout may make a powerful run which should be controlled with pressure on the rim of the reel, and the rod should be held high to keep as much of the line as possible out of the water and so reduce drag. At other times, a hooked sea trout might choose to leap into the air several times. This can cause a leader break if, at the same time, too much pressure is applied from the rod. Most sea trout leap at some stage during the fight and when, in the gloom, you cannot see the fish clearly it makes for nail-biting excitement.

FLIES FOR SUMMER SEA TROUT

Choice of flies depends upon fishing style – of this I am quite convinced. In his book, *Sea Trout Fishing*, Hugh Falkus recommends his Medecine pattern, a sort of 'slimline' Teal Silver and Blue. When fished with a steady figure-of-eight retrieve action, this fly is a good taker of sea trout in both high and low water and especially on the very darkest of nights. However, I find these bright-coloured flies far less successful when sea trout refuse to chase a lure, as so often is the case in warm-water conditions. Then, I get best results with dark flies fished very slowly.

An excellent pattern for this low-water technique is a Butcher tied on hooks of size 10 or 12. Sea trout give an artificial fly a severe testing, so it is well worth checking each hook before tying your sea trout flies. The main area of weakness is at the barb. If the cut is too deep, the point will easily break off. (You could spend a night getting lots of takes and landing no fish!) A single fly is usually sufficient for summer sea

Fig 97   Large tube flies are needed when fishing for sea trout in deep pools at night. Brighter patterns like the Gary Dog (top) and the Hairy Mary (middle) should be fished faster than darker flies such as the Stoat's Tail (bottom).

trouting. When fish are taking near the surface I add a dropper. Then a size 12 Zulu works well as an attractor, although the majority of fish are still taken on the point. Other good point flies for this technique are the Black Gnat, Mallard and Claret and Connemara Black, while any heavily palmered pattern serves as a dropper.

On very dark nights, and when fishing deep with a sunk line, larger flies, lightly dressed on long-shank hooks, sizes 6 or 8, are more successful. On large rivers, tube flies up to 2in or more in length may be necessary to get well down into the deepest pools. Sea trout readily attack such awesome creations. The more flashy flies, such as the Silver Doctor, Medecine and Dunkeld, need to be worked well through the water. If the sea trout refuse to chase a fast-moving lure, try darker flies such as the Sweeney Todd and Butcher. These are patterns which give me better results when fished more slowly.

THE INFLUENCE OF WEATHER AND WATER CONDITIONS

If your available fishing time is strictly limited, you may wish to determine in advance which nights offer best prospects for success. Early in the season many blank days are

Water level		Low: rising falling	−2 −5	Normal	0	High: rising falling	+2 +5
Light level		Bright moonlight	−4	Mid level	0	Very dark no moon	+5
Air temperature		Below water temp	−4	Approx at water temp	0	Above water temp	+5
Weather conditions		Thundery v. unsettled	−5	Changeable	0	Settled high pressure	+5
Month of year	Lower reaches	April/May/ October	−7	June/September	0	July/August	+5
	Upper reaches	April/May/ June	−7	July/August	0	September/ October	+5
Total influencing factor I		Sub-total of nega- tive factors N				Sub-total of posi- tive factors P	

Influence Factor, I = P−N

Fig 98   *The chances of a successful night's sea trout fishing depend on many factors, including luck. Each day is rated according to the factors in the 'Influence Table'. Over a season, weather and water conditions have a great influence on results, as this scatter plot of fifty fishing sessions on the same pool in 1985 suggests.*

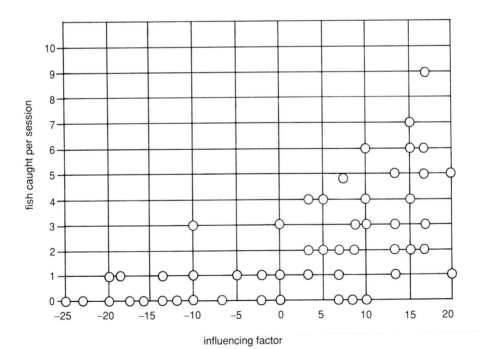

likely, but the quality of early-season fish is a great spur to enthusiasm. As July approaches we hope for a good downpour to be followed by a week or two of settled weather. If such a post-spate period should coincide with a change of moon to give some really dark nights, then vintage sport is in prospect. Worst of all, except perhaps for a really prolonged drought, are those thundery evenings when a sudden stillness descends at dusk. Sea trout do not leap, trout do not rise. Nothing mars the polished surface of the silent pool until first a few spots and then a torrent of rain descends, accompanied by the distant rumble of the approaching storm. Several times have I persisted and fished on through a thunderstorm. Rarely was the fishing good; most often totally fruitless.

Over the past few seasons, I have tried to determine relative 'weightings' for the various factors which seem to influence the degree of success in fly fishing for sea trout at night. On the basis of my collected data, I designed a special 'Sea Trout Fishing Log' which I now use to record results. It serves the dual-purpose of acting as a record for completion of my catch return to the Water Authority and also as data for analysis during the long winter months when I plan strategies for greater success in the coming season. A typical page is reproduced in Fig 98. An overall 'Influence Factor' is determined by subtracting the sum of all negative factors from the sum of all positive factors. For example, an 'Influence Factor' of 13 is very favourable.

In all fishing no firm rules can be applied, and from time to time fish are caught on real 'no hope' days, or not caught when one would expect them to be committing suicide. Nevertheless, results of over fifty sessions on the same 80 yard stretch of water over one season suggest useful correlation between results and 'Influence Factor', as can be seen from the scatter plot in Figure 98.

If you have never before tried fly fishing at night for sea trout then you are in for a surprise and, perhaps, a few shocks. You will be surprised how clearly the sounds of night travel along the river. Every rustle and shriek seems nearer and perhaps a little sinister. Then, just as your resolve is wavering, there is a nearby splash, followed by a whirring sound as a travelling sea trout fans the air with its tail before falling broadside with a shocking crash back into the water. Are you imagining things, or did the bend in your line move imperceptibly? A little late, perhaps, but you strike and the rod is almost wrenched from your hand as the reel begins to scream defiantly and line is stolen at an alarming rate. Your first fight with a big sea trout has begun . . .

15

Fresh Tactics for 'Halfling' Sea Trout

Precious few are those heady days when eager sea trout surge head-long across a pool to seize your fly. On many rivers spring sea trout are late arrivals which all too soon take their leave. Come July and those same sea trout are far from co-operative, while by August, particularly in a dry season, the early runners have settled down for the long wait. They are unlikely to stir until autumn rains fill the main river with the taste of the headwaters. Until then a fly fisher may have to be satisfied with the sparse sprinkling of fresh fish which scurry up through the shallows, their dorsals (and often their backs) exposed as they splash their way up the first few miles before they too take up residence in some turgid pool or sheltered glide.

A fresh sea trout up from the estuary on the evening tide is no match for a competent angler fishing the fly under cover of darkness. But long-stay summer sea trout are a different and altogether more difficult quarry. They are less predictable and less easily tempted. Swing a fly rapidly in front of a stale sea trout and it is unlikely to move a fin. Let a fly drift slowly in front of its nose and it may just follow the lure a yard or two before turning back to its resting place. The urge to feed is something they can resist a few more weeks, at least. They are at the 'halfling' stage between 'nocturnal salmon' and non-migratory trout. To entice one of these fish to seize the fly, and to know exactly when it has done so, demands a fresh look at flies and at tactics.

SOME RULES OF THUMB

Stale sea trout are difficult to tempt. On this, few serious sea trout fishers would disagree. However, there is much less agreement as to what are the best tactics for catching sea trout during a drought. Many persevere with the basic wet-fly method, fishing a team of flies across-and-down, searching the stickles and streamy glides by day, the pools by night. There are a few rules of thumb which have been passed down through generations. For example:

1. Do not cast a line onto the water before dark. This is usually taken to mean when features on the far bank cannot be clearly distinguished. (But with sea trout rivers varying from a few yards to several hundred yards across, this most quoted of guide-lines is surely of dubious practical value!)
2. Use small flies fished near the surface until midnight, switching to a sunk line and larger flies after midnight.
3. If at first you don't succeed, try a larger fly.

These 'hand-me-down' guide-lines would seem to have some merit. They are at least a useful starting-point from which to experiment. You may hear suggestions that such traditional advice is without virtue, and that sea trout can readily be taken on the dry fly in bright sunlight. While some sea trout certainly do revert to feeding in fresh water – in which case normal trout fishing tactics can be very successful (*see* Chapter 19) – in summer these are quite the minority. By mid-September a higher proportion of sea trout may be seen taking natural flies from the surface, and then during the daylight hours a dry fly can be more effective than a wet fly. The majority of summer sea trout either feed sub-surface at night or, more often, they continue to fast. They are best tempted, I suggest, with a skilfully presented wet fly. But what is the secret of presentation which will occasionally cause such a halfling to take the fly?

Over many seasons my results with summer sea trout in drought conditions have steadily improved as I have learned to use a tactic for inducing a response from those lethargic summer fish. The idea evolved not from fly fishing, but from watching and talking with a spin fisherman. At its best, spinning is a challenging technique calling for great concentration and judgement, and this particular fisherman was one of several highly skilled anglers on the lower Teifi in west Wales. We met frequently as we swapped shifts (I was about to start fishing as he began wending his way home-ward). I knew the particular spots he liked to fish, and I took my fly rod to waters undisturbed by his lures.

On one particular evening either I was early or he was late, for there was an overlap. I watched as he dropped his quill minnow within a yard of the far bank, tucking it well beneath the overhanging alders before bringing it steadily back towards the shallows. On three casts out of five, a sea trout followed his lure. Out from the shadows it drifted lazily, following the spinner almost to his feet before turning in the shallows and heading back to safety. Not once did it mouth the spinner. Although its nose was but inches from the deadly treble hook, the jaws of the sea trout remained

Fig 99   The Welsh Dee shows its bones. In such conditions traditional tactics often fail to stimulate sea trout to take the fly.

closed. (At close range you cannot fail to see the white tongue as a sea trout opens its gape to snap at a spinner or fly.) My acquaintance informed me that he had tried just about every pattern in his box. He had varied the retrieve from a bottom-hugging crawl to a surface-skimming dash, and all to no avail. That angler is a true sportsman. He will not continue spinning after dark for fear of foul-hooking sea trout once they leave their daytime hiding places. In the low, clear waters nothing he did would tempt them, and he departed with an empty creel.

Sitting there, waiting for the light to fade in the western sky, I pondered on what I had seen. The same sort of thing must happen when fishing the fly. With the river 'showing its bones' you sometimes see or feel a gentle tapping as your fly swings round slowly in the near slack water of a pool. Strike and you might just be lucky once in a while, but more often you will contact nothing. 'Salmon parr!' I used to tell myself, but changing to a smaller fly made no difference, or perhaps the knocks would cease altogether. Trying a bigger fly gave the same result – nothing! 'They're taking short tonight,' is a cry heard all too often in August. I don't call that taking short, I call it *not taking at all*. I was convinced that many of these gentle taps were nothing more than closed-mouth head butts. There had to be a solution to this problem – a technique for re-kindling the aggression in stale fish, and so provoking a take. I realised that what was needed was something akin to the 'induced-take' nymphing technique which Oliver Kite propounded for nymphing trout.

What is it about a fly that triggers an aggressive response from a sea trout? The wide variety of successful flies would suggest that choice of fly pattern is of little importance when fishing clear water. Size and shape are of much greater significance but, as in other branches of the sport, it is the *behaviour* of the fly in the water (where and how fast it swims and the vibrations it sets up as it does so), which makes the biggest

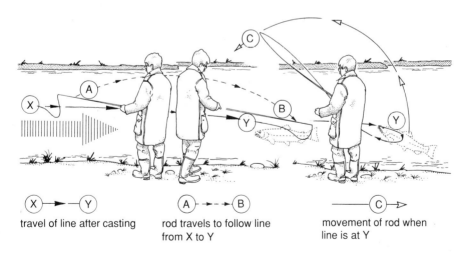

Fig 100 The induced-take tactic for sea trout. The fly is cast to position X and allowed to sink while drifting towards the suspected lie at Y. The rod is lifted upstream so that the fly follows the curve of the line as it is retrieved on the surface.

contribution towards success or failure. Throughout the animal kingdom there is one behaviour pattern which, above all others, incites a predator to strike – fear. Perhaps, I surmised, sea trout in a river can be induced to respond to their predatory instincts by a fly acting like a smaller, frightened fish. If the sea trout ignores a fly which swims across its nose, would it strike at one which behaves like a tiddler swimming steadily towards the resting predator and then darting away upon discovering its peril?

The answer is, *yes!* It may not be so easy to get a spinner to swim slowly into a sea trout lie, then turn around and dash away more quickly, but using fly-fishing gear this is not such a difficult manoeuvre, at least when fishing at moderate range in slowly drifting or static water. I must stress that this tactic is not suited to the traditional across-and-down technique, but to an upstream method of fishing. As the river is flowing very much more slowly, *you* must impart life to the fly. Drag plays little or no part in determining fishing depth, which is determined by leader length and by how long the weighted fly has had to sink. Once you get to know a pool you can readily control fishing depth by timing the fly down from the surface.

AN INDUCED-TAKE TACTIC FOR SEA TROUT

Start by casting upstream and across. Once the fly is near the river bed, begin a slow and steady downstream retrieve. As the fly nears a suspected sea trout lie stop retrieving line, raise the rod tip and swing it gently upstream. Then, as the leader straightens out below the rod tip, begin a fast figure-of-eight retrieve. If you have judged your timing correctly the fly will have performed its 'about turn' just in front of the suspected lie. If a sea trout is in residence this should result in a detectable response. Takes are generally quite positive, but because sea trout have such bony jaws you will need to strike quite hard. If you strike hard initially and thereafter treat your sea trout with the respect it deserves, you should lose few fish during the playing. Some people switch to light, fast-action rods for summer sea trouting. I do not think that they are a good idea, as all too often fish 'come off' while being played and brought to the net. A slower (middle-and-top-action) rod will soon tire a running sea trout, but at the same time it has the ability to absorb the shocks when a summer fish leaps clear of the water and crashes down onto the leader. Remember that, if in playing a fish you can feel every vibration at the rod butt, at least as much shock strain is being applied to the hook hold, and the risk of the fly pulling free must be a serious one. In my experience this is the most common cause of hooked sea trout being lost.

SUMMER SEA TROUT LIES

This method of inducing a stale sea trout to take a fly depends on your being able to turn your fly just in front of an occupied sea trout lie. It is the fly turning tail and running away which does the trick and induces a response. No sea trout, no take, of course! Without the knowledge of where sea trout tend to rest in a pool, the technique is much more hit and miss, but it still beats the traditional across-and-down searching method at this time of year. The alternatives are to wander from pool to pool in the hope of finding the odd fish which is fresh enough to take a fly offered traditionally, or to learn the lies on just a few pools and to concentrate on inducing takes from these known lies.

Naturally, experience with sea trout will strengthen your intuition. You will be able to size up a piece of water and select the areas likely to hold sea trout, but to pin-point lies precisely you need to know the contours of the river bed in detail. It is not necessarily the same sea trout which occupy a lie each night (though the larger fish do stay put for long periods during a drought), but provided the conditions of light, temperature and water-level hold reasonably steady the best lies will be occupied by fish through most of the night. What is even more promising is the fact that if you do find a prime lie in which you induce a large sea trout to take your fly, you can often take several other sea trout from the same spot within a matter of a couple of hours.

Let me quote two examples of reliable sea trout lies. The first is on the River Conwy in North Wales. In its lower reaches the Conwy flows broad and deep between banks of flat meadowland. Just above Llanrwst there is a long curved pool flanked on its eastern bank by a line of leaning willows whose branches trail down to the water. Wading in from a gently shelving gravel bank a side-cast is necessary to tuck the fly well under the canopy. As the fly sinks on its downstream drift I raise my rod to lift as much line from the surface as possible. Occasionally, a sea trout will follow the fly and take it in mid-stream. More often, takes come just as the fly turns to head upstream within a yard or so of the far bank. The large average size of these fish is more typical of the spring run than of the 'summer leapers', as the school sea trout are referred to locally.

Further evidence that the majority of the sea trout from this lie have spent several weeks in the river comes from their dark colouring. Some of the spots, normally black, will have taken on a brown or reddish tinge, so that only their size distinguishes these sea trout from the non-migratory brown trout population of the river. It is a long cast with a single-handed rod, but only when the fly falls hard against the far bank is there any response from the sea trout which by day lie in the shadows of the willow. Casting into the mid-stream channel provokes no response at all.

My second example is a lie much nearer mid-stream, this time on a smaller river, the Teifi. A cast of some 15 yards is needed to bring the fly across a rocky gulley in the scour of the main channel. The depth is 4ft to 5ft which demands both a heavy fly and a long leader. Ideally, this lie should be fished from a position a few yards further upstream, but access is restricted by overhanging trees. Summer fish from this gulley are always larger and darker than average for the Teifi, whose sea trout are generally smaller than those of the Conwy. In most seasons they average around 3lb but four- and five-pounders are not unusual. (On many British rivers the sea trout of summer rarely average above 2lb, and in parts of Eire a two-pounder would be a notable summer fish.)

Finding the lies of summer sea trout need not always be a matter of trial and error. Where there are overhanging trees which you can climb, or high banks which offer suitable vantage points, irregularities in the river bed can usually be pin-pointed by day. Rock gulleys and ledges are but two examples. Any depression caused by the

Fig 101   Summer sea trouting on the River Conwy at Llanrwst.

Fig 102   Rob Salt fishes for sea trout at sunset on the River Towy at Llandovery.

deflection of current – for example, around sunken trees or submerged boulders – can provide an attractive resting place for sea trout. One of my most memorable soakings came one afternoon when, intent on my search for sea trout on the bed of the River Cych, I stepped from one branch of an alder on to what proved to be its reflection in the pool below. I got to know that particular piece of water quite intimately!

SUMMER FLIES

Finally, to summer sea trout flies, another subject on which enthusiasts rarely agree. If discussed in isolation from the style of fishing, I am not surprised at this. Just about any fly will catch sea trout when the conditions are favourable, but we have been discussing perhaps the most difficult of situations – low water and stale fish. The traditional high-water flies such as the Teal Silver and Blue, give best results when fished at

Fig 103   This Dyffryn Demon has been tied to counter the 'short take'.

moderate or high speed, and so they are ideal in spring and autumn. Summer fish are less inclined to exert themselves, and your fly should be fished much more slowly. This is when a dark fly out-performs the more flashy attractor patterns.

In low, clear water I get best results from flies of brown or black with a little red and silver in the dressing. Popular patterns include the Mallard and Claret and the Zulu, but if asked to select a single pattern for summer fishing I would have no hesitation in choosing the Butcher. A size 10 is perhaps the most useful, but I prefer to be equipped with sizes 6 to 14. (Top-quality forged hooks are essential if you want to hold a sea trout on a hook as small as size 14.) The brighter the night, the smaller the fly I use, but if I get no response in the first half hour, I switch to a larger pattern.

For fishing amongst the rocks on the river bed, flies tied dambuster-style help you reduce snagging. In these, an additional hackle is tied in at the bend of the hook and this acts rather like a weed guard to keep the hook point clear of obstructions. As a fry-shaped outline, dambuster flies are less effective than simply reversing the tying, when the hackle represents the caudal (tail) fin rather than the pectorals. For this reason, perhaps, dambuster flies with their more bulky silhouette are less effective as lures than are the traditional sea trout tyings. In my experience, they catch fewer snags *and* fewer sea trout. In particular, I have noticed that more takes are missed altogether. The hackle certainly would not prevent a sea trout from firmly seizing the hook. I conclude, therefore, that the reason for so many missed takes is that sea trout seize the fly beyond the bend of the hook, in which case striking will simply pull the hook free.

Fig 104   Fishing the 'sea trout induced take' at close range from a position of concealment.

I am now convinced that summer sea trout rarely attack a fly from the side, but more often follow and seize it from behind. As a result, few summer fish are hooked in the scissors. Most often, the hook point is embedded in the bony upper jaw, a plight from which a lightly hooked fish can readily escape. Experimenting with fly patterns and styles, I find (as, no doubt, have numerous sea trout anglers before me) that tying the body of the fly to finish well above the bend of the hook is the best cure for *genuine* short-takes. Unfortunately, there is no effective way of tying dambuster flies in this way, since to provide good snag resistance the rear hackle must be tied in at the bend.

These low-water flies work well after a summer spate has brought fresh fish up from the sea, but they really come into their own in real drought years on those difficult nights when sea trout ignore flies fished by traditional methods. Then, induced – take tactics make all the difference between an exciting night's sport and *complete* peace and quiet.

PART IV
AUTUMN TACTICS

16

September on a Rough Stream

It had not rained since the last week in April. May had given way to June when I met an elderly farming friend. He was slumped across a gate, surveying the far from lush pasture, and remarked woefully: 'Well, Pat, that's all the grass we're going to get this spring, and there won't be another until at least September.'

Two springs in one year? But I know what he meant, and river trout fishing seems to follow a similar pattern. The season awakens in March and activity rises in step with the grass, reaching a peak with the Mayfly hatches and the haymaking. From late June onwards, things get much more difficult, and fly fishing for trout would be a nonentity some days were it not for the blessing of the evening rise. Through July and August the fly fisher's skill is tested more than at any other time of the year. (I will confess to switching much of my attention to sea trout during these dog days . . . well, nights actually!) So, despite the approaching close season, September must be welcomed for providing an echo of the spring and, hopefully, a few 'glowing embers' to recall through the winter ahead.

SEASON OF MISTS

My diaries over several seasons show that while for quantity May and June are way ahead, September has consistently provided trout of the highest average size. Shortening days and cooler nights bring lower water temperatures and improved daytime hatches of fly, but it does seem that fish location and behaviour are more variable with the onset of changeable weather and preparations for the spawning period ahead. In selecting tactics for late-season trouting it is necessary to consider how the river is changing and how the fish might react to these changes.

One big advantage of fishing the smaller streams is that, while the main rivers may stay high and brown for a week or more following a heavy flood, the brooks and small streams soon fall back to a useful level for fishing. On the lower reaches of the Teifi and Towy in West Wales, anglers often lose the last couple of weeks of the season, whereas tributaries such as the Cothi, Gwili and Cych provide some of their best brown trout and sea trout fishing at this time of year. Most rivers fish quite differently 'on the way up' compared with 'on the way down', so it is well to have tactics to suit both rising and falling water levels available.

Fig 105   Early autumn, and the overhanging vegetation is home to numerous small creatures which will be washed into the stream when the river rises.

Fig 106 Side-cast, roll cast and (particularly) the catapult cast are the order of the day when fishing in confined places like this small rough stream.

FISHING A RISING STREAM

Unless over-keepered, quite tall vegetation should by now have collapsed to overhang the edge of the stream, with fronds swaying and dipping on any breeze. With the first of the autumn rains the rising water will wash all sorts of creatures out of their summer residences. Beetles, spiders and caterpillars suffer this fate and the trout soon learn where to look for them. (It is not just to avoid the increasing force of the current that fish collect in eddies hard against the banks!) So, on a rising stream it pays to fish close into the side. Avoid heavy footfalls, keep well back from sight and ensure that the flash of a flailing rod does not give the game away.

The rod must be kept very low when casting, and the problem is how to avoid getting caught up in all the vegetation during the back cast? The best solution that I know is to use the 'catapult' cast. This short-range technique is ideal for fishing within about two rods' distance. Note that by flexing the rod to the left or the right instead of vertically it is actually possible to cast 'round corners', but beware! It is easy to crack a rod against a tree in this way. Whether or not you are ambidextrous, this is one style of casting which you will find just as easy with either hand holding the rod. In fact, when wading to fish under the banks of very heavily overgrown streams, you are virtually condemned to fishing only one side unless you can handle the rod with either hand.

Fig 107   A short length of 10lb nylon tied loosely around the thumb, with the free end looped over the hook bend, reduces the risk of hooking the thumb when using the catapult cast.

Observe a likely lie from well down stream for a minute or two and note the position of any good rise. Keeping low, approach the lie quietly until the rod tip is at the edge of the bank and a yard below the fish. A catapult cast from this position should land the fly about a yard upstream of the rise. Listen for a splash and strike without delay. (Do not show head and shoulders in an attempt to watch your fly, for when you can see the fly the trout will almost certainly see you, and at such short range that will prove disastrous.)

As might be expected, the daddy-long-legs is an excellent fly for this style of fishing. Also useful are furry caterpillar imitations (mine are green and brown), black spiders and beetle patterns. When using small flies on a cold day, gripping the fly to catapult it across the water can be difficult. A short length of 10lb nylon tied loosely around the thumb, with a free end looped to hold the hook bend, avoids the risk of catching your thumb or finger when using the 'catapult' cast.

FISHING A FALLING STREAM

At the peak of a flood, a stream is a torrent of debris-strewn chocolate and there can be no fly fishing. It is worth remembering that the shorter a stream, the more quickly it

Fig 108   A fallen tree creates a back eddy in which trout will rise to flies amidst the flotsam as the water fines down after an autumn spate.

fines down, so, unless continual heavy rain persists, it is usually possible to find a feeder which can be fished at some time of the day. On a falling water, fishing generally improves steadily and it is at its best when the silt has settled but a degree of colour remains. (The ideal colour varies from 'weak tea' to 'bottle green' depending on the terrain through which the river flows.)

While the water level is still well above normal, wet-fly techniques are effective by day. In the swift current you may need to use a sink-tip or a slow-sinking line to get the fly down to where the fish are resting. This is a time when inevitably you will lose a few flies. Late-summer and early-autumn spates rarely have the strength to scour the river beds thoroughly, but, as the water level falls, so debris brought down from the head-waters is deposited to form small underwater obstructions quite sufficient to snag a fly. Fishing 'deep' on a falling spate calls for guarded flies – for example, flies tied dambuster-style. A second hackle is added just in front of the bend of the hook and this helps the fly to climb over rocks and debris without snagging. Whereas most fly tiers use hen hackles for wet flies, this is one case where a really stiff cock hackle is essential.

'Big flies for big water', is an old, but seemingly quite apt, saying. Flashy patterns such as the Peter Ross, Bloody Butcher or Silver Doctor tied as sizes 8 or 10 are killers in fast coloured water. As soon as possible, I like to change to a floating line, lengthening the leader or casting slightly upstream to aid sinking. More subdued, imitative patterns are preferred as the water fines down. The Mallard and Claret, Blue Dun, and Black Gnat in sizes 12 to 16 are good all-rounders, taking both brown trout and sea trout at the end of the season.

CLEAR-WATER TACTICS

With the algal bloom of summer having been washed away by the first of the autumn spates, the stream soon fines down to a crystal clarity unmatched at any other time of the fly-fishing season. This is the time for stalking rough stream trout with tactics more often associated with chalk stream fly fishing. When there is cover, make full use of it. When there is no cover, move slowly and keep as low as possible.

How Low can you Get?

An angler who stands, say, 6ft tall, will be about 4½ft tall when kneeling upright, and a little under 3ft tall when crouching as low as he can without discomfort. This will allow him to get nearer to the edge of the river without being seen by the trout. Being nearer to the trout may make casting a little easier, but it does not make it any easier for the angler to see the fish, of course! The real enthusiast might decide to stalk a good trout by getting down on all fours, or even by slithering along on his tummy – a position from which casting is far from easy.

How Near can you Get?

Below a grazing angle of 10° very little light penetrates the surface, and a trout is unlikely to see a fly fisher or his rod if the angle between the edge of the trout's

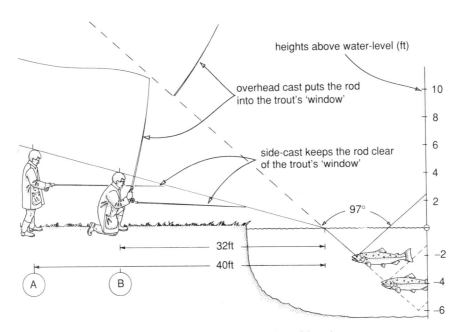

heights above water-level (ft)

overhead cast puts the rod
into the trout's 'window'

side-cast keeps the rod clear
of the trout's 'window'

Fig 109 Keeping low and using the side-cast enable the angler to fish at closer range without rod or angler being visible in the trout's window.

window and the top of the fisherman's head or his rod is less than 10°. Fig 109 shows an angler approaching and casting to trout which are lying at various depths in the water. Here, the river bank is just 1ft above the water level. A trout lying just under the surface will be able to see the top of the angler's head at position A, a distance of 40ft. By kneeling, the angler will be able to move to position B, 8ft nearer his quarry, *but he must crouch as he moves from A to B*. Simply to walk to B and then kneel down is of no use at all.

For trout lying further below the surface, the minimum safe distance (MSD) must be increased. For practical purposes it is sufficiently accurate to allow an extra foot of distance for every foot of depth. *But beware* – the effect of refraction gives a false impression of depth; water is always deeper than it appears. You will have noticed how a stick appears broken at the surface when you immerse it in water. It is the refraction of light as it leaves a rare medium and enters a denser one which causes this effect, and makes us underestimate depth.

If the bank is more than 1ft above water level, simply add 6ft to the MSD for every foot of height above the surface. A simple formula, then, can give us a guide to how close we can approach a trout:

$$MSD = \text{depth of trout} + 6 \times (\text{height of bank plus angler})$$

Clearly, when stalking trout, there is no substitute for getting down to it!

The Value of Side-Casting

It is interesting to do this simple sum for an angler who is 6ft tall and making an overhead cast with a 9ft rod. Let us keep the bank just 1ft above water-level and see how close he can get to a trout before the top of his rod appears in the trout's window. When the trout is lying just under the surface, the MSD is around 90ft. The angler would need to cast a full 30-yard fly line to reach the fish!

This might appear to make the overhead cast redundant for all but tournament champions, but trout do get used to seeing things moving on the river bank 30 yards away. They do not dart for cover every time a branch sways in the wind or a bird flies by. Yet, in crystal-clear water it is not unusual to see trout sent scattering by the waving of a rod in bright sunlight at a distance of 20 yards or more. I know, for despite my best intentions it happens to me far too often.

Wearing thigh waders, you reduce your height above the surface substantially, particularly if you side-cast. For example, an angler 6ft tall, wading in water 2ft deep should be able to get within 24ft of a trout resting on the river bed without appearing in the trout's window. This reduces the required casting distance to a mere 8 yards.

Wading is particularly helpful in reducing the MSD on streams where the banks are high. For example, an angler lying prone to peer over a bank 8ft high would be visible in the window of a trout almost fifty feet away.

Short-Range Tactics for Surface Feeders

Once you have seen a good trout rise and marked position, watch for a while. If it rises frequently, there must be a good supply of surface food and it is likely that the trout will hold station just under the surface. If, on the other hand, it takes surface flies very occasionally, with periods of a minute or more between rises, then it is likely that it will choose to settle deeper in the water where the current is less strong and where, more importantly, it can survey a larger area of surface. In both of these instances you can, if you are careful, move within the theoretical MSD.

First, let us consider the frequent feeder lying just sub-surface. There is an abundance of food passing over, and all that it has to do is turn slightly to the left or to the right, poke its nose up and gulp down the fly. Its eyes are focussed at short range, so objects at great distance appear as shapeless blurs. An angler, moving slowly into the picture, will pass undetected provided that he blends reasonably well into the surroundings. The trout sees nothing more than a gradual change in the hue of the blurred background against which he eyes passing food morsels.

Choice of clothing is important. Against a background of green bushes, a white shirt with arms waving would instantly attract the trout's attention. A momentary shift of focus and the game would be over. When fishing, wear drab clothing, preferably without chromium buckles or other fittings which might glint in the sunlight. Move

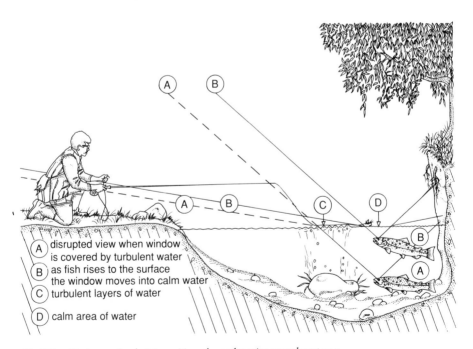

A   disrupted view when window is covered by turbulent water
B   as fish rises to the surface the window moves into calm water
C   turbulent layers of water
D   calm area of water

Fig 110   Moving cautiously into position, the angler gains concealment as a result of the light-scattering effects of turbulent water between himself and his quarry.

slowly, and cast gently, with your rod as close to the surface as possible. Then you will be able to catch frequent risers at remarkably short range.

One thing which does make it difficult for a trout to see you is surface turbulence. Seen through streamy water, stationary objects on the river bank appear to be broken up into horizontal slices, all moving, one relative to another. The effect is that a tree, a fence and an angler all look very similar, until the angler moves quickly!

In Fig 110, an infrequent riser at position A observes the surface from a depth of several feet. The trout's window is large, but light from the angler has to pass through the turbulent water, and so the image is confused. The angler casts a fly onto the surface so that it alights in the calm water near the high bank. As the trout rises to the surface, its view of things on the other bank clears. It is no longer looking through turbulent water. If the angler moves at all, during the rise of the trout, he will give the game away. Instead, he must cast and then freeze until his fly is either taken by the trout or ignored, in which case he should let it drift downstream before lifting off to re-cast.

I have watched many an angler cast to a trout in some quiet back eddy. As the trout rises towards the fly the angler sees it and reacts in some visible way, perhaps by turning his head or by raising his rod in readiness. At the last moment the trout turns away, perhaps with a splash of its tail. This, the angler mistakes for a rise to his fly. The fly is wrenched from the surface, the fish bolts for cover and another opportunity is lost.

The secret of this tactic, then, is to creep very slowly into position, to cast your fly, *and to freeze immediately*, until the trout has taken the fly. Only then should you react by pulling line back through the rod rings, and finally raising the rod as your fly makes contact with the jaws of the trout.

THE SEA TROUT IDENTITY CRISIS

By September, sea trout which entered the river system in spring have changed considerably – the flanks have lost their silver sheen and taken on an olive or bronze hue, the spots have grown in size and paled to mid-brown, with perhaps a hint of red, but most remarkably, many of these brown trout look-alikes have begun to feed. Their feeding habits – and hence the means of their downfall – are much the same as those of their non-migratory cousins.

The smaller sea trout feed throughout the day, taking flies from the surface and nymphs as they ascend from the river bed. Larger fish, from about three pounds upwards, are infrequent risers, although they can sometimes be tempted to the surface as dusk descends. The very biggest fish very rarely, in my experience, take surface flies, but they can be taken on imitative patterns fished near the river bed, both by day and after dark. (Traditional lure-fishing tactics remain the most effective means of taking fresh run sea trout, of course.)

In autumn, there are three kinds of sea trout in the river: fish of the autumn run, darker than the springers, but firm and fresh from the sea; leaner halflings, which have spent a month or two in the river; and spring runners, many of which have reverted to behaviour more in keeping with non-migratory trout. Whether you use trout tactics or sea trout tactics, you would be well advised not to fish too fine as the trouting season draws to a close, for there is no way of discriminating between migratory and non-migratory trout at this time of year.

In rivers and streams having a run of sea trout, size 12 flies are quite small enough. With a little colour in the water, there is no need to fish with a very fine point to your leader. Five-pound nylon and a size 12 hook will be fully tested if you make contact with one of those double-figure sea trout which vie for water space with the wild brown trout.

17

Autumn Miscellany on a Chalk Stream

My camera, complete with zoom and close-up lenses, preceded me through the dense growth of rushes as I slithered on my belly, determined to capture, in emulsion, the beautiful blue, green and brown damselflies so intent on their courtship rituals. It was not easy. A dozen times or more I would get within ten inches and the whirr of my auto-focus lens would send a flurry of iridescent bodies and wings wheeling above my head to join an increasing throng behind me. Then, at last, I got within range of a fine blue damselfly, apparently asleep in the grass beside a dead twig. Through my lens I saw the twig move – it was his lady friend. I zoomed back to bring both flies into the frame, and the disturbance sent them aloft where they collided. The female fell to the water, where she struggled helplessly, trapped by her wings in the surface film.

Before I could reach out to free her, a blue line flashed before me as her mate swooped down to the rescue. Gripping the thin brown abdomen with his legs, he beat his wings furiously in an attempt to lift his young lady bodily from the clinging surface. In this he failed. Undaunted, he proceeded to drag her across the water until she was able to climb onto the tangle of marginal rushes. The male hovered for a few seconds and then came to rest a safe distance from me. If I could have read his thoughts, no doubt I would have been made to blush! I took my leave of them, hoping that, free from further disturbance, they would mate successfully before, perhaps, some cunning old trout made a meal of them. If it did, well I would try to do the same to it, for I know that damselfly imitations are useful autumn flies on several of the chalk streams.

FIRST FIND YOUR FISH

If rough stream trout must survive on Autumn's table d'hote menu, then their chalk stream cousins enjoy à la carte treatment. Increasingly, during the day, cooler weather brings more prolific hatches of upwinged flies. These are supplemented by afternoon and evening sedge activity together with the emergence of stone-flies of several species. The top of the menu must be those large flies of autumn which help trout stock their larders ready for the ordeal of winter spawning. I am thinking, in particular of the crane-flies, the damselflies and, on some streams, the unpredictable but very welcome, second hatch of Mayflies.

The large evening sedges, such as the Caperer and the Large Cinnamon Sedge, as well as the daddy-long-legs, the damselflies and, to a large extent also the Mayflies, all have an affinity for the margins – some because they hatch from silt trapped among the roots of marginal plants and others because they arrive on the water due to 'pilot error' in windy conditions. In either case, there is every good reason for concentrating your efforts on those narrow strips of water beside the banks of the stream.

During the day, surface activity may be confined to the pools on bends in the river. Throughout the summer, trout have a habit of taking up lies in close proximity to one another and the majority are in or near these deep water pools. The streamy glides, which held fish in spring, may have appeared devoid of fish during the hot summer days, but once the autumn sedges emerge, huge brown trout often lurk there.

Trout Spotting

On warm bright days it is as if high summer has returned – the river is calm, unruffled by wind and seldom dinted by rising trout. Blustery days bring more fish to the surface, but the rises can be difficult to spot. The secret, of course, is to look in the right places and to know what you are looking for.

On rough streams, trout take up lies where some irregularity in the river bank or bed creates a holding feature. The problem with chalk streams is that there are, it may seem, too many features. The river bed is a patchwork of dips and mounds created by the action of fast-flowing water between the wracks of weeds. Then, particularly on smaller streams, there are numerous foot bridges whose pilings break up the flow of water, natural and man-made weirs, groynes and pipe dams. All these add holding features which may well outnumber the stock of trout. As chalk stream trout often have more than one lie, a fish noted earlier in the day may well move to a new position which it prefers once the sun has moved round. Perhaps it can more comfortably survey a food channel from this lie. The problem, then, is finding an occupied lie.

There can be a visible indication of a favoured lie, whether trout are present or not. The fanning action of the tail of a fish, as it holds station against the current, sweeps away any algae and leaves a bright patch of clean gravel. This lighter patch shows up clearly against the darker background. (This observation, reported by Goddard and Clarke in *The Trout and The Fly*, is equally applicable to rough stream trout and sea trout.)

The first lesson in fish spotting is: do not expect to see fish. You may see part of a

Fig 111   The River Test near Stockbridge, where trout usually feed more on nymphs than on flies during autumn days.

fish but more often you will see the effect of the fish on its surroundings. Far too often you will see the effect of your approach – signs of a departing fish.

What parts of a trout should you look for? The parts which show up most clearly are the vertical line of its tail, the white tongue when it opens its mouth, and the part of its flanks below the lateral line. You may see a brief flash of gold from the flanks of a trout as it turns from its lie to seize a nymph. Scan the water very slowly, for it is movement which betrays life. Do not be in too much of a hurry. Allow enough time and most trout will make some movement, either forward or to one side. Then note some landmark against which you can pin-point your quarry. This is most important. Otherwise, your perception of where your quarry is lying will drift downstream with the surface pattern of the water.

The effects of a trout on its environment are often easier to spot than the trout itself. The most obvious is that of taking a fly from, or just beneath, the surface. You may hear the splash or see the rings radiate from the centre of the disturbance. (Remember that the trout will return to a lie some distance upstream of where it took the fly.) Reflections on the surface may shimmer as a trout turns beneath the surface. On very calm water, a trout taking a nymph at a depth of 3ft may well betray its presence to the experienced eye. In shallower water the signs are all too obvious. Often, as you cast a line on to smooth water, a series of 'Vs' surge upstream – a message to you that there were trout lying unseen in the tail of the pool. These harbingers of doom forewarn other, often larger, trout that all is not well in the neighbourhood. Your quarry may not bolt, but it may sink a little lower in the water, and cease feeding for a while.

But there are other, more subtle signs which can help the observant angler stalk an infrequent riser. Silt rising from the river bed as a fish noses amongst the weed and gravel for nymphs and freshwater shrimps, the unexpected movement of bank-side reeds during a lull in the wind, a few fronds of a submerged weed bed moving against the general trend, are all things to look out for.

Shadows of fish can sometimes be easier to spot than the fish themselves. The light brown back of a trout feeding on a gravelly run can be very well camouflaged, but its shadow sometimes shows up clearly on the river bed. (Fig 40 illustrates how polarised sunglasses improve the visibility of both trout and their shadows.)

Large trout have an effect on the other fish in the stream. If you see small fry splashing on the surface in a confined area, expect there to be a predator – perhaps a trout – responsible for the panic. Trout feeding on small fry will, occasionally, take a well-presented nymph or an artificial shrimp.

Despite your best intentions, you will spook the occasional fish as you make your way upstream. Note the position from which it bolts and where it goes to, because it may simply move to another of its feeding lies. Return a little later, this time approaching with more caution, and you may yet turn the tables on it.

CALM DAYS

On most chalk streams, duns of the Small Dark Olive and of the tiny *Caenis* fly hatch sporadically through the day in August and early September. Trout rise splashily to

218

Fig 112 This old built-cane rod has an ideal action for dry-fly fishing at short range. It would be overstretched when casting more than fifteen yards.

these upwinged flies and can be tempted with a suitable imitation. A long, fine leader is needed in calm conditions. On occasion, where the surface is very smooth and very big trout are not to be expected, I will use 15ft of leader tapering to a 2lb point. On major chalk streams, however, 2lb nylon is not strong enough to keep a hooked fish under enough pressure to prevent it diving into the weed. It may be more difficult to deceive your quarry on 3lb or 4lb nylon, but do always use a strong enough leader to minimise the risk of breakage.

A stiff rod is no good at all for this type of fishing, as the shocks when the trout leaps arc transferred directly to the leader rather than being absorbed by the flexing of the rod. Built-cane rods are still very popular on chalk streams, and with good reason. Most of them have a softness of action which, in synthetic materials, would be synonymous with poor recovery and inaccurate casting. The best cane rods, although heavier than their modern counterparts, show little evidence of such drawbacks provided they are used at short range. As general-purpose river rods they are, I feel, outclassed by the best of carbon technology, but for casting a Caenis imitation 8 or 10 yards across a chalk stream I can find nothing better.

Later in the day, Blue Winged Olives are likely to hatch. On cool afternoons they may take a little longer to get airborne, and the trout manage to thin the hatch considerably. The spinners return in the evening, and they appear to be preferred to the duns when both are on the water at the same time. (It may be that the orange in the body of the spinner catches the light of sunset and is more visible.) I have taken many fine trout in early evening with a size 14 Sherry Spinner fished on a 3lb point. Again, stronger nylon is a definite deterrent.

In early evening the emerging nymphs of the Blue Winged Olive often bring trout on to the feed. At first all you see is a slight upwelling at the surface as the trout rises

Fig 113   A Silver Sedge is cast beside the reeds to the lie of a trout on the River Alre.

slightly to take the nymph soon after it leaves the safety of the roots and gravel of the river bed. As the sun sets, the fish seem to need longer to spot a hatching nymph, for the bulges are nearer the surface. Grease up your leader accordingly so that your nymph is fished at the depth at which the trout are feeding. Eventually, nymphs are taken from right under the surface, and a swamped fly is a better imitation than an artificial nymph. To swamp a dry fly, simply immerse it and the last 2in of your leader in leader 'sinkant' (or washing-up liquid).

As dusk approaches, splashy rises suggest that egg-laying spinners are on the menu. Finally, as the last of the light fades the river turns to burnished lead. Just occasionally, the mirror distorts its image of the trees and the clouds as a trout slashes at a hatching sedge fly, and this is your best chance of a really big trout. Cast your own sedge (I find the Silver Sedge pattern a useful one in autumn, because it catches the afterglow of evening so well) beside the reed beds. This is usually a much better place than mid-stream, as large trout shun the areas of fast current when sedges are available. If nothing happens in the first few seconds, give your fly a gentle twitch four or five times over half a minute before lifting off and re-casting.

WINDY DAYS

A good breeze is an upstream breeze, but any breeze is better than none in bright sunny weather. You will find fish-spotting much more difficult when the surface is choppy, and polarised spectacles will make little difference, except that they reduce the strain on your eyes. With a good surface ripple, concealment is virtually assured provided that you move slowly. To a trout below the surface, everything on the river bank will appear to be chopped into distorted pieces which dance about. Its only area of relatively clear vision will be directly overhead, so it will still pay you to keep your rod low when fishing at short range. I use the side-cast if trying to tempt fish within three rod lengths from the bank, and I find that the trout are rarely spooked by my casting.

The emerging olives are still worth imitating, of course, and a few female spinners will also get back to the water in anything but a full gale. But the joy of a breezy autumn day on the chalk streams is the opportunity to see how the trout react to terrestrial flies and, in particular, to the daddy-long-legs. They love them! A daddy-long-legs will even bring a nymphing trout to the surface on occasion.

An important advantage of the daddy-long-legs as an artificial fly is its relative freedom from the problem of drag. Such a large floating fly acts as a 'sea anchor', resisting, to a large extent, the pull of the leader. Indeed, a little drag appears to be of no concern to the trout. (Perhaps they accept it as evidence of the struggle for life of the fly as it tries to break free from the clinging surface.)

I used to think that damselflies and dragon-flies were too big a mouthful for a trout. Not so! Damselflies, in particular, are prone to the occasional forced landing on water. In a calm, they sometimes manage to take off again, but when a wind ruffles the surface they are more likely to get swamped. Small trout sometimes nose uncertainly

Fig 114   Damselflies are not too big a mouthful for chalk stream trout. This one is the male of Enallagama cyathigerum.

Fig 115   Battling with a brown trout on the Test, near Romsey.

at a spent damselfly, but larger fish have no such inhibitions and take them from the surface with great precision, sucking them down with little more disturbance than they do a spent spinner.

Black gnats (of various *Bibio* species) are also blown on to the water throughout the fly-fishing season. Most years they are still around in reasonable quantities in September. One example is the Heather Fly, which is prevalent at this time of year on most upland streams. This species also frequents the chalk regions of Hampshire and Wiltshire where it gets blown onto the water in sufficient quantities to justify the use of a general Black Gnat representation.

I recall one September evening on the Test when I came upon three trout all rising steadily beside the bank along a 10-yard stretch. The 'tail-end Charlie' was hard against the reeds and I presumed, rightly as it turned out, that it was taking sedge flies. It was a good fish of around 2lb and I got it first cast. It helped me by turning downstream where I played and netted it with little difficulty. I had kept my rod low, and the other two fish continued rising, apparently unaware of the goings on a few yards below them.

The second fish was more difficult. Its rises were gentle sips, so, despite seeing no spinners on the water, I offered it a Sherry Spinner. It ignored it several times and I rested it while changing to a size 14 Black Gnat. The first time I offered it, it rose to it and turned away. Thereafter, it would have nothing to do with it. It succumbed, finally, to a smaller version, and gave me a few anxious moments when, having been weeded, I had to hand-line it free. I estimated that trout as just over the pound, and released it without lifting the net from the water.

The third neb looked a much better proposition. The light was difficult and I had only the rise form to guide me, but these were deep throaty sploshes, a sure sign of a large fish feeding on surface flies. It ought to have been easy, but there was so much fly life in and around the water and I could not tell what it was taking. I decided that trial and error had to be the order of the day. Variety being the spice of life, there was no reason why he shouldn't take the first fly I offered him, was there? Well, obviously there was. I went right through my fly box, but to no avail. The surprising thing was that the trout continued to rise despite several less than delicate offerings on my part. Whether this was one of those '*gut shy*' trout, as Skues used to call them (trout which have felt the hook a few times through the season, got used to seeing anglers and gained enough experience to tell a real fly from an imperfect imitation), I will never know, for I left it feeding contentedly and crept away to dry out the contents of my fly box.

18

The Indian Summer Wine

September marches on relentlessly, and a growing sense of foreboding hangs over the river fly fisher. His ever-shortening days are numbered. On many rivers, trouting will close at the end of the month, yet it is too early, many say, to seek out the shoals of winter grayling. The main chance, surely, rests with migratory Salmonids, and, if sea trout are your quarry, the river can be a pretty daunting sight at this time of year. Gone is the silence of the still, pellucid pool. It has been replaced by a swirling debris-littered eddy. The gentle run now churns and roars; the silent summer glide is a race of turbulent white water, and each defies its domain to all but the weightiest of wet flies.

But these are magical days, when sea trout shake off their summer lethargy and cruise in broad daylight. No longer need they hide away beneath roots and crevices. Liberated from their inhibitions, they move up from pool to pool with their own sense of urgency and purpose. But they are not so single-minded that a well-presented fly will go unnoticed!

AUTUMN SEA TROUT

Within the shoals of autumn sea trout will be fish which left the sea many months ago and fish which did so on the last tide. The more recent runners are a little easier to catch, but neither are anything like as willing to take a fly as the bright silver sea trout of spring. Autumn fish are leaden both in coat and in humour. Their black spots may have turned to brown with more than a hint of the red of the native brown trout, and there is little doubt that some specimen 'brown trout' are incorrectly identified sea trout.

The late runners can be seen feeding in fresh water throughout the day and, whenever the water level rises, they run steadily through the river system, populating the smallest of feeder streams and brooks, many of which are dry in the summer months.

FISHING BY DAY

I have had greatest success during daylight hours working a fly through the runs of fast broken water in search of sea trout resting temporarily during their upstream struggle.

Fig 116   Playing a late-run sea trout on the River Teifi. This fish took a size 12 Teal Silver and Blue in fast water during the afternoon.

Fig 117   Mike Davies fishing the River Towy, which vies with the Dovey for the title of Wales' premier fishery for large sea trout.

Most runs contain some sub-surface undulations which can provide some respite from the force of the current. Outcrops of bedrock, boulders or sunken trees create swirls which shift the gravel to one side, leaving a depression of slack water which sea trout find attractive. Unless there is plenty of cloud cover, avoid searching the open water. Instead, work your fly down under the trees where there is plenty of shade. On smaller rivers you may be able to wade down a run in mid-stream, casting both to the right and to the left to comb the water on either side.

There is no place here for bushy flies, which would be pushed up by the current to skate across the surface. Lightly-dressed sombre patterns such as the Butcher, Connemarra Black or Mallard and Claret score well in fast clear water. These should be tied on heavy forged hooks with an under-dressing of lead foil. Even then, you may have to fish a long line to minimise drag across the stream. In very fast water a sinking line may be necessary. Try casting upstream and across to allow more time for the fly to sink before working it steadily away from the bank. Allow the fly to swing right round to the dangle before retrieving and casting again. Takes often come from fish

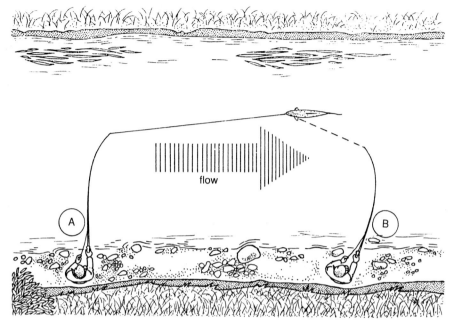

Fig 118   A sea trout hooked from position A should be played gently until either it swims upstream or the angler moves down to B. Then it is safe to apply pressure as the hook will be pulled further into the scissors of the fish's jaws.

which have followed the fly out into mid-stream, even though fish would rarely choose to lie there in bright sunlight. I have taken numerous sea trout at the moment of lifting off to re-cast.

When fishing across-and-down after sea trout in fast water, fish usually hook themselves. Even so, I play the fish gingerly until I can get below it and make a firm strike to set the hook past the barb. Of course, it isn't always possible to get downstream of a running fish, especially in broken water where wading must be a slow and cautious business. What if a sea trout makes a downstream dash? I would reserve the tug-of-war approach as a very last resort. A better way is to turn the fish and get it to beach itself. This is nowhere near as difficult as it may sound, since sea trout tend to run against the direction of applied strain. All you have to do – indeed, all you can do if the water downstream is too deep for wading and you cannot get out on to a clear bank – is apply just enough side strain to get the fish running across the river towards a shelving bank.

When all attempts to turn a fish fail, and the fish is estuary-bound, you may have to resort to desperate tactics. Strip off line from the reel so that it forms a belly downstream of the sea trout. If it feels the pull of the line and turns to resist it, all you need do is reel in steadily until you have it on a tight line upstream of you. Let the fish fight the current as well as your rod, and it should not be long before a glistening flank tells you that it is ready for the net. I must confess to awarding myself premature praise for this tactic when I turned a monster of a fish in very fast water. I breathed a sigh of relief as a great 'V' surged up past me into the pool above the run. I raised my rod to slow the running sea trout, and it had not the slightest effect. With my finger sore from braking the rim of the reel I watched in awe as my line ran straight through the pool and into the run above it before dropping back limply, my leader having parted under the drag of a full line. I learned an important lesson that day – when there is a great length of line in the water, the tension on the leader is far greater than the pressure you apply to the rim of a fly reel. With 30 yards of fly line trailing behind it, the drag created by a running fish can be enough to snap 8lb nylon.

FISHING BY NIGHT

Sea trout will leave the broken water as dusk approaches, and so should you. Like your quarry, move to the pools. Sea trout shoal up at the head of a pool as soon as the sun leaves the water, but in the cooler flows of autumn they soon move back from the

Fig 119   A 2lb sea trout comes to the net. The fish was taken from a debris-strewn back eddy following an autumn spate.

shallows and into the deeper eddies. This concentration of fish in just a few places in the pool can work to your advantage, of course, but there is a snag, or rather, there are lots of snags. With the first of the autumn rains, the debris of summer is washed into the river and collects, inevitably, in the quieter back eddies. Great rafts of flotsam make large areas of water quite unfishable. Elsewhere, waterlogged material on the bed of the stream lies in wait for your fly. Conventional fishing methods and conventional flies can result in frustration beyond description. Extraordinary tactics are called for.

Occasionally, it is possible to drift a fly beneath a raft of debris. Look for eddies on an outside bend where you can cast into the run above the pool. If necessary, sink the rod tip below the surface to keep your line clear of surface obstructions. Remember, if you get a sharp take when your rod is submerged, there will be nothing to absorb the initial shock except the stretch in your line. For this reason, when fishing a short line, I hold a loop of line lightly between my fingers and allow this to slip during the take. Remember, also, not to raise your rod rapidly, as you could break it. Instead, use the 'reel hand strike' technique and follow it with a steady lift of the rod in a direction which will keep your line clear of the debris. This might well mean keeping your rod tip below the surface until the sea trout is well clear of the flotsam, as, if it leaps upwards through the debris, you are surely finished!

To fish a fly effectively in deep water, you will need to overcome (quite literally) the many obstacles on the river bed. Ordinary flies have a magnetic attraction towards sunken branches, unless they are tied with some sort of weed guard. Once again, dambuster flies can be effective if fished slowly through water of slow to moderate flow. A more effective solution for heavy flows is the use of a keel hook together with a strong nylon loop to guard the hook point. When using these types of flies, do not expect fish to hook themselves. You will have to strike firmly to set the hook at the first indication of a take.

BROOKS AND FEEDER STREAMS

It is often said that the size of a river is a guide to the size of the fish it holds. Certainly, this seems to apply to the native trout of very small streams. It is hard to imagine how a fish can live for five years and weigh no more than an ounce, but I know many mountain streams well stocked with trout none of which reach a length of 6in. However, no such generalisation should be applied to sea trout. I have seen fish well into double figures in a stream I could step across. A good example is Pennard Pill, a tiny brook on the Gower Peninsula in South Wales. This stream winds its way over no more than 200yds, between high banks, before opening out into the sands of Three Cliffs Bay. Tall reeds and grasses overhang the banks, leaving the narrowest of channels for fishing. Yet sea trout of 5lb and more rest in the dark recesses of those undercut banks, emerging at dusk to cavort noisily on the surface. By day they are uncatchable; by night the stream is almost unfishable.

Short-range fishing is essential. The only way that I have found of fishing these types of waters is to take up position on the outside of a bend so you are looking along

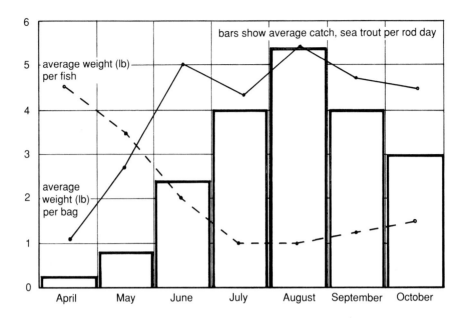

Fig 120   A chart of the author's sea trout catches during the 1985 season. Despite the presence of shoals of small whitling, an increasing number of larger sea trout raised the average weight towards the end of the season.

the centre of the main channel. Cast a weighted fly upstream, allowing it to sink to the river bed and then bring it steadily back towards you down the middle of the stream. Start with a cast of one rod's length and gradually extend your line, a foot each cast, until you have covered all of the water up to the next bend. Move steadily upstream searching the water thoroughly. If the fish are taking, you will not be disappointed. My favourite fly for this style of fishing is a long-shank version of the Night-Shift Nymph. I choose this pattern for no other reason than its ability to sink rapidly. Fishing as darkness descends, this upstream technique has accounted for some out-standing sea trout from waters which I am quietly confident have never before been fished by artificial fly at night.

19

Sea Trout in Coloured Water

Over the past five days I had reluctantly passed the river on my way to work. Last weekend's spate water had fined down to that dull greenish grey which spells perfection to the autumn sea trout fisher. Only vaguely, during a fitful night's sleep, had I registered the howl of the wind and the drumming of heavy rain. Now, on Saturday morning, I stood despondent before a river running like dark chocolate, frothing and foaming at the weir, swirling angrily through bank-high pools. The storm had put paid to my one chance of a day's sea trout fishing. In frustration, I stomped off back to the car. Another weekend ruined. With little more than a fortnight to the end of the season, my chance of contacting one of those late-run leviathans was receding rapidly.

Slamming my car door, I revved the engine hard, ground a few more slivers of steel from the crowns of reverse gear and spun the tyres in a shower of gravel. Fortunately, the nagging tongue of sanity prevailed. I was in quite the wrong frame of mind to be let loose on the public highway. A breath of fresh air was necessary, and, for an angler, inevitably, this means a walk beside the river. Already the water had fallen 6in. Another twelve and it might just be fishable. After ten minutes at a brisk pace, I rested on a rickety stile, listening to the comforting lilt of Nature – the gentle sighing of the wind in a tall sycamore, the steady lapping of water scouring the high outer bank of the pool beneath my feet, the irregular plopping and splashing of . . . The what? Cautiously I crept to the water's edge and peered into the pool. Plop! There it was again. Tell-tale rings spread from beneath an overhanging briar further up the pool. It wasn't what I had intended, but an hour's trouting would certainly ease the pangs of disappointment.

Returning with trout rod and dry flies, I crept cautiously to within 10 yards of the briar and waited for the fish to rise. I had seen no hatching flies, and so presumed the trout to be feeding on terrestrials blown in from the bank side. The rises had ceased, but, undaunted, I tied on a Silver Sedge and cast close against the bank. Immediately, my offering was engulfed by a swirling rise. As I lifted my rod, down went the tip, almost to the surface, and with a violence I was not expecting. A half-pounder from that stream is a very good trout, and anything over a pound almost unheard of. A piercing screech from my reel told me this was a much bigger fish. With an olympic leap, a sea trout of well over 2lb broke the surface. As it smashed back to the surface the 3lb point of my leader suffered a similar fate and the prize was lost. I shook my head in disbelief, raised my eyes to the lowering skies, and let fly with a few well-chosen words for that unfeeling iconoclast.

SEA TROUT AND THE DRY FLY

The realisation that sea trout will rise to a surface fly, and will do so because they want food, should have occurred to me earlier. All the evidence was there. Having taken the occasional fish on a surface lure or 'wake fly', I had, wrongly I now believe, assumed that stimulated aggression was the reason for its success. I recall a September morning when trout fishing with angling writer and journalist, Steve Windsor. Steve caught his first sewin (sea trout) that day (barely a half-pounder) and it rose to a tiny dry Greenwell's in coloured water. Brown trout were rising occasionally, but I had not seen the sea trout taking natural flies from the surface, and so again I assumed it had been annoyed by the presence of the Steve's fly. Now I know better, and when I see or hear a good rise on a sea trout river in autumn I make sure that my tackle is suited to the task.

Sea trout certainly do feed after a long stay in the river, and as a consequence the great majority of them are in fairly good condition after spawning and survive the migration back to sea. A 10lb sea trout may have spawned a dozen times, whereas the majority of atlantic salmon are in very poor condition and die after spawning. (It is rare for a salmon kelt to survive even if it does reach the sea and multiple spawners of this species are relatively rare.)

In recent seasons, I have made a special point of observing the behaviour of sea trout on a small river near my home. In spring and early summer they rarely rise to the surface during the day, but from late July or early August the summer resident fish begin rising to the hatching sedge flies as soon as the sun goes off the water. (I have also seen school sea trout behave like immature brown trout, rising repetitively in an attempt to intercept thistle down as it rolls across the surface in the autumn breeze.)

WHEN AND WHERE WITH THE DRY FLY?

Very occasionally, a spring sea trout will rise to a near-surface fly. More often it is mid- to late-July, as the water warms up, when the fish take in the top foot or so of water. I now know when it is worth trying a surface fly, for it coincides with the school sea trout moving into the shallows just after dark. Small sea trout are shoal fish, and shoal fish are not individuals in the way multiple spawners are. The school sea trout will move into the shallows when they are ready. They do not come in dribs and drabs – they either all come or none come. If they do, they will come right up close to you if you stand still and avoid shuffling your feet. There have been seasons when I have had to wait until well into August for this, but most years it is some time in July. Then they can be caught with no more than your leader on the surface.

When the shoals move in to the shallows, larger sea trout also move from the depths to hover in shallower water (not usually in the margins, but at least they move out from those deep holes and trenches so impenetrable to fly-fishing tackle). Favoured lies for the bigger autumn sea trout are those with plenty of tree shading and a depth of 3–4ft. On a dull day, a dry fly cast upstream to drift beneath the trees can take a fish or two when a wet fly will be ignored. These fish are rarely the monster sea

Fig 121   A shaded pool is an ideal place for tempting autumn sea trout with the dry fly.

Fig 122   Deep water in a shaded gorge. Before ascending the rapids, sea trout rest here and take surface flies trapped in the swirling eddies.

trout of 6–10lb, but more often second or third spawners, worthy adversaries which average around the 2–3lb mark.

Only in the most heavily coloured water have I taken sea trout from slowly drifting pools in bright sunlight. Then the dry fly is most definitely worth a try. Indeed, experience suggests this is the one circumstance where the dry fly can be counted on for better results than the wet fly. Pay particular attention to the quiet back eddies at the head of a pool, or where a fallen tree has left a scour hole. If you see a rise in an eddy, cast to it, but if you rise a trout rather than a sea trout, move on to another likely spot.

DRY FLY AT NIGHT

As the water fines down after a spate, sea trout will rise to the dry fly well into the night. A small dry fly cast upstream and across under the trees will sometimes tempt a fish before dusk. Later, especially if there is no moonlight, sea trout will move around the pool, hovering periodically in mid-stream. This is when a large bushy dry fly can be used to attract their attention. I have had some success in seasons past with a large Silver Sedge, although I am far from convinced that the pattern is at all important. For me, the Silver Sedge has one important quality – it is very easy to see, either in black water (the reflection of surrounding trees) or silver (the reflection of the sky). Another useful 'bi-visible' fly is the Black Gnat, tied with white wings. A size 8 is not too large for sea trout fishing, although on bright nights a size 10 will often be preferred.

One important warning about small flies. Dry flies are usually tied on fine wire hooks, as these provide for better buoyancy than do heavy forged hooks. Below size 10 it is very difficult to obtain fine wire hooks strong enough to give any reasonable chance of beating a 3lb sea trout. Of course, if you tie your own flies there is no problem. You simply use forged wet-fly hooks for tying flies of size 10 or smaller.

FISHING THE WAKE FLY

As dusk approaches, sea trout slash eagerly at hatching sedge flies. Often a fish will make two or three swirling lunges at a skittering sedge before either the fly takes off or it is finally captured. The surface disturbance of the struggling pupa can be simulated by dragging a dry fly or surface lure. Although some impressive results have been reported with large cork-bodied lures, I have had little success with such creations, and far better results with the Soldier Palmer dressings or deer hair patterns such as the G and H Sedge, in sizes 10 and 12. Fished across and down to create a wake in the surface, they are particularly attractive to sea trout in the witching hour.

One thing that demands great control is delaying the strike. You must wait until the

Fig 123   A large bushy fly, such as this G and H Sedge, can be used to attract the attention of sea trout at night.

fish has turned down from the surface. If you tighten too soon either you will fail to make contact altogether or the hook point will meet the bony upper part of the jaw where penetration beyond the barb is unlikely. When you delay striking until the sea trout have turned, you hook most of your fish in the scissors, and the hook rarely pulls free.

In very muddy water, surface fishing can be successful all through the day. I find it most effective on stretches with some natural shade. As the colour fines down, best results come during the hour or so after the sun dips below the horizon. As dusk approaches, it may be necessary to change to a larger fly to improve visibility. Any bushy pattern will do. Colour is unimportant since the fly is seen only in silhouette. To attract the attention of the fish, give your fly an occasional twitch as it drifts or drags across the suface. I will confess that, perhaps because I have no faith in surface lures for clear water fishing, it still comes as a great surprise to me when my fly is taken from the surface. I am hardly ever ready for the take, and this helps me delay that all-important tightening. I lose very few sea trout tempted in this way.

WET-FLY TACTICS

'Clear water, dull fly; coloured water, bright fly.' This old salmon angling saying is certainly borne out by my experience with sea trout. In the far north of Scotland,

Fig 124   In the boulder-strewn rivers of the south-west of England, sea trout are notoriously shy, but a bushy dry fly cast upstream in fast water is well worth a try on autumn evenings.

where there is little or no darkness on mid-summer nights, sea trout are taken throughout the twenty-four hours on bright flies such as the Teal Silver and Blue. Further south, the contrast in light level between day and night is much greater, and sea trout are more difficult to tempt during daylight.

FISHING AMONGST THE BOULDERS

Amongst the most challenging sea trout fishing is that of the rivers of the West of England. The River Dart, in Devon, has good runs of sea trout, but they are notoriously difficult to tempt by day. The exception, perhaps, is just as a spate is fining down. Then, a bright fly contrasts well with the peaty water, and can be used to tempt peal from their boulder lies. Cast your fly to swing across a submerged boulder, or to drift beside an exposed boulder. Then make a smooth upstream retrieve for a few yards before lifting your line from the water to re-cast. Takes generally come as the fly moves through the lie, but I have had sea trout follow for a yard or two before snatching at the fly and turning back to the lie. Almost invariably, these fish hook themselves. Unless the spate is a heavy one, a floating line should enable you to sink your fly a foot below the surface. This is usually deep enough to provoke a response.

A word of caution if you get the chance to fish boulder-strewn rivers like the Devon Rivers Dart and Avon. The thousands of years since glaciers left these boulders stranded in mid-stream have not been enough to remove all of their sharp edges. Some of them will cut through 4lb nylon like a knife through butter, so don't use too fine a nylon point on your leader. Otherwise, when a good sea trout makes off downstream with your line threading this way and that between the boulders of its watery domain, you and your quarry will soon part company. Eight-pound nylon may seem like overkill, but it is not. (I confess to learning this lesson the hard way.)

PART V
WINTER ACTIVITIES

20

Winter Work on the River

Each season of river trouting brings with it new experiences, perhaps some new skills and, for the diligent pupil, an increased understanding of Nature's ways. The lessons are there for all to learn; the teacher is the ever-patient river itself. But the learning need not stop at the close of the fishing season. There are so many things we can learn from the stream in winter which will help us achieve greater success in our fly fishing in future years. And, while you are at the waterside, there are a few ways in which you can help keep the stream in good heart.

A MANAGED WILDERNESS

Trees, so vital to the quality of fishing on a trout stream, need a little attention most years to provide a workable compromise between the 'wilderness' element and the need for some reasonable prospect of presenting a fly to the fish. Have you noticed how the overhanging branches do not actually reach the water at the beginning of the season, yet later in the year new growth will have trailed down below the surface? The river does its own pruning during spates, albeit rather unselectively, tearing off branches and straining the tree roots as it does so. It is far better if we carefully remove such hazards in early winter before the floods have a chance to damage the anchorage of the tree, leaving the bank unprotected against erosion.

When fishing the stretch of river which I look after, I usually carry a pair of pruners so that I can attend to small matters as required. Before taking any such steps, it is, of course, essential that you or your club obtain permission for the work from the riparian owner. In the past, I have found little difficulty obtaining approval once the purpose and scope of the proposed work have been fully explained. It is equally important to dispose of driftwood and prunings properly, and not to leave them strewn across the meadows. Weighted down with heavy rocks, trimmings can be very useful for helping to fill scour holes, especially those which form due to erosion behind old trees. If allowed to remain unattended, the eventual result is that the tree will be left with insufficient hold via its roots and will fall, either in a gale or in a heavy

Fig 125   Preventing bank erosion on a spate river is a major undertaking, in which the land drainage authorities must be consulted. Here, on the Towy, rocks are used to reinforce the outer bank on a gentle curve in the river.

spate. Once a large tree turns sideways on in a flooded river, it is almost certain to get stuck somewhere on its downstream passage. Wherever this happens considerable bank erosion is bound to ensue. It is surprising how these casualties always seem to come to rest in the best of pools and never in straight, featureless stretches of water where they might at least create a few holding lies!

TREE SURGERY

Amongst the many varieties of trees which line British rivers and streams two predominate – the alders and the willows in their various guises. Sadly, both of these are prone to premature demise. Alders, for reasons quite mysterious, suddenly die and rot to almost nothing in less than three years. Willows, which grow very quickly by the waterside, are often unable to support their own weight and either topple over or split in high winds. Every bit of willow which touches wet soil then takes root, and in no time at all an impenetrable jungle of bushes replaces the once-graceful tree. Fortunately, these problems can be avoided by pollarding. This is a technique of beheading trees at an early age so that, like hydras, they grow new heads which their trunks can support. The beautiful old willows seen gracing many of the more exclusive chalk streams received this sort of attention at the age of fifteen or twenty years, with periodical minor surgery since then.

Except when a tree is damaged in a gale, when urgent attention may be essential, pollarding is best left until winter when the sap is down. The sequence of cuts is important. First, the 'leaning' side of the trunk is cut, about a third of the way through, about 10in above the place intended for the final cut. This is to prevent splitting of the trunk under the weight of the branches as the lopping cut proceeds. Then the lopping cut is made, a further 6in above the first. Finally, a clean cut – sloping so that the rain will run off – is made at the location of the new crown of the tree. A coat of tree surgery paint is applied to the wound to reduce bleeding.

Within a few weeks, fresh growth emerges all the way up the trunk. If necessary, the tree will have to be protected by fencing for two or three years until the new growth has reached a height where cattle cannot graze it off. Throughout the growing season for the first few years, side shoots must be removed to encourage branches high up in the new crown. In three years time, the pollarded willow will have a span of ten to fifteen feet and will be a haven for flies, spiders, caterpillars and many other insects which may eventually end up as food for the waiting trout beneath.

Any major jobs, such as the removal of mature trees, should only be done in conjunction with the Water Authority who, in most cases, will carry out the work themselves using plant suited to the task. It is my experience, however, that where trees have been removed by the Water Authority 'roots and all' in order to fulfil its statutory obligation to maintain adequate land drainage, quite severe erosion has ensued with more tree casualties occurring further down the stream. For this reason, even when dead alders are removed, I cut them off at ground level leaving the roots to protect the bank. It is then possible to plant a replacement sapling just behind the old stump which provides protection from the scouring winter floods until the new tree

Fig 126   High winds can damage or uproot tall willow trees. Pollarded trees, like these on the author's stretch of the River Cych, are less vulnerable to wind damage. They also harbour many insects which may become food for the trout resting in the shade beneath.

*Fig 127   The author's river-keeping tools: an ancient tractor, a chain-saw, a
bow-saw, a pair of long-handled pruners, a billhook and (most useful of all), a
grass-hook.*

becomes firmly established. On streams prone to very heavy flooding it may be
necessary to brace the sapling, via straps, to mature trees either side of it, at least for its
first winter.

Many of the major jobs in maintaining a stream would be very time-consuming
without the use of tractors, chain-saws and other specialist tools, but a few simple
hand tools can achieve tremendous improvements and make for a safer fishery, particularly for the elderly or disabled. Other tools useful for small river-keeping jobs
include the grass-hook, billhook and slasher (a blade on a very long handle used for
reaching high up or across the stream). Of these, the grass-hook is undoubtedly the
most valuable as it can cope with nettles and brambles as well as small branches.

BANK MAINTENANCE

On at least one side or the other, and sometimes both, the banks of a river are being
eroded constantly. Earth from the surrounding high ground pushes to replace the lost
soil in a gradual process which fills the ocean beds with silt and reduces the height of
mountains and hills. Occasionally, a tree topples into the river, and with its root ball
goes a large quantity of soil, leaving an ugly scour hole. The pollarding of old trees can
extend their life, but eventually all must die. Unless the dying tree is cut off at ground-
level, a scour hole will inevitably result.

Fig 128   This young alder has been washed out during a flood. Now, while the river is low, is the time to remove it and repair the bank before a large scour hole develops in later spates.

To fill a scour hole effectively you should build a wall of large rocks at the upstream end of the scour. The void behind the wall can be filled with brushwood and topped off with a layer of heavy stones. In subsequent spates the river will deposit silt and eventually firm soil will be built up behind the rock wall. If you prefer, a layer of soil can be added on top of the stones. It is better to finish off by laying turf rather than to try to secure the new surface by seeding. Either way, there is always a risk that this top layer will be lost if the next heavy spate occurs before the repair had become firm.

The Flag Iris is a useful plant for firming up scour repairs or consolidating the bank in boggy areas. Its roots spread and intertwine to resist further erosion, and in autumn the dying foliage traps silt so that the soil level builds up gradually. (And, of course, they do happen to provide the most ideal cover from behind which you can cast a fly to an unsuspecting trout!) Flags are easily propagated by root division in winter or early spring.

FOOT-BRIDGES

Bridges over ditches or boggy land are relatively easy to construct and can ensure safe access in wet weather. Choice of materials is as important as the design of the

Fig 129   Llandysul Angling Association's suspension bridge at Abercerdin requires annual inspection and treatment of timbers, and periodic replacement of the steel hausers to ensure safe passage by anglers.

structures themselves. Foot-bridges over substantial feeders are best made from metal girders with heavy oak planking. Three or four steel-reinforced concrete fence posts, with a suitable handrail above them, make a secure walkway over small brooks. For crossings over ditches, rough hewn willow planks are fine and last many years. Ash is another useful timber if treated with a suitable preservative. Larch trunks provide nice straight handrails, and will normally last a decade even without preservative treatment.

Because it is readily available by the riverside, alder might suggest itself as a construction material. Have nothing to do with it! An alder bridge would be unsafe within two years due to decay of the timber.

STILES AND SEATS

On sea trout fisheries (where people walk the banks at night) secure stiles are not a luxury, but, from a safety point of view, an absolute necessity. The elderly angler will appreciate a stile that does not wobble, as much as he will value the occasional rustic seat where he can rest and survey the river, or sit whilst changing fly. The best times for sinking posts deeply into the ground are after spring or autumn rains have softened the earth to a good depth.

Fig 130 Ten-inch diameter posts
driven 2ft into the ground ensure that
this well-used stile is as steady as a rock.

Thin posts, even if strong enough to support a person's weight, make for rickety stiles and collapsing seats. In wet weather they rock back and forth, producing an ever-wider hole. Stout posts, soaked with a good preservative before being driven into place, can take a lot of punishment. The stile in Fig 130 is used several dozen times a day during the fly-fishing season. Its 10in diameter posts go 2ft into the ground, and the rails and treads are as steady as a rock.

STOCK ENHANCEMENT

Where a stream has been seriously polluted, restocking is the only way to re-create a sport fishery quickly. It takes many years, however, before plant, insect and fish life return to a proper ecological balance, and this means that stocked fish may find little to sustain them. The result, inevitably, is that the fish migrate either upstream or, more often, down. There is growing evidence that pond reared brown trout and rainbow trout, have a tendency to migrate to sea, if stocked into spate rivers. The brown trout return, either to the river in which they were stocked or to another river system, to spawn as sea trout. The rainbow trout also run to sea, but when they return, as steelhead trout, they generally find the rivers unsuitable for spawning.

On rivers with an ample stock of both resident and migratory Salmonids, stock enhancement programmes need very careful thought. Pre-season stocking with large

*Fig 131   Re-stocking must only be carried out with approval from and
supervision by the river authority. Here, Artie Jones and Gwilym Jones of
Llandysul Angling Association prepare to plant brown trout into the River Teifi.*

brown trout can provide good sport in the early months of the year, but at what cost to existing stocks? How many trout and salmon fry are eaten by half-pound brown trout before either the trout is caught or a spate carries it away to sea? There must also be intense competition for food, especially in streams of poor to moderate fertility (where stocking might be seen as the route to improving the quality of the fishing). Consequently, there is currently much debate amongst fishery managers as to whether trout should be stocked into migratory fishing waters.

Enhancement of migratory fish stocks is a different, but equally confusing issue. Salmon parr and smolts released into a river system should, if possible, be the progeny of the native salmon of the river; otherwise, only a very small proportion are likely to return as adult salmon to the river into which they were stocked. (Salmon from many rivers had to be stocked into the Thames before a strain which would remain loyal to the river was found.) Some salmon stock enhancement programmes, although costly, have been very successful. Sea trout restocking has received less attention. Peter Jarrams, a leading expert on sea trout and fishery management, suggests in his book, *Sea Trout Run*, that releasing sea trout smolts from a hatchery may prove costly and provide very little overall benefit to the fishery.

IMPROVING THE HABITAT

There is little doubt that long-term improvements in a river fishery cannot be obtained by means of short-term actions. Sewage effluent has to go somewhere, and it will take much concerted effort, as well as the political will, before there is adequate treatment capacity to cope with peak output. Encouraging progress has been made in recent years, however, and on many rivers the real damage is not from the steady release of treated sewage, but from episodic leakages, often due to poor control technology or human error. In dairy farming areas, releases of slurry have a serious effect on feeder streams. The move away from hay and towards silage for winter fodder carries with it the risk of highly dangerous liquid run-off from storage pits. We have the technological capability to deal with these types of problems; the requirement is for better education and strong enforcement of the law. At present, the water authorities take little notice of pollution incidents where no fish kill is evident. Unfortunately, the damage to insect life is difficult to detect, but this may well be responsible for the shift to main river spawning on many spate rivers. (Spawning in a restricted area can be deleterious to fish stocks if, as a result, over-cutting of redds occurs.)

The starting point in the food-chain is plant life. Without algae, mosses and weed there would be little for insects to feed on. The back-breaking work of weed cutting on chalk streams is balanced by the equally tedious task of weed propagation on spate rivers and rough streams. Much more could be done in this respect. I have significantly increased the aquatic insect population on my stretch of the River Cych by propagating water crowfoot. Root cuttings are the quickest way of establishing a new bed, and the planting is very straightforward, but it is most important to choose the site carefully. Watching the river in winter is the key to success. Look for sites which are covered by at least 6in of water when the river is low, and where the current does not change direction as the level rises. For example, eddies at the sides of weir pools are usually unsuitable, as the current usually changes its direction between low and high water.

Ideal places are wide, shallow gravelly stretches. Plant small beds with a clear channel of 2–3ft between them. Do not plant this type of weed hard against the banks as it can cause erosion when fast water pushes between the weed and the bank. A flat rock, partly sunk into the gravel, will help protect the weed bed until it becomes established.

Summer is the time for planting, when the risk of heavy rain washing out your work is minimum. (On no account should you plant weed in winter. You could disturb the gravel in which fish have already spawned.) At first you might make a few mistakes, but, with practice, you will get better at choosing your planting sites and the majority of your weed beds will take. Once established, they enhance the appearance and the fertility of the fishery.

BEGINNER'S LUCK

Despite all the stories about 'beginner's luck', by and large, newcomers to our sport have a pretty lean time, especially when river fishing. In earlier chapters I discussed the importance of the choice of artificial fly and of skill in its presentation, but beginners do also spend a lot of time casting to empty water, not knowing where the trout are likely to be lying. Much can be gleaned from watching others fishing and from reading books and magazine articles, but this must be supported by first-hand experience. Each pool, glide and run of every river and stream is unique and needs to be observed in all its moods before its closely guarded secrets will be revealed. Summer is the time for fishing; winter, I suggest, is for watching.

Working and walking the banks in winter give you ample opportunity for observations which can help your fishing in the coming season. At no other time of year does the river depth vary so greatly or so rapidly, and these changes in water-level allow you to study the surface and sub-surface currents which so greatly influence the trout in their choice of lies. Fig 132 shows a typical small-stream pool, with the strength and direction of surface currents at three widely differing water levels within the range 'summer maximum' to 'summer low'. On these maps, I have marked the lies of trout as found both from observation and from fishing results.

LIE DETECTION

For the patient fly fisher, an hour or so spent up a tree, above a pool, looking straight down into the water gives a far better view than that obtained from an oblique angle on the bank side. As you climb, fish will inevitably dart for cover. It takes up to an hour for the fish to settle after such a disturbance, but it is well worth the wait. By this means, I once found some hidden and hitherto unsuspected undercuts in a pool which

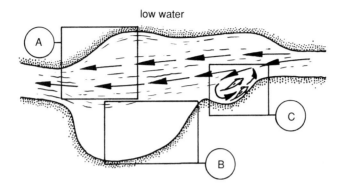

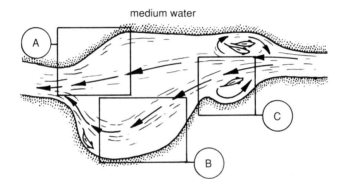

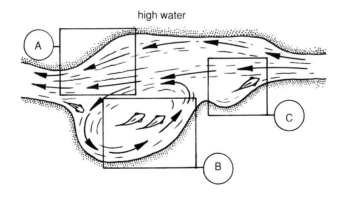

Fig 132   A pool on a small stream at low, medium and high water. Region A: only fingerlings in residence at all times. Region B: devoid of fish except at high water. Region C: hot spot in all conditions.

has since yielded several good brown trout and a sea trout of over 5lb. The sea trout was taken during the daytime in a spot which I would not have bothered to try but for my 'inside information'.

In pools where the depth changes gradually from the head to the tail and across the width of the pool, I find that the sub-surface currents are in the same general direction as the surface water flow. Exceptions to this are well worth looking for as they often provide food funnels with a nearby slack-water lie so sought after by wild brown trout. Familiar examples are waterfalls beneath whose sills there are always quiet zones between the crashing white water and the reverse-flow or undertow. These are very difficult places to fish but I have, on occasion, been amply rewarded after tossing a very large and weighty nymph actually on to the face of the falling water so that it joins the 'race'. A steady pull on the rod lifting the nymph up from the undertow will pull it through the slack water and if a trout does take, there is certainly no need to strike!

Swirls around sunken boulders provide similar opportunities and are much more easily spotted in winter when they have been scoured of their summer camouflage of algae. (Anyone who has fallen into a lamprey redd while wading in summer will know just how quickly such depth anomalies become concealed by algae.)

Bank-side undercuts near the river bed are not scoured out by the winter floods as I once thought they were. They generally occur at or near the low-water level and are the result of the year-round erosion of sand or gravel strata invariably on the outside of bends in the stream. They may, of course, be located by probing with an 'L'-shaped bar worked from the bank above, but such activities might take some explaining during the close season. Instead, let the trout show you where the undercuts are. Creep carefully to a suitable vantage point and peer over the edge of the bank to spy on the fish below. The slight movement of an arm is enough to send the trout darting for their hide-outs. Try to see exactly where those heading for the bank disappear. Next spring these undercut lies may be occupied by their bigger brethren, freshly returned from the spawning redds . . . and you can be there to welcome them!

Appendix

TROUT AND SEA TROUT FLIES

Dry Flies

G and H Sedge (John Goddard and Cliff Henry)

The best sedge pattern I have come across for the later stages of the evening rise.

Hook   8–12 longshank.
Tying silk   Green.
Body   Deer hair, spun on and clipped, tapering towards the eye to give a sedge shape.
Hackle   Two rusty cock hackles, the stems used as antennae.
Under body   Orange or green seal fur.

Ginger Quill (G.E.M. Skues)

A fly of the chalk streams, the Ginger Quill is reputed to be the best imitator of the Pale Watery dun.

Hook   14, 16.
Tail   Pale sandy dun cock fibres.
Body   Pale-orange seal fur on hot-orange tying silk.
Rib   Gold wire.
Hackle   Pale sandy dun cock.

Gold Ribbed Hare's Ear

A competitor, with Greenwell's Glory, for the best all-round olive representation. It can be fished dry or 'swamped' in the surface film to represent an emerging dun.

Hook   12–16.
Tying silk   Black.
Tail   Guard hair fibres from hare's face.
Body   Hare's ear.
Legs   Long hare's body fibres picked out.
Rib   Gold wire.

Greenwell's Glory (Canon William Greenwell and James Wright)

This most famous of trout flies can be used to imitate any olive. It will fool all but the most fastidious of selective feeders.

Hook   12–16.
Tying silk   Primrose.
Body   Primrose tying silk.
Rib   Gold wire.
Hackle   Light furnace cock.
Wing   Blackbird or starling.

Iron Blue Dun (Frank Sawyer)

The Iron Blue often fills in when no other upwinged flies are hatching, so a couple of imitations in your box are a sound investment.

Hook   14, 16.
Tying silk   Crimson.
Tail   White cock hackle fibres.
Body   Pheasant tail herls.
Hackle   Light purple cock.

Sherry Spinner (William Lunn)

A close match for the spinner of the Blue Winged Olive, this pattern will cover for many other spinners, especially during the evening rise.

Hook   14, 16.
Tying silk   Pale orange.
Tail   Light ginger cock hackles.
Body   Deep-orange floss.
Rib   Gold wire.
Wing   Pale-blue dun hackle points, spread in the spent position.
Hackle   Rhode Island Red cock.

Blue Winged Olive Dun (David Jaques)

A closer match than a general representation such as the Greenwell's or GRHE, this pattern sometimes convinces fastidious feeders.

Hook   12, 14.
Tying silk   Orange.
Tail   Dark-olive cock hackle fibres.
Body   Dark-olive ostrich herl overlaid with olive PVC.
Wings   Coot.
Hackle   Dark-olive cock.

Grey Duster

I rate this as the best all-round pattern for imitating the many species of autumn hatching stone-flies.

Hook   10–16.
Tying silk   Black.
Body   Blue-grey rabbit fur.
Hackle   Badger cock.

Yellow Sally

A fly which hatches on hot summer days when the rest of the insect world sleeps. Trout will occasionally break their siesta to take this tiny mouthful.

Hook   14, 16.
Tying silk   Primrose.
Body   Palmered, dyed yellow cock hackle.
Hackle   Yellow cock.

Grannom (Pat Russel)

A very important early-season sedge on both chalk stream and spate river. This is a daytime fly, so if fish are rising in April, the Grannom may well be what they are taking.

Hook   14.
Tying silk   Green.
Tip   Fluorescent green wool.
Body   Heron herl.
Wing   Blue dun cock hackle fibres.
Hackle   Ginger cock.

Silver Sedge (Taff Price)

A sedge fly hatches of which appear on some chalk streams and many rain-fed rivers from June to September.

Hook   12, 14.
Tying silk   Grey.
Body   White or grey floss.
Rib   Silver wire.
Wing   Grey squirrel tail fibres.
Hackle   Grizzle cock.

Black Gnat (Jack Hughes Parry)

A general label for several of the *Diptera*, I like this simple Welsh pattern.

Hook 14, 16.
Tying silk Black.
Body Grey floss silk.
Hackle Black cock.

Daddy-Long-Legs (Geoffrey Bucknall)

The crane-fly, in various sizes, is about the meadows throughout the trout fishing season, and on breezy days an imitation is well worth a try.

Hook 10 long-shank.
Tying silk Black.
Body Brown floss.
Legs Knotted 15lb dark nylon monofilament.
Hackle Ginger cock.
Wings Ginger cock hackle tips tied in the spent position.

Wet Flies

Coch-Y-Bonddhu

This pattern, an imitation of the familiar red and black beetle, is of Welsh origin. It makes a good general representation of other small beetles.

Hook 12, 14.
Tying silk Black.
Tag Gold tinsel.
Body Bronze peacock herl.
Rib Red floss silk.
Hackle Coch-y-bonddhu.

March Brown Spider (Roger Wooley)

Hook 12.
Tying silk Orange.
Body Sandy hare's neck fur.
Rib Yellow tying silk.
Hackle Light brown partridge.

Partridge and Orange

A trout and grayling fly from the north of England. A good pattern to use late in the season when stone-flies are hatching.

Hook   12–16.
Tying silk   Orange.
Body   Orange tying silk.
Hackle   Grey partridge.

Black and Peacock Spider

A popular stillwater pattern which is as effective on rivers. Cast beneath overhanging bushes on a breezy day, the Black and Peacock is deadly fished just sub-surface.

Hook   8–12.
Tying silk   Black.
Body   Bronze peacock herl.
Hackle   Hen hackle.

Butcher (Jewhurst and Moon)

Hook   10–14.
Tail   Red ibis.
Body   Flat silver tinsel.
Rib   Oval silver wire.
Wing   Blue Mallard.
Hackle   Black.

Sweeney Todd (Richard Walker and Peter Thomas)

Hook   6–14 longshank.
Tying silk   Black.
Body   Black floss.
Rib   Flat silver tinsel.
Throat   Daylight fluorescent neon magenta wool.
Wing   Black squirrel tail or bucktail.
Beard hackle   Crimson hackle fibres.

Teal Silver and Blue

Hook   8–14.
Tail   Golden pheasant tippets.
Body   Flat silver tinsel.
Rib   Silver wire.
Wing   Teal flank feather.
Hackle   Bright blue cock hackle.

Dyffryn Demon (Derek Hoskin and Pat O'Reilly)

This pattern has taken dozens of sea trout from spate rivers with rocky beds. The keel version has good anti-snagging properties.

Hook   6–10 longshank (Keel hooks for guarded version).
Tying silk   Black.
Body   Black floss with an under-dressing of lead wire along front half of body.
Tip   Daylight fluorescent magenta wool, tied to finish before the bend of the hook.
Optional Wing   Black squirrel tail (sparse).
Hackle   Black cock (as option to winging).

Alexandra

This pattern was once thought to be so lethal that its use was banned on some fisheries. It is still a popular sea trout fly.

Hook   8–12.
Tail   Red ibis (or substitute).
Body   Flat silver tinsel.
Rib   Oval silver wire.
Hackle   Black hen.
Wing   Peacock swords flanked with red ibis.

Nymphs

Tom's Green Nymph (Tom Chapman)

This is an excellent imitation of the cased caddis with algal coating, and should be fished slow and deep.

Hook   6–10.
Tying silk   Black.
Body   Dark olive seal fur.
Thorax   Dark olive seal fur.
Optional rib   Flat gold tinsel.

Longhorn Pupa (Richard Walker)

Hook   12, 14.
Tying silk   Brown.
Body   Rear two-thirds, pale sea green ostrich herl. Front third, chestnut ostrich herl.
Rib   On rear section only. Fine gold thread.
Hackle   Two turns, brown partridge.
Horns   Two strands, pheasant tail fibres slanted over back.

Mayfly Nymph – Improved (Richard Walker)

Deadly when fished induced-take-style at the beginning of the Mayfly season.

Hook   Longshank 8.
Tying silk   Brown.
Tail   Pheasant tail fibres.
Body and thorax   Cream ostrich herl.
Rib   Brown nylon.
Wing case   Pheasant tail fibres with the ends left protruding and turned down to represent legs.

Night-Shift Nymph (Pat O'Reilly)

A very simple construction which makes a good plop on entry. I devised this nymph for trouting by moonlight, but have also taken several sea trout on it.

Hook   8–12 longshank.
Tying silk   Black.
Tail   Pheasant tail fibres.
Body and thorax   Dark-orange baling twine (or raffia as substitute) tapered towards tail.
Wing case   Baler twine doubled back and tied in at head.

The Plummet (Pat O'Reilly)

A fast-sinking nymph which I devised for fishing the induced take in the undertow beneath waterfalls.

Hook   8–12.
Tying silk   None.
Tail   Pheasant tail fibres.
Body and thorax   BB or swan shot (according to hook size), pinched on behind eye of hook and varnished, overwound with peacock herl and copper wire to form tapered body.

Bibliography

The selection listed in this brief bibliography includes a sample of the many fine works of writers of an earlier age – an age when skill and perception had to make up for severe limitations in tackle. Others are here because of the clarity of their instruction in areas beyond the scope of this volume. I have also included a further group for the sheer enjoyment they have given me, and in the hope that, if they are new to you, you will enjoy them too.

Fly Fishing Past

Carter-Platts, W., *Modern Trout Fishing* (Black, 1938)
Dunne, J.W., *Sunshine and the Dry Fly* (Black, 1924)
Halford, F.M., *Dry Fly Fishing in Theory and Practice* (1895)
   Modern Developments of the Dry Fly (Routledge, 1913)
Hills, J.W., *A Summer on the Test* (Hodder & Stoughton, 1924)
Skues, G.E.M., *The Way of a Trout with a Fly* (Black, 1921)
   Nymph Fishing for Chalk Stream Trout (Black, 1939)

Entomology

Goddard, J., *Trout Fly Recognition* (Black, 1966)
   Waterside Guide (Unwin Hyman, 1988)
Harris, J.R., *An Angler's Entomology* (Collins, 1952)
Smith, R., *Life in Ponds and Streams in Britain* (Jarrold, 1979)

Salmonids, Their Physiology and Behaviour

Ade, R., *The Trout and Salmon Handbook* (Helm, 1989)
Clarke, B. and Goddard, J., *The Trout and the Fly* (Benn, 1980)
Jarrams, P., *Sea Trout Run* (Black, 1987)
Sosin, M. and Clarke, J., *Through the Fish's Eye* (Deutsch, 1976)

Trout Fishing

Kite, O., *Nymph Fishing in Practice* (Jenkins, 1963)
Lapsley, P., *River Trout Flyfishing* (Unwin Hyman, 1988)
Sawyer, F., *Nymphs and the Trout* (Black, 1974)
Wilson, D., *Fishing the Dry Fly* (Unwin Hyman, 1987)

Sea Trout Fishing

Falkus, H., *Sea Trout Fishing* (Witherby, 1975)
McLaren, C.C., *The Art of Sea Trout Fishing* (Oliver and Boyd, 1963)
Morgan, M.J. and Harris, G., *Successful Sea Trout Angling* (Blandford Press, 1989)
Oglesby, A., *Fly Fishing for Salmon and Sea Trout* (Crowood, 1986)

Flies and Fly Tying

Morgan, M.J., *Fly Patterns for the Rivers and Lakes of Wales* (Gomer Press, 1984)
Roberts, J., *The New Illustrated Dictionary of Trout Flies* (Allen and Unwin, 1986)
Veniard, J., *Fly Dresser's Guide* (Black, 1979)
Wakeford, J., *Fly Tying Techniques* (Black, 1980)
Williams, A.C., *A Dictionary of Trout Flies* (Black, 1949)

Reading for Pleasure

Bailey, J., *Travels with a Two-Piece* (Crowood, 1985)
Currie, W.B., *Days and Nights of Game Fishing* (George Allen and Unwin, 1984)
Haig-Brown, R.K., *A River Never Sleeps* (1946)
Plunkett-Greene, H., *Where the Bright Waters Meet* (Deutsch)
Sawyer, F., *Keeper of the Stream* (George Allen & Unwin, 1952)

Glossary

Over many generations, our sport has gathered around itself what may appear to the newcomer as an impenetrable barrier of abbreviations and jargon. The terminology is the entry to a wealth of entertaining and informative literature. This glossary of commonly used terms should help you find the key.

Action   The distribution of stiffness along a rod. Fast- or tip-action rods flex mainly in the top section, while slow- or soft-action rods flex throughout their length.
AFTM   A scale of fly line weights. The line and rod must be matched for optimum casting.
Alevin   A recently-hatched trout or salmon.
Attractor   A bright fly not representative of any particular insect. In particular, a bushy fly used on a dropper when fishing for sea trout.

Backing   A monofilament or braided line joined to the reel before the fly line is attached.
Bulging   Action of a trout feeding on nymphs before they reach the surface. Water wells up as the trout rises to seize the hatching nymph.

Cast (1)   To use a rod and line to project a fly onto or into the water.
Cast (2)   A leader to which flies are attached. Also a leader with a team of wet flies attached ready for fishing.
Chalk stream   A spring-fed stream rising from a chalk aquifer and maintaining a near constant flow throughout the year.
Char   A group of Salmonids including the arctic char and brook trout, inhabiting cold northern rivers and seas.

Diptera   The order of two-winged or true flies.
Dog Nobbler   A large lure with a heavily weighted head.
Double-haul   A casting technique which increases line speed. Used for distance casting and to improve accuracy in windy conditions.
Double-taper   A fly line with a level middle-section tapering over a 10ft length at each end.
Drag   Action of conflicting surface currents via a fly line and leader such that a dry fly skates across the surface of a stream.
Dropper   A nylon link on a leader to which an additional fly is tied, usually when fishing with wet flies.
Dry Fly   An artificial fly designed to float on the surface of the water.

Dun   The first winged stage in the life cycle of an Ephemerid or upwinged fly.

Ephemeroptera   The order of upwinged, or Ephemerid flies, which includes the Mayfly.

False-cast   Casting a line back and forth in the air whilst lengthening the line.

Figure-of-Eight   A method of retrieving line by bunching it into the palm of the hand in such a way that the fly swims at a nearly constant speed.

Finnock   A sea trout.

Fry   A young fish between alevin and parr stage.

Grayling   A fresh-water Salmonid (*Thymalus thymalus*) which spawns in spring rather than winter.

Greendrake   A Mayfly dun.

Greydrake   A Mayfly spinner.

Grilse   A young salmon which returns to the river after just one winter at sea.

Hackle   The feather from the neck of a game bird, tied to represent the legs of an insect.

Hatch (1)   A wooden shutter which can be raised or lowered to regulate the flow of water in a (usually chalk) stream.

Hatch (2)   A large quantity of flies of one species changing into their winged form together.

Herling   A young sea trout which has spent a few months at sea before returning to the river.

Imago   The spinner, or final phase in the life cycle of an insect.

Induced take   Drawing an artificial nymph towards the surface so that a trout is deceived into taking it as a hatching nymph.

Kelt   A sea trout or salmon which has survived spawning but has not yet returned to sea.

Kype   The hooked lower jaw of a male Salmonid, especially pronounced in the breeding season.

Larva   A nymph

Lateral line   The line of vibration-sensitive dots along the sides of a fish.

Leader   The thin nylon connection between fly line and fly.

Lie   The place in which a fish chooses to settle whilst feeding or resting.

Lure   A large attractor fly designed to trigger a predatory reaction from a fish.

Mayfly   The largest of the Ephemeroptera or upwinged flies hatching in British waters. The term Mayfly is sometimes applied to upwinged flies in general.

Mending   Lifting a fly line from the surface, by a flick of the rod tip, so that on its return to the water it lies upstream of the fly, and so reduces drag.

Midges   Chironomid flies of the Diptera order.

Milt   The roe of a male fish.

Mirror   The region surrounding the circular window through which a trout can see above the surface. In the mirror, the trout can only see a reflection of objects on the river bed.

Neb   The nose of a trout as it breaks the surface to take a floating fly.

Nymph   The larval stage of aquatic insects between the egg and the pupa or fly. Nymphs crawl or swim around the river bed, and can be imitated with artificial nymphs tied on hooks.

Olive   A general term for several flies of the upwinged order, whose duns have olive-coloured bodies.

Ovipositor   Part of a female fly used to place her eggs on the surface.

Parachute fly   A dry fly with hackles tied in the horizontal plane to provide increased realism and more delicate presentation.

Parr   A juvenile trout or salmon growing in a fresh-water stream.

Peal   A sea trout.

Point   The final, and usually the finest, section of a nylon leader.

Priest   A cosh for killing fish which are to be kept for the table.

Pupa   The final stage of a sedge or midge before the adult fly emerges.

Redd   A nest in the gravel of a river bed in which a fish lays its eggs.

Rise   The action of a fish swimming to the surface to take a fly. Also, the period of time during which trout take flies from the surface.

Salmon Trout   A sea trout.

Scissors   The intersection of upper and lower jaws of a fish, providing a very secure hold for a hook.

Sedge fly   The winged insect form of the caddis, many of which hatch at dusk and contribute to the evening rise.

Selectivity   Action of repeatedly taking flies of one species in preference to any other when more than one type of fly is hatching.

Shooting head   A length of fly line, tapered at one end and connected to a thin backing line. Used for casting a fly over great distances.

Sink-Tip   A fly line, all of which is designed to float except for the last few feet which are of higher density, so that the fly swims below the surface.

Smolt   A young sea trout or salmon ready to make its first migration to sea.

Snake rings   Rod rings consisting of semi-circles of steel wire which provide minimum resistance as the fly line passes through them.

Spate   A substantial rise in water level caused by heavy rain in the catchment of a river.

Spate river   A fast-flowing rain-fed river prone to flooding during wet weather.

Spent gnat   A dead spinner or imago of the Ephemeroptera or upwinged flies; especially of the Mayfly.

Spey cast   A method of casting a long line in a continuous motion such that the line does not extend behind the rod.

Spinner   The final (imago) form of an upwinged fly.

Steelhead   A migratory rainbow trout (*Salmo gairdneri*)

Stone-fly   Aquatic insects which are important elements of trout diet on many spate rivers and upland streams.

Sub-imago   The dun of an Ephemerid or upwinged fly.

Take   The seizing of a fly by a fish.

Team   Two or more flies fished by means of droppers on a single leader.

Terrestrials   Flies or other small creatures of non-aquatic origin blown onto the water.

Tippet   The final section or point of a leader.

Treble   A three-pointed hook which provides improved holding power. Used, in particular, with tube flies.

Tube fly   A wet fly dressed on a plastic or metal tube, usually fitted with a treble hook.

UDN   Ulcerative dermal necrosis. A fatal disease which ravaged stocks of salmon and sea trout in British rivers in the 1960s and 1970s.

Wake fly   A lure which is dragged through the surface to attract the attention of sea trout.

Weight-Forward   A fly line whose weight is concentrated in the forward section, with a thin running line to help achieve long-distance casting.

Wet fly   A fly designed to swim below the surface.

White trout   A sea trout.

Window   The circular base of an inverted cone of water above a fish and through which it sees a distorted image of what is above the surface.

Index

Note: Entries in bold refer to flies for which tying details are given in the Appendix.

Ade, R   261
alevin   17
Alexandra   47, **259**

Bailey, J   262
bank maintenance   245–6
Black and Peacock Spider   42, **258**
Black Gnat   43, 125, 209, 223, 235, **257**
Blagdon Buzzer   45
Blue Winged Olive   39, 219, **255**
Butcher   148, **258**

Caenis   40, 173, 175, 219
Carter-Platts, W   261
casting
   catapult   73, 207
   double haul   71
   false   71
   overhead   67–70
   roll   73, 187
   side   72, 109, 211–13
   spey   74, 187
   tuition   64
Chapman, T   43, 259
Clarke, B   24, 216, 261
Clarke, J   261
clothing   58–60
Coch-y-Bonddu   47, **257**
Conwy, River   144, 197
Cove, A   85
crane-fly   45, 216
Currie, W B   262
Cych, River   199, 206, 250

daddy-long-legs   45, 97, 216, 221, **257**
damselfly   46, 216, 221–3
dapping   132
Dart, River   237
drag   95, 112
droppers   90
dry fly
   fishing tactics   157–9
   fishing techniques   85
   patterns   254–7
Dunne, J   261
Dyffryn Demon   148, **259**

evening rise   159, 167, 177

Falkus, H   188, 262
flies (artificial)
   sea trout   147–8, 188–9, 199–201, **254–60**
   trout   49, 110, **254–60**
flies (natural)   33–46
fly lines
   AFTMA rating   54
   profiles   53
   quality   54
fry   17, 117

Ginger Quill   38, **254**
Goddard, J   24, 40, 216, 254, 261
Gold Ribbed Hare's Ear   40, 128, **254**
Greenwell's Glory   37, 40, 128, 232, **255**
Grey Duster   42, **256**

Haig-Brown, R K   262
halfling sea trout   192–201
Halford, F M   261
Harris, G   262
Harris, J R   261
Hawthorn fly   45
Hills, J W   261
Hoskin, D   148, 259

induced take   157
insects
    natural   34–46
    stone-flies   41–2
    sedge flies   42–4, 216
    terrestrial   45, 98
    upwinged   34–40
Iron Blue Dun   37, **255**
Itchen, River   29, 129

Jarrams, P   261

kelts   19
Kite, O   175, 195, 261
knots   51

landing nets
    designs   57
    use of   88–90
Lapsley, P   262
Large Dark Olive   37, 94, 128
leaders   51, 219, 237
Lunn's Particular   38

March Brown   37, 94, 128, **257**
Mayfly   34, 38, 130–4, 154–5,
    216
Mayfly Nymph   **260**
McLaren, C C   262
Medium Olive   38
mending line   76
mirror (trout's vision)   23
Morgan, M J   262

Night-Shift Nymph   168, 230,
    260

Nymph
    fishing tactics   111–12, 155–7,
        163–70, 175–7
    fishing techniques   83–5, 102
    patterns   111, 163, 259–60

Oglesby, A   262

Pale Watery   38
parr   17, 117
Partridge and Orange   42, **258**
Pheasant Tail Nymph   37, 175
playing and landing   87, 188
Plummet Nymph   **260**
Plunkett-Greene, H   262
pollarding   243–5
Priest   58, 89

Red Spinner   37
redd   17
reels   57
rise form   173–5
rivers and streams
    acidity/alkalinity   25
    chalk streams   28–32
    management of   242–51
    oxygen content   25
    rough streams   26
    spate rivers   26–8
Roberts, J   262
rods
    action   55, 219
    AFTMA rating   56
    brook fishing   61, 107–10
    river fishing   61–2

salmon   16
salmonids   16, 117
Sawyer, F   85, 175, 255
sea trout
    feeding habits   21, 213
    fishing tactics   146–8, 181–7,
        192–6, 225–37
    fishing techniques   136–50
    identification   18–19

lies   138–44, 146, 196–9,
    251–3
life cycle   19
sedges
    G and H   99, 178, 235, **254**
    Grannom   98, **256**
    larva   43
    pupa   43, 167–8
    Silver   220, 234, **256**
    Walker's Longhorn   43, **260**
selectivity
    feeding   172–5
    fishing   118–20
Sherry Spinner   40, 219, 223, **255**
shrimps (freshwater)   47
Skues, G E M   29, 223, 254
Small Dark Olive   173, 175, 218
Smith, R   261
Sosin, M   261
stock enhancement   248–51
striking   86, 108, 147
Sweeney Todd   148, **258**

Teal Silver and Blue   47, 148, **259**
Teifi, River   27–8, 197
Test, River   32, 217, 223

Tom's Green Nymph   **259**
Towy, River   15, 206
trout
    brown   16, 248
    educated   127–8
    lies   94–8, 112–16, 121–5
    life cycle   17–18
    rainbow   16, 248
    senses   22–4

Veniard, J   262

wading   188
Wakeford, J   262
weather   102, 189–91
wet fly
    patterns   257–9
    tactics   100–3, 159–61
    techniques   79–83
Williams, A C   262
Wilson, D   262
window (trout's vision)   23, 109

Yellow May Dun   40
Yellow Sally   42, **256**

Other fishing books published by the Crowood Press

Match Fishing – The Winner's Peg *Paul Dennis*
An instructional, anecdotal journey through a match fishing season with some of Britain's leading match fishermen.

Angling Afloat – A Complete Guide for Coarse Fisherman *Stephen Harper*
The first book devoted exclusively to freshwater boat fishing which will appeal to newcomers as well as experienced boat anglers.

Grayling – The Fourth Game Fish *Ronald Broughton*
Grayling experts give details on methods, tactics, tackle, locations and recount personal anecdotes.

Perch – Contemporary Days and Ways *John Bailey and Roger Miller*
Suggests alternatives to standard methods of fishing for perch, describing more exciting and successful innovative tactics.

In Wild Waters *John Bailey*
A book which inspires enthusiasm for wild water fishing in every angler, expert or novice by one of Britain's best-known fishermen.

Reeling In *Arthur Oglesby*
Offers a unique insight into the angling career of one of the sport's giants, Arthur Oglesby.

To Rise a Trout *John Roberts*
A unique guide to the techniques and tactics of dry fly fishing for trout on rivers and streams.

Barbel *Barbel Catchers and Friends*
Every river, every method and every bait is covered with each chapter written by a man who is an expert on his water.

The Handbook of Fly Tying *Peter Gathercole*
Provides a thorough grounding in the basics of fly tying, and takes the novice to a point where he or she is able to tackle even the most tricky methods.

Travels with a Two Piece *John Bailey*
A collection of writing inspired by the author's journey along the rivers of England with an ancient two piece fly fishing rod.

River Fishing *Len Head*
How to read waters and set about catching the major coarse fishing species.

Boat Fishing *Mike Millman, Richard Stapley and John Holden*
A concise but detailed guide to modern boat fishing.

Stillwater Coarse Fishing *Melvyn Russ*
A guide to the maze of tackle, baits, tactics and techniques that surround the cream of coarse fishing in Britain

Beach Fishing *John Holden*
A comprehensive insight into the fish, their habitat, long distance casting, tackle, bait and tactics.

My Way with Trout *Arthur Cove*
Outlines the techniques and tactics employed by the master of nymph fishing on stillwaters.

In Visible Waters *John Bailey*
John Bailey reveals the deep insight that he has gained over nearly thirty years closely observing the lives of coarse fishing species.

Imitations of the Trout's World *Bob Church and Peter Gathercole*
Describes advanced fly tying techniques and explores the link between the natural and the artificial.

Bob Church's Guide to Trout Flies
Covers some 400 flies, with advice on how to select the right one and how to fish it.

Fly Fishing for Salmon and Sea Trout *Arthur Oglesby*
The first recent really comprehensive work to deal almost exclusively with fly fishing techniques.

Tench *Len Head*
Natural history, physiology, distribution, tackle, tactics and techniques are discussed in this most comprehensive study of the species.

Pike – The Predator becomes the Prey *John Bailey and Martyn Page*
Twenty top pike anglers' experiences of all types of waters.

Carp – The Quest for the Queen *John Bailey and Martyn Page*
Combined specialist knowledge from twenty-six big fish men.

Long Distance Casting *John Holden*
A guide to tackle and techniques of long-range casting in saltwater.

The Beach Fisherman's Tackle Guide *John Holden*
Covers rods, reels, accessories, rigs and maintenance.

An Introduction to Reservoir Trout Fishing *Alan Pearson*
Covers tackle, casting, flies, bank and boat fishing, and location.

Rods and Rod Building *Len Head*
A manual of rod building, giving guidance on design and the selection of rods.

Further information from **The Crowood Press (0793) 496493.**